A call to NEEDLES

A Call to NEEDLES

ACTS of CRAFTIVISM and CRAFTED KINDNESS in THE AGE of TRUMP

Dee Ann EISNER

Published by Proving Press

Copyright © 2022 by Dee Ann Eisner

All rights reserved. This book, or parts thereof, may not be reproduced in any form without permission.

LCCN-2022915015

Print ISBN: 978-1-63337-660-1

E-book: 978-1-63337-661-8

1 3 5 7 9 10 8 6 4 2

PREFACE

"Some believe it is only great power that can hold evil in check, but that is not what I have found. It is the small everyday deeds of ordinary folk that keep the darkness at bay. Small acts of kindness and love."

—*The Hobbit* (movie version)

I HOPE YOU FIND INSPIRATION and kindred spirits in these pages. As you enter, please consider that knitters, and crafters in general, like the broader population, can be found on all points of the political spectrum. All are welcome in these pages—the political and the apolitical; those who bleed liberal blue; far-right conservatives; moderates and independents with no party affiliation; Trump supporters, former Trump supporters, and Never-Trumpers, as well. I will quickly make my spot on the spectrum clear, and while you may not agree with me, you still may find something here that will compel you to pick up your needle(s) of choice. Because crafters are nothing if not kind—always willing to create something to be given to someone in need. Blankets to warm those who are cold, chemo caps for people with cancer, and prayer shawls for comfort will continue to be needed. That is our common ground on which to build. In the *Age of Trump*, Americans chose sides and political divides grew wider, but I think that attempting to talk to each other and understand each other and standing together on common ground (no matter how small the patch) is the only way we will find our way closer to "united." Needlework can be an important, bold, clear voice in these conversations.

As we navigated our way through the days and then years of the Trump presidency, many impressive crafting opportunities emerged. In some cases, creativity was inspired by a particularly offensive policy the forty-fifth president enacted by executive order. In other cases, official presidential tweets that insulted allies while defending enemies—or attacked journalists, immigrants, or people of color—inspired our creative action. The refusal of the Trump administration to recognize, let alone act, on climate concerns, also served as inspiration. This book discusses many of the craft projects, initiatives, and opportunities that were a direct result of executive actions taken since January 20, 2017.

To be clear, *Acts of Craftivism and Crafted Kindness* are not mutually exclusive efforts, but have important distinctions, sometimes overlapping. Most acts of craftivism originate in feelings of frustration over the absence of kindness or compassion we observe in people who have the power, but lack the will, to improve the lives of others. When words and votes are ignored, people will look for other ways to get their attention.

Crafters and artists know that strong emotions, passion for a cause, even depression can inspire our work. The darker the world, the bigger the need to make something beautiful or compelling, to make a statement, start a conversation, support a movement, drive the change, or create something we can give to someone in need when we feel helpless. When those drives collide with your needlework skills, a craftivist is born. And if there was ever a need for a *Call to Needles*, this became the time.

Crafters and artists know that strong emotions, passion for a cause, even depression can inspire our work.

CONTENTS

Preface v
Contents vii
Desperate Times Call for Creative Measures 1

Part I

1: Craft, Hobby, Art, or Science? 5
2: Is Creativity a Teachable Skill? 15
3: It's Always Personal 21
4: A Brief History of Craftivism 27
    War-Crafting on the Home Front 27
    Crafting in Harm's Way 29
    Suffragists and Feminists 31
    Post-War Crafting Intersects with Second and Third Waves of Feminism 33

Part II

5: Modern Craftivism 37
6: Resistance Crafting 43
    Protest is Patriotic 43
    The Pussyhat Project 47
    Yarn Bombing 49
    The Kudzu Project 52

 Pears with a Purpose 55
 Cross stitch and Other Acts of Embroidery 58
 Knitting Nannas Against Gas (Australia) 66
 DIY Techniques 68
 A Stitch in Time 71
 The Protest Banner Lending Library 73

7: CRAFTED COMPASSION 75
 Little Sweaters for Little Penguins 76
 Warm Up America! and Made with Love 77
 The Giving Doll 79
 Sharing Our Heart(s) 80
 Knitted Knockers 81
 Et Cetera, Et Cetera 83

8: BeCAUSE CRAFTING 85
 The Welcome Blanket Project 86
 The Mourning Project 89
 The Tempestry Project 91
 Talking Heads 94
 Menstrual Craftivism 97
 The Violet Protest 101
 The Social Justice Sewing Academy 103
 Or . . . You Can Just Show Up and KiP (Knit in Public)! 107

9: METAPHORIC QUILTS 111
 Quilts Made by Enslaved People—Legend, Folklore, Art 114
 World War and Post-War Quilting 117

Narrative Quilts—The Modern Storytellers and Craftivists 117
One Last Quilt Metaphor 125

10: Arpilleras 127
Chile 127
USA 130

Part III

11: Crafted COVID Kindness 133
The Mask Makers 134
Finding Community in a Pandemic 139

12: The White Elephant in the Craft World 143
"Can we just go back to making pretty things?" 148
"The road to change is paved with yarn" 149

13: Self-Care for the Weary Craftivist 157
The Cognitive Impact of Crafting 158
Knititation—Meditation in Motion 160
Wrap Yourself or Someone Else in a Shawl 164
Yoga for the Needle Clenchers 165

14: Seeking Closure 187

Citations 193

Photo Credits 201

Acknowledgments 203

x

DESPERATE TIMES CALL FOR CREATIVE MEASURES

Knit on with confidence and hope through all crises.
—Elizabeth Zimmermann, *Knitting Without Tears*

I AM FAIRLY CERTAIN that the writers for *Saturday Night Live* had access to our living room on the night of November 8, 2016, as the results of the presidential election were posted. Much like the sketch *SNL* did in the first episode after that election, we hosted an election night watch party, expecting to celebrate, among other things, the first female president ever elected in the United States and the shattering of an enormous glass ceiling. We had a bottle of pink champagne chilling that later headed to the back of a pantry shelf to await the appropriate celebration, hopefully in the not-too-distant future.

I am also quite certain this was a scenario that played out in many homes across the country, with occupants expecting a different outcome and experiencing feelings of shock and dread. Even Michelle Obama, in her book *Becoming*, wrote that she went to bed early that night, when she suspected the outcome because she could not deal with what appeared to be happening. Many Americans knew exactly what type of person Donald Trump was and believed he was unfit for the Oval Office. Too many of us believed it could not—would not—happen. But it did. SNL encapsulated what many of us felt when that post-election November 12th episode aired with the cold open—Kate McKinnon, in a significantly feminist white pantsuit, at the piano, singing "Hallelujah" by Leonard Cohen.

Another experience that I believe played out in various ways across the United States came soon after the election. Good friends of ours who voted for Trump attempted to empathize with our post-election angst, and assured us that it would be fine. "He'll surround himself with good people who will have expertise in the areas he doesn't. It will be OK—you'll see." (*I filed these under "comments that didn't age well."*)

When the election was called by the networks on election night 2016 and Trump was declared the winner . . .

YES, all the liberal snowflakes melted in puddles of disbelief and denial. But the next day, the resistance arose from those puddles and started thinking about how to protect our democracy, all in our own ways. Plans began emerging for the Women's March on DC, to be held January 21, 2017, the day after Donald J. Trump would be inaugurated as the forty-fifth president. For knitters and crocheters, the Pussyhat became a phenomenon and pink yarn was suddenly very hard to find on store shelves.

In 2003, Betsy Greer, author of *Knitting for Good!: A Guide to Creating Personal, Social, and Political Change Stitch by Stitch*, popularized the term "craftivism" (combining the terms craft and activism), which, early on, focused largely on feminist and climate concerns. Craftivism existed before it had a name and its brief but impressive history can be traced back further than the *Age of Trump*, but Mr. Trump may have given craftivism a twenty-first century boost and new life. So . . . thanks?

The Craftivism Manifesto, created by Greer and a dozen other craftivists, is well worth viewing at www.craftivism.com/manifesto/. It begins by describing a craftivist as "anyone who uses their craft to help the greater good. Your craft is your voice." This public declaration also reminds us that "craftivism does not expect you to come with skills but with willingness" and "my craftivism can be different than your craftivism and that's okay." I take a closer look at what modern craftivism is and what it is not, and why that has become an important discussion, in chapter 5.

After the Pussyhats created a sea of pink at the Women's March came the Welcome Blankets for refugees and immigrants, the brain hats for a Science March, and the Mother's Dream Quilt Project to remember and honor victims of gun violence. Patriotic hat and scarf patterns became popular among progressives as a reminder that protest is patriotic, a concept disputed by extreme conservatives who believe in a blind, unquestioning form of patriotism rooted in authoritarianism and nationalism. ("If you don't like it, you can leave!") Resisters often created their own designs to share messages about topics that mattered to them, like voting rights. Do-it-yourself techniques are covered in chapter 6.

Although many of the projects described in this book reflect anger, fear, and frustration, they often include acts of kindness, intended to right observed injustices. Some endeavors began long before Trump became a politician, but they have a place in this era as well.

Although many of the projects described in this book reflect anger, fear, and frustration, they often include acts of kindness, intended to right observed injustices.

Desperate Times Call for Creative Measures

The more I researched the subject of *Crafted Kindness*, the more I found, and the more inspired I became. The chapters covering *Crafted Compassion* and *BeCAUSE Crafting* describe some of these efforts and represent several spots on the broad continuum of craftivism, some resembling a fusion of protest art, kindness, and activism. The intent of this book is to inspire you to find what calls your name and your needles to action, and to help you find ways to get involved.

Quilts have their own chapter in this book because they have become such an important tool for craftivists and crafters of kindness. Once a necessity for warmth and comfort, then as artistic expression, quilting became a leisure art, sometimes moving from the bed to the wall. Quilters have access to a sizable industry providing colorful, themed fabrics, tools, patterns and shops devoted to the medium. That branch of the quilting family tree continues to thrive, but more and more we see that quilts have become metaphoric, public-facing narratives for stories people feel compelled to share, much like the arpilleras in chapter 10. These two branches of the same tree share common roots but tend to keep a distance between them, rarely intertwining those branches.

I never imagined writing chapter 11. I was well into researching and writing this book when the pandemic entered our lives. Crafters and craftivists set aside everything to become the mask-makers, and I have included other pandemic-related projects that I believe deserve to be documented.

In chapter 12 you will read about people of color who have used social media in recent years to call out the inequity and demand change in the white-dominated craft industry. Racism is something that has been very difficult for white crafters, collectively, to acknowledge, let alone face with intention and make the necessary changes. I encourage those who have not yet recognized the white elephant in the craft industry to be willing to step out of your comfort zone with a sense of urgency, take a closer look with an open mind, and when you see it and feel it, find a way to "be (part of) the change."

✕✕✕✕✕✕

Another factor influencing our *Call to Needles* in this era is that needlework can be very soothing to a wounded soul. The need for that comfort may have played a role in so many people turning to their craft of choice in the *Age of Trump* to cope, distract, or feel useful. As a coping tool, research shows positive, meditative effects when people do the repetitive motion of needlework. So, it is also the mission of this book to remind readers of the importance of self-care in times of turmoil. As a registered, certified yoga teacher and therapist, I have included some rationale for turning to yoga if yoga has yet to find you, with some simple stretches for the areas of the body most affected. *Let's stop clenching those needles!*

✕✕✕✕✕✕

Before moving on, let's be clear about defining the *Age of Trump*, because we may have given too much credit to the man himself. We need to recognize and accept that what led to his 2016 victory holds some hard and surprising truths about our nation's demographics. Obviously, a widely diverse combination of beliefs, concerns, attitudes, and misinformation, already deeply ingrained, propelled the reality TV star and self-proclaimed billionaire through the primaries to become the nominee of the Republican Party. Those voters will be the subject of analysis and study for decades to come. But most of us know, from personal experience, that they were not made up solely of racist, misogynist, or uneducated people. I expect we will discover, in hindsight, that the movement toward an authoritarian, nationalistic type of leader was decades in the making, and it may take decades to right the ship of state.

The historic presidential ticket of Joe Biden and Kamala Harris won the 2020 election by a sizable, comfortable, declarative margin. And people danced in the streets, here and around the world, as if a dictator had been overthrown, because they knew how close we had come to fascism and the point of no return for our surprisingly fragile republic. Many of us held our collective breaths and stayed hypervigilant during the oh-so-many days between the election and the inauguration of our forty-sixth president, as lawsuit after lawsuit attempted to overturn the results of the election. The Stop the Steal rally on January 6, 2021, appeared to devolve into chaos, but apparently it was carefully and willfully planned. It will continue to be investigated and prosecuted for years to come—remembered as the day we almost lost our legislative branch to a mob.

The impact of the fear and anger that Trump and all of his party's enablers tolerated and stoked lingered long after he vacated the people's house. The healing of our country, even the world, will take a long time, and it will require a resolve to work together with common goals and a willingness to compromise on both sides. Time to toss out the "win-lose" philosophy.

Healing family and personal relationships will be equally challenging and will require listening to each other with the intention of truly hearing what is said without our political filters altering the messages. After the Vietnam War, the healing of damaged family relationships and friendships took years. Some of those wounds never healed.

The world always watches us closely. During the four years of the Trump administration, I believe most of our earth-mates were hoping we would find our way out of the mess we became mired in because the country that usually leads and inspires the world suddenly felt like it was on life support. I would like to believe the world needs us to survive and watches and prays for us the way we, as individuals, stand vigil over a loved one fighting for their life. The reality of historical context would indicate that the world may not need us to survive, and perhaps we won't, since efforts continue to restrict voters' rights and sow the seeds of doubt about the validity of the election process. If we don't resolve this, another country will emerge as the leader of the free world—democracy, or whatever version of leadership dominates in the future—much like we carry on even when that loved one does not survive. Time will tell.

During that time, as I discuss in this book, putting our feelings and beliefs into packages softened by fiber or fabric can often open a path to the uncomfortable conversations that help us face our history and help lead us to healing and reconciliation.

Part I

CRAFT, HOBBY, ART, OR SCIENCE?

Anything women enjoy always has to be designated a hobby and not a real form of art or political movement.

—Cathy de la Cruz, *Knitting for Good*

Creating necessities with available fiber-like substances and tools has been a thing since baskets were first woven from grass or rope. Crafted fishing nets and sails were important tools for fishermen and explorers. Wearing animal pelts for protection and warmth, the next step was spinning animal fur and hair into threads and manipulating them to better cover and protect. And even when basic survival issues were the daily priority, people seemed to yearn for and create items that adorned and brought aesthetic values to life. Evidence has been found that Neanderthals, both female and male, wore decorative objects and used cosmetics.[1]

Various forms of fiber arts have always served as reflections of the society or the culture in which they were created and have often had religious or political intent. Even the needles themselves were important players in history. Simple sewing needles, once made from bone or wood, can be traced back at least twenty-five thousand years. Once made by blacksmiths, the journey of the sewing needle predictably made them treasured gifts among the wealthy, especially when crafted from silver or gold. During the Industrial Revolution they were able to be mass produced and became a common object.[2]

Knitting needles made an equally interesting journey. Traced back to socks found in Egypt in AD 1100, these sticks, and the knowledge of various ways to use them, traveled to Spain, Italy, and Eastern Europe on their journey to becoming another common object, typically made from copper, wood, ivory, bamboo, tortoise shell, or iron. Again, predictably in hindsight, it was predominantly men who made a comfortable, middle class living knitting garments and other necessities for the wealthy. In France, the first knitting guilds were created to pass the craft on and maintain a set of standards. Many a knitter's lucrative employment supplied the wealthy, the church, and the military with stockings, socks, and other garments, even rugs. Peasants knit what they needed, unpaid, to keep their families warm.[3]

The making of various types of needles and the development of ways to use them were underrated game changers, moving humanity forward from wrapping themselves in animal skins to more comfortable, practical, washable, and reusable garments. These advancements also gave voice to creative ideas for purely aesthetic appeal.

With historical context in mind, writing about the debate over whether our crafts are a hobby (or something more) compels me to provide some background on how my own attitudes and views developed, since I believe I share a needlework *herstory* with many others who learned their favorite craft technique from grandmothers and mothers. And I am confident our attitudes toward our needlework have evolved along with societal and cultural norms.

xxxxxx

My two grandmothers, and possibly a few genetic factors, get most of the credit for my interest, passion, and . . . possible obsession with needlework. I can almost claim that I was born with a needle in my hand.

After raising nine children on a farm in southeast West Virginia, my maternal grandmother, Maude, developed a form of reproductive cancer. She was part of a study at the nearest large hospital, in Charlottesville, Virginia. But it was 1952 and there was still much to learn about cancer. Medical efforts failed, but I like to think her struggle helped them build on the science we use today. As she slowly faded away at home, my mother and father helped care for her. My father's skills as a pharmacist's mate in the navy meant he could administer shots to ease her pain. Her goal was to live long enough to see me play in her flower beds, and she was still alive when I took my first steps. Knowing that has always made me feel a connection to the woman I cannot remember. My other connection to Maude Humphreys is the stuff of family legend. While I was still an infant, this grandmother placed *(carefully, I assume)* a sewing needle in my tiny hand, and I predictably closed my fist around it. Folklore was that an item placed in an infant's palm would become their life's work. I've often thought there might have been more interesting items she could have used, but I'm also sometimes completely in awe at how well it worked. *Then again, how risky was it to predict a woman would obtain needle skills in the 1950s?*

Grandma Maude's plan for my future may not have been successful without the influence of my paternal grandmother, Susan. Maybe it was the skills she passed on to me and maybe it was her example as a strong, get-it-done woman, but she was a force, helping manage a forty-acre farm with her second husband. Her first husband, my father's father, was killed in a car accident in 1933. Imagine the plight of a widow in the 1930s with three children to raise. Baby Bea, child number four, died in early childhood from some type of fever. This grieving widow had no marketable job skills, so she was forced to make some very difficult choices. She sent her two boys to live on a friend's farm nearby and her daughter to live with friends in Georgia. She then found a way to earn a modest income preparing meals and selling them to miners as they headed to work. She was eventually able to reunite her wounded family, but not long before the boys joined the navy following the attack on Pearl Harbor. The oldest son did not come home, "still at sea" aboard the USS Indianapolis. Thankfully, my father did come home, and my mother's first impression was that he was the cutest sailor she had ever seen.

A few years later, with two grown children out on their own, Susan Martin met and married "Miller," as we always called him, a widowed farmer. In my memories, I entered their lives at age four. Mom, Dad, and I lived in a small house on land adjoining this farm, until my father, like so many other postwar male breadwinners, had to go where the jobs were and moved us to Cleveland where he worked for the railroads.

Susan C. Miller. *I. Did. Not. Like. Her* at first, and I'll never understand why, since I didn't send future me any illuminations into my thinking at the time. Maybe it was because she wasn't the ideal 50s feminine soft-spoken woman the era demanded. I know that's likely the very reason Miller loved and married her. She was a warrior and a survivor, very unladylike qualities for that time. I eventually bonded with her completely, possibly because she was such a skilled needleworker, poking holes in the wall I had built between us until it completely crumbled.

Susan Miller could make elegant clothing for my life-sized Rosemary doll in the evening after killing a chicken and cooking it for dinner. My memories of childhood summers at their farm are as warm and comforting as her handmade quilts that I slept under in the farmhouse with the tin roof (with the possible exception of the memory of the chicken killing. There was an ax and blood—but I digress). Her quilts were functional as well as decorative, with snips and pieces of dresses, shirts, and aprons I had seen her wear. She was the woman who

Grandma Susan and me on the farm, 1957.

taught seven-year-old me to knit and crochet, as well as some basic hand sewing techniques and a little practice on her treadle sewing machine, which sits next to me as I write this.

As hard as everyone worked on the farm, from dawn until dark, the farmhouse was always clean and welcoming. The large round table in the dining room meant there was always room for one or two more for dinner, especially on Sunday. The small, functional house had a sun-porch that was my grandmother's "soft" spot in the home and where I learned to love reading. If you're not sure why there's a connection between reading and crafting, or why it matters, you've obviously never tried to follow pattern instructions. This sunny spot invited you in with softly cushioned wicker furniture and shelves of books. The view of the mountains from this little nook was spectacular, and at the time, as an only child (my long-prayed-for baby sister would join us a few years later), I spent many hours there reading books from her shelves, especially on rainy days. I discovered and devoured all of her *Reader's Digest Condensed Books* and developed a list of favorite authors. Four of the books I discovered there were written by my grandmother's cousin, Edith H. Shank, who was born in the same town in West Virginia as my grandmother but later settled in Maryland and became the poet laureate of Frederick, Maryland, and one of the "Contemporary Poets of Dorrance," as named by the publisher of her books. I am almost convinced she was a time traveler when I read some of her poems in the context of today. I selected this poem from her last book, *Threads of Time*, published in 1961, because it fits nicely into this work, but also as a tribute to a woman I wish I had known.

THREADS OF TIME
By Edith Shank
Some are coarse and some are fine,
Some are beautiful and frail,
Some reveal a long life-line,
While others seem to fail.
Some threads of time show much strength
To bear the burdens of great weight,
While others boast of length
To stretch from date to date;
But all the threads of time must be
Woven into one great plan
Which fits into eternity,
The final goal of man.

I discovered that my other favorite reading spot was a few branches up in a peach tree in the farm's chicken yard. It was the perfect place to keep an eye on the long gravel driveway and be the first to know if visitors were arriving. There is still something powerful about reading outside for me, with some of the same background noises of nature, now often trapped in apps to soothe you while you meditate. The chickens made their own gentle chorus of odd little clicky sounds as they meandered beneath me looking for food. Add the sounds of other farm animals and the gentle whoosh the wheat made when a breeze came through the field. If I was lucky enough to be there when the peaches ripened, that only added to the sensory pleasure.

When I wasn't reading and the beauty of the surrounding hills called my name, I could be found out in the rocky fields, wearing one of my grandmother's skirts, touching the ground when worn on little me, wrapped in a shawl, intrepidly heading west in a wagon train on some days, and on others, simply searching for undiscovered treasures on land the glaciers sculpted. Spending time on that farm allowed me to discover my creativity and ways to use it and I will always be grateful for all I learned from Grandma Susan, her husband, Miller, and their forty acres.

xxxxxx

My mother, Garnet, was the other strong woman in my life. While my father was in the Pacific and then Normandy during World War II, his future wife worked for the Celanese Corporation, which, at the time, was manufacturing nylon for parachutes. She was part of a generation of women who set their lives aside for the war effort. In her case, that meant leaving high school at sixteen to work in the factory, in an era when women were expected not to work outside the home unless they were "spinsters." When the war ended, most of them had to step aside and return to their roles as girlfriends or homemakers so that returning soldiers could go back to their jobs. I find myself wondering at times what that felt like, but I missed the opportunity to ask my mother when I had the chance.

Garnet enjoyed sewing, and the clothes she made for her children were likely motivated by a combination of thrift and fun. I remember her excitement when she got her first "modern" sewing machine. It was the early 60s and it was the trendy new Singer Slant-O-Matic 500 Rocketeer. I don't remember ever seeing her sit down with knitting or any other needlecrafts, but she did enjoy sewing.

Having learned some skills as a child, by the time I hit my teens and took my first home economics class, I had a legitimate passion and used that Singer more than she ever would. While my friends found more traditional part-time jobs, I made money sewing for people. I did alterations, made custom curtains, sewed doll clothes and custom clothes for my customers. And I'm sure somewhere in the archives of "awkward family photos" often seen today on greeting cards, there is a picture of my mother, grandmother, sister, and me wearing the matching long pink gingham quilted robes with white eyelet trim that I made for all the women in my family one Christmas.

xxxxxx

I obtained my bachelor of science degree in education and started my career as a home economics/family and consumer sciences teacher (and all the other iterations of "home ec" through the years) in the Cleveland Public Schools. Yes, I taught "stitchin' and stirrin'," but so much more! I felt like I was part of a dying breed, as school districts started worshipping at the altar of the test and slashing electives. In districts across the country, as those of us teaching these life skills retired, we were not replaced, and eventually the courses were cancelled. Today, many school districts and parents want to see these courses reinstated. I will always declare to anyone willing to listen that we taught math, science, and logic in our classes, and students were able to find creative ways to think and work that enhanced the major subject areas.

That was my career, but at home I always had, always have, and always will have several fiber arts projects going simultaneously. Referring to them affectionately as WIPs (work in progress) sounds slightly less obsessive. *Other crafters understand this affliction . . . Amirite?*

But I have struggled my entire adult life with attitudes (mine and others') regarding my profession, as well as my needlework, and I assume I'm not alone. I acknowledge the advantages I've had as a white American since birth. But I will also acknowledge that, as a woman born in the 1950s, I have often been at a disadvantage, due to outright misogyny at one end of the spectrum and outdated role expectations at the other end. The women's liberation movement of the 60s and 70s was a dramatic turning point in our herstory. Here, in the first three decades of the twenty-first century, however, we seem to be living through an era that wants to take women back to the 1950s in terms of who makes decisions for and about us, especially decisions related to our own bodies. Male authoritarianism seems to always find its way to the surface for air, despite gains made by women for equity over the years, but I believe that most women and progressive-thinking men who are aware of this backsliding trend are also aware that most of the power to change it rests in some form of intelligent, peaceful activism—and, of course, the VOTE. Most of us choose to work within those parameters to bring about change and protect the progress we've made, using the skills and gifts we possess.

My decision to be a teacher, and specifically, to teach home economics, was actually a rather cowardly choice on my part. While I have no regrets and would not trade my journey for anyone else's, truthfully, it was the *safe* choice. It included areas of concentration in which I felt I already excelled. My choice of college major was made in the late 60s and early 70s, when my parents were unable to understand my drive to go to college. I never burned my bra, and I lingered at the younger end of the women's lib movement, more observer than participant, but much like the MeToo movement today, it was always in the news and became too iconic not to notice. Or, to quote Helen Reddy, it showed up "in numbers too big to ignore." *(Roar!)*

At the same time, much like what we see today, older, more established forces kept pushing back. During college, I had to pass a physical for a summer job at my dad's place of employment, and during the exam, the doctor (you would be correct to picture an old white guy) said to the air in the room, "I don't know why your father is paying to send you to college. You're just going to get married and have children and it will be wasted." There was no mention of my mother, who had recently left her role of full-time housewife and entered the workforce. That did not change her role as full-time housewife, it just crammed it into a part-time role. I wasn't the person—then—to

We seem to be living through an era that wants to take women back to the 1950s in terms of who makes decisions for and about us.

explain anything to an authority figure such as this doctor, but it stung. I was there to make my own money and pay for the college I chose to attend, rather than the state school my parents thought they could afford.

When I began teaching at a large high school in the city of Cleveland, my principal referred to me, daily, on sight, as either Pots and Pans or Needle and Thread rather than remembering and using my name. He was otherwise so awesome in so many ways that I excused it. But it fed the beast that lived inside me, whispering that that was all I was worth. Journalist and author Connie Schultz once tweeted a reminder for women to stop using the word "just" when talking about anything they do, and it made me wonder how many times in my life I've used that term in response to the question "What do you do?" And if I didn't say out loud that I was *"just* a home ec teacher," was it spoken internally (which may have been just as damaging)?

xxxxxx

The same flawed thinking often causes us to call our needlework a hobby or something to fill the time of those with nothing more interesting to do. Mention knitting to someone who doesn't knit, and they may be quick to point out that you seem too young to be knitting. To consider it an art might be perceived as attempting to elevate your skills to an undeserved level.

Dig back far enough in history to the roots of education around the world and you'll be reminded that men were taught to read and write while women were taught to manage home and hearth and were expected to learn necessary life skills like knitting and other forms of needlework to clothe their families.

I make my quilts as fast as I can to keep my family warm, and as beautiful as I can to keep my heart from breaking.

That quote is attributed to a pioneer woman on the lonely prairie in early America, and it has always resonated with me. Imagine the desperate need to have something aesthetically pleasing in such a harsh, lonely environment and consider it as one piece of evidence of the artistic side of needlework. Other efforts in this book describing various needle skills may remind you of this quote.

Sewing, knitting, and other forms of needlework were survival skills in early times. But if you were a wealthy and entitled woman, those skills were meant to occupy your time and give your life some purpose while creating beautiful household heirlooms. Early American samplers (rare and valuable finds today) were a rite of passage for young women, evidence that they had mastered their needlework skills as well as the alphabet. Include the skills for managing the household staff and a woman of privilege would be prepared for all that was required of her in that era. Some of those early samplers, as well as treasures like altar cloths and wall hangings, reside in places of honor in museums around the world as historical artifacts, but many crafters still have a difficult time thinking of their handiwork as art. After the election of Donald Trump, art museums, typically apolitical, began to recognize and display fiber art as important political statements that document history. The following list is a tiny representation:

- The Pussyhat was part of the Rapid Response Collection in London's Victoria and Albert Museum in February 2017, shortly after the Women's March in DC.
- The Fuller Craft Museum in Brockton, Massachusetts, began collecting Pussyhats for their Revolution in the Making exhibition to memorialize a movement that saw more than a million hats made. The Pussyhat, to date, is considered the biggest act of craftivism in modern history.[4]
- A large collection of work from the Welcome Blanket project (chapter 8) had a home at the Smart Museum of Art in Chicago and later at the Museum of Design Atlanta.
- Juilee Decker, an art historian and author, and Hinda Mandell, author and craftivist, used the two years after Trump was elected to create a curated exhibition of acts of craftivism. Upon publicizing an international call for art and craftwork created after 2015, they received more than one hundred submissions and selected over thirty of the works for the exhibit. The Anthony Mascioli Gallery in the Rochester (New York) Public Library housed the exhibit from August–October 2019, but it lives on in their book *Crafting Democracy: Fiber Arts and Activism*.

What drove this change? Why are more museums choosing to display fiber arts created in protest of a specific issue? Things like posters and banners carried at protest marches are usually considered the garbage left behind. After the Women's March in DC in 2017, abandoned posters became part of the leftover debris. But the Pussyhats, which involved more human investment than a poster or banner, lived on to march another day. That did not go unnoticed.

Mary Worrall and Shirley Wajda wrote a chapter in the book *Crafting Dissent: Handicraft as Protest from the American Revolution to the Pussyhats* titled "Curating Craftivism and Rethinking Collection(s)" that sheds some light on this. Both are involved in the research and curation of textiles, especially in the context of social justice, at Michigan State University. They see the value of challenging old ways of looking at their mission, redefining protest art and craft as meaningful craftivism.

After all, quilts and similar handmade objects of protest and affiliation are deliberate, well-thought-out, time-consuming, artistic and oftentimes skilled labor . . . typical attributes of the objects American Museums have historically collected. (p. 213)

As the nation's museums and libraries reconceive themselves as sites of civic engagement and social conscience, curators, educators, and other staff are rethinking what they collect and how they collect, reexamining their relationship with the communities they historically have served and the communities they wish to engage . . . How does the idea of craftivism redefine practices of historical communities and how do we, as museum professionals, rethink our collections. (p. 214)

For me, being open to seeing things in a new way seems like progress and helps us see our own craftwork as something of value. Perhaps we can wrap our minds around the idea that crafts can be hobby and art at the same time *and* that we incorporate logic, math, and science in the process of creating. All these things can be true.

I've noticed an increased awareness that the designing of needlework requires math and science skills. It was a thrill to find Kate Buckner's 2015 article "How Knitting is Like Coding" on Medium. "Hours of staring at knitting and crochet patterns, and a bit of time writing and editing my own and researching best practices for doing so, has led me to look for knitting-like patterns in my code and coding-like patterns in my knitting." Buckner cites this example:

"Don't Repeat Yourself" is a fundamental programming principle which encourages programmers to recognize and eliminate duplication. Well-written knitting patterns have this down:

Round 4: k 5, * k1, y0 k1, k4, p4, k4, rep from * around.

The notation k[knit] 5, instead of saying k1, k1, k1, k1 and the often-used repeat from * creates a loop and saves much repetition in patterns.

Another reference to coding and crafts can be found in Christina Koch's "The Computer Science of Knitting," from her blog *Enthusiasms*. She explains how knitting is binary, like coding, which uses 0s and 1s. Knitting relies basically on two stitches in various combinations, knit and purl. Koch also looks at the patterns within knitting patterns: "Knitting patterns are like a program, where the input is a single string of yarn (almost like streaming text from standard input) and the output is some kind of knitted object. The compiler and interpreter is, of course, the knitter. This gets especially computer-sciencey when your 'program' or instructions are written as a chart." Crafters, imagine the charts for a delicate lace, a colorful Fair Isle design, or a cross stitch pattern for this analogy.

xxxxxx

If you are a fan of illusion knitting (chapter 6) you are probably familiar with Steve Plummer and Pat Ashforth, dubbed the "mathekniticians." This husband-wife team spent their careers teaching mathematics in the UK. Their original foray into knitting was the result of a commission from a US yarn company to create a geometric design. That job led them to realize that textile art could be "used for making mathematics more accessible" and added this tool to the toolbox during their teaching careers. Afghans and wall hangings were found to be very conducive to teaching math concepts at all grade levels. They were regular presenters at mathematics conferences, promoting the concept that craft and mathematics play well together and can help more students (especially visual and kinesthetic learners) find success. In 2000, they "produced a small booklet for schools which was quickly adopted in many parts of the UK for use in formal mathematics and technology classes and for school craft clubs."[5] Although Ashforth died in 2021, the work continues at Woolly-thoughts.com with designs, pattens, tutorials, and other aids for teaching math concepts. The website includes a link to an article the couple wrote titled "Mathematical Knitting and Crochet" for anyone interested in a deeper (mathier) dive into this subject.

Looking forward, we now see yarn grown from human skin cells called fibroblasts being knitted, knotted, braided, woven, or twisted, to create human yarns and textiles for repairing organs, tissue grafts, and creating tubes, valves, and membranes. A fibroblast is a type of cell found in human connective tissue that helps maintain structure and is helpful in healing. And, unlike synthetic substances, the body will not attempt to reject this natural tissue or react with an inflammatory response. Nicolas L'Heureux led this research at the French National Institute of Health and Medical Research in Bordeaux. "With the yarn, any textile approach is feasible."[6] Research on animals has been very successsful and lends hope to finding its way to caring for humans soon.

xxxxxx

Call it craft if that is where it fits in your comfort zone, but the evidence is clear that it should be recognized as art and science, as well. An adjustment in the regard some of us have for our own work is critical if we wish to be effective craftivists or protest artists. We cannot expect the hoped-for impact if we don't set the right intention and see it reflected in our work.

Call it craft if that is where it fits in your comfort zone, but the evidence is clear that it should be recognized as art and science, as well.

2

IS CREATIVITY A TEACHABLE SKILL?

Creativity is intelligence having fun.
—Albert Einstein

When reading a good book, do you ever find yourself in awe of the creativity it took to devise the plot or create such complex characters? Which came first, the ending, a particular character, a specific event or crime? Or was it all built at once in an outline? I have a similar experience when following a complex knitting pattern. Stephen West of Westknits designs the most interesting shawl patterns I have ever seen, and as a teacher, I'm always impressed at how he creates the instructions to implement his vision, in an "explain it to me like this is my first knitted shawl," user-friendly kind of way. There are thousands of shawl patterns available to knitters online, many quite unique, and all were created using only two stitches, knit and purl. I can usually follow a set of well-written and illustrated instructions, but that doesn't mean I always understand the *how* of every pattern. *Sometimes, that is part of the fun on the journey. Look at that! How did my needles do that?* Is there something different going on in the brains of those who create? Is it a product of nature or nurture and can it be learned or taught?

Creativity is defined as:

- the ability to transcend traditional ideas, rules, patterns, relationships, or the like, and to create meaningful new ideas, forms, methods, interpretation, etc., originality, progressiveness, or imagination (Dictionary.com)

- the act of turning new and imaginative ideas into reality . . . characterized by the ability to perceive the world in new ways, to find hidden patterns, to make connections between seemingly unrelated phenomena, and to generate solutions (creativityatwork.com)

Words related to creativity, via Dictionary.com: talent, ingenuity, genius, resourcefulness, originality, imagination, cleverness, inventiveness, vision, inspiration. I have seen all of these words living in the actions of designers and makers in the craft world in which I exist, and I cite many of them for inspiration in this book.

I taught high school family and consumer sciences (FCS, a.k.a. home economics), a large tent covering subjects that included family living, dynamic living (life skills), food and nutrition, child development, home management and maintenance, consumer education, and fiber arts. Course names and curriculum changed regularly through the thirty-five years of my career to reflect the needs of our students and societal norms. By the end of the twentieth century, sewing was no longer considered a necessary skill because the cost of buying patterns and fabric became more expensive than buying clothing made for pennies in faraway places. Processed foods and microwaves made home cooking unnecessary. At the same time, both pursuits became "leisure arts" and outlets for creativity, with an entire media network created around food preparation, while a variety of crafts could be found on public broadcasting channels and YouTube. I have no doubt these advances contributed to the demise of FCS courses, but most of the blame goes to the testing obsession that invaded every school district in the nation, originating in the US Department of Education. The misguided belief that core subjects were all that mattered, and therefore electives should be related to math, science, English, or social studies, left precious little room in student schedules for traditional electives like art, music, or FCS. If we are teaching students how to pass a test, we are not teaching them to think or attempt to be creative. The required curriculum, designed to prepare for the tests, made it nearly impossible to teach thinking skills, no matter how creative the teacher.

Creativity was always an important component in the elective courses I taught, especially sewing and related types of needlework. Before beginning my teaching career, I worked as a home economist for a fabric store chain. We would often display an article of clothing made from a specific pattern on a mannequin, in a fabric that the company wanted to promote. And even though the fabric line came in several colors and print variations, the fabric used for the display invariably sold out first. I tend to do the same thing in yarn stores. We are faced daily with so many options for every decision we make, mundane or important, maybe seeing one option displayed is a relief. But, maybe in some cases, we simply lack the trust in our own creative process, which can get in the way of considering other possibilities.

In my last eight years working in the Cleveland school district, I was one of several teachers selected to work with high school students who were considering a career in

Maybe in some cases, we simply lack the trust in our own creative process, which can get in the way of considering other possibilities.

teaching. It was a state-supervised career-tech teaching professions program, which allowed students to explore college-level work that required a standard of reading, thinking, and creativity to which our students had seldom been exposed. It was the most productive and satisfying part of my career. I was teaching about teaching, and the students were interested, engaged, and involved with neighborhood elementary schools as teacher's aides and tutors, often teaching lessons provided and guided by local Junior Achievement offices.

In order to be considered completers in the program, students were required to create a portfolio of short essays based on areas in which they would need to show competence to become a teacher in our state. It was incredibly difficult for them to take their school and life experiences, apply them to the pedagogy of teaching, and get the right words from brain to paper. We were asking high school students to do college-level thinking. This process relied on a skill set that was new to them, involving creatively arranging words, making it seem like an impossible task until they had the opportunity and encouragement to try.

Testing aside, here is how I think we failed our students generally in public schools: by dumbing down the curriculum and stifling creative thinking. First, I must say, I worked with incredibly talented and skilled educators, as well as intelligent, accomplished students. In a large urban district like ours, many students, unfortunately, started kindergarten at a disadvantage, having reached that age living in poverty, and often found themselves on a very uneven playing field. Their access to free public education did not improve their outlook. Financial issues experienced by large public school districts meant overcrowded classrooms in crumbling buildings, with outdated books and equipment, along with unrealistic expectations for teachers who had to deal with factors beyond their control. This often resulted in using classwork to control behavior, keeping them busy to prevent problems. Group work and project-based learning that would allow creativity to flow could be very difficult to manage in an overcrowded classroom—and therefore was often avoided.

By the time they reached high school, most of my students (there were always exceptions) did not like to be asked to think or be creative. These were foreign concepts to many of them because they had so few creativity opportunities in school. When I required them to participate in state competitions by creating posters or displays on a chosen theme, I heard comments like "I'm not creative," "I've never been creative," and these assignments really seemed to stump them.

✕✕✕✕✕✕

On the question of whether creativity is a phenomenon of nature or nurture, as with most things in life, we realize that it is a combination of genes *and* environment. And, if environment is a factor, does that mean creativity can be taught?

George Land, a general systems scientist, author, and consultant, designed a creativity test for NASA in 1965 to help identify the most innovative candidates for jobs in engineering and science. NASA was very pleased with the results, so Dr. Land then decided to see what he could learn about whether creativity is a skill that could be learned. He applied the same test to sixteen hundred children, ages three to five, who were enrolled in a Head Start program. He retested the same children at age ten, and again at age fifteen. The results led Dr. Land to conclude that "non-creative behavior is learned."[7] In other words, the creativity is taught out of us.

- Test results among 5-year-olds: 98%
- Test results among 10-year-olds: 30%
- Test results among 15-year-olds: 12%
- Same test given to 280,000 adults: 2%

Every child is an artist. The problem is to remain an artist once they grow up. –Pablo Picasso

The Artist's Way, by Julia Cameron, a bestseller in the 1990s, linked creativity to spirituality, as a God-given gift (nature). Building on that concept with the tools of nurture, the author set up a twelve-week program designed to encourage creativity and develop imagination. One of the basic principles in *The Artist's Way* is that "creativity is the natural order of life. Life is energy: pure creative energy."

Michele and Robert Root-Bernstein wrote about their belief that creativity *can't* be taught, at least not directly, in an April 2011 post for their *Psychology Today Creativity* blog titled "Can Creativity Be Taught?"

We believe that certain habits, behaviors, and strategies associated with the creative process can be modeled in classroom learning. We believe that classroom curricula can promote and sustain nurturing environments for creativity. But we don't believe that creativity itself can be taught. Not directly.

This idea supports my observations that some of my students, given the time, materials, opportunity, and encouragement could sometimes tap into their inner creative genius. The Root-Bernsteins continued:

We believe that it is possible to teach almost anyone how to use carpentry tools or knitting needles . . . it is possible to teach people how to use the imaginative "tools for thinking" described in our book Sparks of Genius. *You can't make anything as a carpenter or as a knitter if you don't know how to use craft materials and implements. By the same token, you can't imagine and make a new and useful sort of sweater or a chair if you don't master the thinking tools that such creative outcomes require.*

This perspective on thinking tools and imagination illustrates the point I was making about fabric store customers seeing the sewing pattern made up on a mannequin and wanting to make an exact replica when there were so many other options and possible outcomes.

The main reason the Root-Bernsteins believe creativity can't be taught is that "creativity is not simply a set of skills . . . not simply a body of knowledge." They believe, as do I, that school districts need less focus on testing and more on opportunities to think, problem-solve, and create, whether they're learning to knit or designing a robot. In another *Psychology Today* blog post from May 2015, "Shop Courses, Crafts and Creativity," they recommend that "if society wants to foster innovative scientists and inventors, it will have to put those shop and crafts classes back into the curriculum." **THANK YOU!!**

And pandemically speaking, when the stay-at-home orders of March 2020 closed schools in most parts of the world due to COVID-19, classes suddenly went online, and traditional ways of teaching had to change. Sports and events like prom and graduation had to be cancelled. I was amazed and impressed to observe the way teachers, administrators, and students found creative ways to keep moving forward. I understood how disappointing it was. I taught public high school, and commencement was my favorite, if quite emotional, event of the year, partly because I knew how much some of my students had to overcome to wear that cap and gown and I was so very proud of them. But I was also honored and proud to be part of a profession that, when forced to teach from beyond the classroom, did their best to make it work, and their best was pretty damn awesome. Suddenly, those dreaded tests were necessarily cancelled, and teachers created lesson plans that covered the chapters and drill work, but also brainstormed creative ways students could learn at home by doing, using what they had available.

Kudos to teachers and principals who found creative ways to keep in touch with their students. The teacher who was supposed to run a marathon that was cancelled instead running past each of her student's homes as she covered those miles; the principal who visited each senior's home for a selfie and presentation (properly masked and distanced, of course); and the districts, like Cleveland, that equipped idle school buses with Wi-Fi and parked them in neighborhoods with public housing so students could log in and keep up with their work. But for me, the most impressive efforts came from the students themselves. Children making masks for front-line workers, high school seniors Zooming unique versions of prom, concerts, and group projects for school.

My daughter-in-law teaches fourth grade, and I know she struggled with the need to deliver education in this uncharted format. At least when the March 2020 shutdowns came, the teachers and students had been together face-to-face since the school year started, to develop those oh-so-important relationships. But she was not alone in longing to be in the classroom with all of her kids.

The 2020–2021 school year will, of course, be analyzed, criticized, and documented with data for years to come. It was not successful for everyone. I have only considered the topic of creativity here. I hope we address the fact that taking education online for everyone did not work for everyone, since not everyone had a computer or access to Wi-Fi. With other factors involved as well, where it failed, it failed big. That needs to be fixed! Despite attempts to provide a more normal school year, 2021–2022 got off to a rocky start in many districts. Strong disagreements over vaccines and masks created a new set of problems for staff, parents, and students. But ultimately, those who suffered most were the students. And isn't that always the predictable result? Adult problems = consequences for the children.

It may have taken a pandemic to notice what was wrong with the way we were delivering education in the traditional setting, and I'd like to think at least some of the ideas will go back with them to the classrooms when everyone returns to the new normal. And maybe . . . they'll forget to test them every month. *Shhhh!*

xxxxxx

Getting back to the subject of needlework, although some of us learned the skills from family or friends, some from classes, and some from YouTube videos, many of us can say we have learned in all these environments. That doesn't mean we can create something with sticks and string or needles and fabric without a pattern to follow.

I find myself in awe at the vast number of ways people find to be creative crafters and craftivists, linking their concern, passion, and intention to make a difference in someone's life, to reach out a helping hand and heart, amplify a cause, or fight an assault on the rights of others, confirming for me that they learned the skills first and were then propelled by their passion and determination to find and use whatever creativity may be needed to get there.

I find myself in awe at the vast number of ways people find to be creative.

3

IT'S ALWAYS PERSONAL

*Just because we enjoy doing something, it doesn't mean
we don't take it seriously or aren't really good at it.*

—Cathy de la Cruz, *Knitting for Good*

CRAFTERS TYPICALLY HAVE MULTIPLE WIPs (works-in-progress)—three to five, minimum. We may start a quilt, but need a break, so we start a hat to keep a homeless person warm. And much like a dog distracted by a squirrel—*"Oh, look, what a pretty yarn"*—we start something new to nourish our souls. And many crafters find we need something to manipulate in our hands as we watch TV, sit through a work meeting (especially a Zoom meeting), stand in line, or sit in a waiting room. Needles are our very productive fidget spinners. But our projects tend to become personal.

I look at something I've made and immediately feel the energy in that item that was generated by what was happening in the world or in my world as it was being created.

Most people involved in any type of needlework can tell you what was going on in their lives when they knitted that scarf or crocheted that afghan. Milestones in their lives, whether it involved witnessing birth, death, suffering, or celebrating—personally, remotely, with people they know, or with strangers on their screens—were made even more memorable to crafters by the project they worked on during that time. I offer a few personal examples here.

I have a large amount of soft, knobby white yarn, knitted into the beginning of a shawl, which I have not yet been able to finish or repurpose. When my mother was in a hospital in South Carolina and my sister and I went to spend what would turn out to be our last days with her, I knew I needed something to occupy my hands, heart, and mind, so I headed for the nearest craft store and purchased white yarn and knitting needles with the idea of making my mother a shawl. At the time we were hopeful she would be transitioning from the hospital to skilled care. Garnet was always the biggest fan of my work (more on that in a moment), although this project was as much for me as for her, a way of coping and a labor of love. She had been suffering through Alzheimer's for many years and seemed to know I was someone important to her but could not always come up with my name or my role in her life. Still, she always greeted me with love, and that had to be enough. She died before I could finish the shawl.

A couple of decades before the white shawl, as a young married woman, I completed a large, elaborately designed counted cross stitch portrait of a mother holding an infant. At the time, I was going through infertility treatments and decided that every stitch would be a prayer for a child of our own. After many failed attempts to conceive, we adopted two older children who were biological siblings and we became a family. But that cross stitch project, which sustained me through the agonizing infertility treatments, resulted in a stunning finished product that I gifted to my sister, mother of three, who had long admired it. It hangs in her home today, which makes me happy as well.

More recently, during the time that my grandson, at age nine, was beginning a three-year battle with leukemia, I was taking a quilting class at the University of Akron taught by a master quilter. Making a quilted wall hanging was a requirement for the class, and mine is full of sunflowers, with a very Tuscan vibe, and had no association to my grandson's illness. He is now a cancer-free teenager, but during a time when my heart ached for what he and his mom, dad, and little brother were going through, my thoughts, prayers, hopes, and fears traveled through my nervous system and flowed right into the fabric as I focused on one stitch at a time, one day at a time, knowing he was dealing with one pill at a time, one infusion, one side effect, one complication at a time.

Stitches have often been considered prayers in all cultures, especially on items like altar cloths or clerical garments. Working with fibers, textiles, and their tools can give us a more direct pathway to our hearts and minds than we usually experience.

As we live through significant moments in history, we may connect those events and moments to one or more handmade projects. What did your needles create during the COVID-19 pandemic, the Black Lives Matter protests, the 2020 election, or the insurrection that followed? What personal event in your own life was made more bearable or memorable with a project-in-progress?

xxxxxx

A second aspect of the personal nature of needlework is the *why*. Some people create with needles purely for the act itself. They need to be busy and find that making items to share with family and friends or to donate to those in need is a win-win endeavor, benefitting the recipient as well as the maker. While not mutually exclusive, others see their work as part of a legacy. We have looked at incredibly beautiful pieces of needle art and declared them so stunning that we are sure they will be family heirlooms, treasured and passed through generations. Rita's Quilt, which you'll read about in chapter 6, is an example of a legacy piece, although it took an unexpected and fascinating route to become one.

Somewhere in the mix of intentions regarding the *why* is the feeling for many crafters that the time and creativity put into a knitted sweater, for example, is not fully recognized by the recipient. There are basically two types of giftees. There are those who truly treasure the idea that you made something just for them and appreciate, even cherish, the handmade gift above the store-bought, even if, and sometimes because, they have no needlework skills themselves. The other type of recipient has no idea what went into the gift making. Not the planning that comes from an idea or concept, the sizing, finding the pattern, choosing fibers and colors, and the weeks, even months spent working on the item. Without that awareness, they may never be able to truly appreciate the effort, which is one reason I believe it's always personal.

On the other side of this coin, we can find our sometimes misplaced intentions. We may create what we perceive as a family heirloom, or an act of love and caring, that is not at all appealing to those we choose to gift. (Think bunny costume in *A Christmas Story*.) Tastes and preferences are also very personal, and we don't always read the room correctly. *I could survey my family and friends on this, but I don't think I'm ready to know, let alone share that data.*

xxxxxx

A third area of personal interest involves needleworkers, particularly knitters, who police movies and TV shows, on the lookout for their next project, and apparently more importantly, fake knitters. From *A Handmaid's Tale* to a John Stamos commercial, we know when you're fake knitting and when you're really knitting—you are not fooling us. Or maybe we could keep in mind it's acting and move on because I doubt there is a line item in most producers' budgets for a knitting consultant.

Wouldn't that be fun? (There are exceptions, including one we will soon see in this chapter.)

Since knitters rarely take on projects one at a time and usually have at least a mental queue of the next project, and the one after that, there is always room for another must-make. When we spot an actor wearing something that looks handmade we've been known to blow up the internet to find the pattern. And find it we will. If not, someone will soon replicate the design and post the pattern to fill that void. Katniss's one-shouldered wrap, spotted in *The Hunger Games*, was something I had to make for one of her biggest fans, my granddaughter. (In hindsight, I may have overestimated that "need," but I found it and I made it.)

Hunter Cowl by Diana Burk, available on Ravelry.

Outlander, *Little Women*, and other period pieces often tease us with knitted treasures. *Outlander Knitting: The Official Book of 20 Knits Inspired by the Hit Series* by Kate Atherley was published in 2020. *Harry Potter: Knitting Magic* by Tanis Gray was released the same year.

Fibreworkshop in the UK sometimes provides hand-knit items to be worn in movies. The shawl worn by Beth in *Little Women* (2019 movie) is one example and the pattern can be purchased on Ravelry. (www.ravelry.com/patterns/library/beths-shawl-3)

Beth's shawl pattern caught my attention for the bigger picture. The designer was happy with her small, but important, contribution to the authenticity of a film heavy with themes of feminism, creativity, and independence. But in the style of a true craftivist, this maker decided to use the pattern as a fundraiser for the Barefoot College Solar Mamas (www.barefootcollege.org/solution/solar/), "an international charity that trains women from rural communities to become solar engineers bringing light and power to their remote village communities." These incredible women, now operating in eighty countries and villages around the world, need more *light* on their efforts.

Beth's shawl in *Little Women*, 2019.

If you have found yourself paying more attention to what appears to be a handmade garment or accessory than to the actual storyline in your favorite television series, you may be interested in *Fandom Knitting and Crochet* (www.fandomknittingandcrochet.com) or *Fandom Knits: A Geek Driven Blog* (www.fandomknits.com). Go for the fandom and stay for the patterns, like a Dr. Who fez, a LOTR's smaug, baby Groot, or Sherlock's deerstalker hat. Brooke Ali at *Geek'd Out* (www.geekd-out.com) delved into the authenticity of colors and yarns used in the knitted garments in period pieces like the latest movie version of *Little Women*, with links to patterns.

Perhaps these are all just versions of product placement by the yarn industry, but even with that cynical view, would it be a deal breaker for the average knitter?

An extremely personal phenomenon in the world of those who engage with yarn is the curse of the boyfriend sweater. Knitters are not, by nature, superstitious types, but when this one is mentioned, cue the knowing look with the ominous background music. The curse claims that if you are in a relationship and you decide you care enough about this person that you want to knit your love into a sweater for them, it may well doom the relationship. In fact, the making of the sweater often lasts longer than the relationship. Many knitters have stepped forward with personal evidence attesting to this curse, which does not seem to apply to married people, but does also hold true for same-sex relationships. Alanna Okun wrote a book titled *The Curse of the Boyfriend Sweater: Essays on Crafting*, and the phenomenon is well documented in other books on knitting.

We could analyze this further and probably conclude that "relationships are complicated" and "look at the number that fail where no sweater making was involved," or we could lower the risk by respecting the curse, putting the sweater further down the to-do list, and making that special person a scarf or hat instead. *Just sayin'.*

✖✖✖✖✖✖

For a final perspective, there are those rare individuals who are called by their needles to take something completely impersonal and make it personal. When Lea Stern saw a small knitted green sweater at the *Hidden Children* exhibit in the US Holocaust Museum in Washington, DC, in 2003, she felt that she had a duty to find a way to replicate the sweater and share its amazing journey. The child-sized sweater once belonged to Krystyna Chiger who, in 1943, hid with her parents and brother in the sewers below the Lvov ghetto in Poland, avoiding transport to the Janowska camp and certain death. During the fourteen months the family spent in the sewers, barely surviving, aided by a city sewer worker who brought them food, Krystyna wore the sweater her grandmother had made for her. This child had already witnessed her grandmother taken away to the camp where she was killed by the Nazis, making the gifted sweater even more of a cherished treasure. The family, and the green sweater, survived, eventually settling in America, where many years later, Krystyna reluctantly donated her sweater to the US Holocaust Museum.

Original green sweater.

Green sweater recreated by Lea Stern.

The determined Stern searched extensively for the pattern with no success, but she was now on a mission, and with persistence she was able to see and study the sweater after contacting the head of textiles at the museum. What do you do when you want to replicate a knitted item but can't find the pattern? You reverse engineer it by studying the original, which is exactly what Stern did. She carefully studied the sweater, took extensive notes and pictures, and eventually re-created the pattern. Experienced knitters can imagine her search for the right shade and type of green yarn, and the many swatches made to get the correct gauge and finished size. Now it was personal—an act of humanity and a way to honor history. "The sweater talks about the war."[8]

In 2014, it became even more personal when Stern traveled to New York to meet Dr. Krystyna Chiger-Keren and share her completed mission. Stern presented her with a copy of the new pattern and let her choose from several test-knitted sweaters, the one that looked most like the original. Donating the sweater had been painful, but she was thrilled and grateful and told Stern, "Now I have my sweater back."[9]

If you would like to knit a bit of history, this pattern can be found on Ravelry. You can search for it on the Ravelry homepage as "the-green-sweater" or search for designer Lea Stern.

The pattern is also sold at the Holocaust Museum Bookstore, with proceeds donated to the museum. Since 2014, more than a thousand copies of the pattern have been sold, and Stern has received requests for adult-size versions of the pattern. In 2019, the *Times of Israel* summed it up nicely in a posted article, titled "Knitters Worldwide Recreate Sweater Worn by Girl Who Survived Holocaust in Sewer."[8]

I think the personal nature of crafting serves us well as craftivists. The issues and actions that most disturb our souls are observed and felt on a very personal, even visceral level. The skills we possess to take needles and fiber and use them to voice our concerns can be quite powerful for the *makers*. The hope is, always, that on another level what we make will inspire thought and action in others.

xxxxxx

I mentioned earlier that the biggest fan of my needle art was my mother. As part-owner in a counted cross stitch and framing shop during the 1990s, I stitched up many samplers to use as pattern promos in the store. When a pattern was no longer available, the framed example became ours to keep. After weeks of looking for one that I had stitched and was ready to hang at home, I gave up looking. Then on a visit to my parents' home, I discovered that my mom had "borrowed it" to show off her daughter's work. While I would have made an excellent, highly accomplished Early American wife, I take more pride in believing I now make a formidable craftivist. (And apparently my mother could have been an art thief.)

This sampler (the one my mother "borrowed") does not reflect the typical message of a cross stitch sampler, which, if including a message beyond the alphabet, numbers, and date stitched, would have likely been more biblical in nature.

This one drew my attention and time with a perfect description of my philosophy on needle arts. I regret I cannot credit the designer as I no longer have the pattern, but it was likely inspired by this Marshall McLuhan quote, found on What's My Quote (www.whatsmyquote.com):

Whence did the wond'rous mystic art arise,
Of painting SPEECH, and speaking to the eyes?
That we by tracing magic lines are taught,
How to embody, and to colour THOUGHT?

The sampler that got away.

4

A BRIEF HISTORY OF CRAFTIVISM

An interesting journey from stitching the internal to the external; a journey from the hearth to the collective voice of the world.

—Marjorie Agosín, *Stitching Resistance*

ART HAS OFTEN BEEN AN ACT OF PROTEST OR RESISTANCE. If you have something important to say but have no voice in society, you will look for a way to express yourself that people will be able to see, hear, and feel (tactilely, intellectually, or emotionally). Graffiti gave a voice to young, disenfranchised people throughout the world who felt no one was listening to them.

Throughout history (and herstory) the snail-paced evolution of the role of women in society forced many women to use more acceptable forms of communication, when their voice was not welcome in conversations regarding anything of importance in their lives. They still found ways to participate in important moments in history in interesting and relevant ways.

Knitter and author Betsy Greer popularized the term *craftivism* in 2003, after hearing a friend use it in a knitting circle. She was attracted to the concept that two terms with negative stereotypes, like craft and activism, could be a good fit. A few years later, in her book *Knitting for Good*, Greer talked about "the universal voice of craft . . . Craft can be a profound way to transmit messages and emotions across the globe when we cannot communicate verbally or through written word . . . Craft allows us to transform emotion into a tangible object . . . I can hold your dissent in my hands" (pp. 114, 115).

The journey from dutiful women creating needed wearables and home decor to today's craftivists has been a long road with many stops and starts, and even a few steps back occasionally, but craftivism now seems to have become part of the American lexicon.

War-Crafting on the Home Front

Wartime crafting was always conducted on two fronts—one at home, distanced from battles, and the other in the arena of war, which was also, often, someone's home. On the home front, *Little Women* reminded us that the US Civil War called those with needle skills to make and send socks, scarves, and mittens to soldiers (gray or blue), as well as to the families unable to obtain basic necessities once husbands, fathers, and sons went to the fight.

As American soldiers fought in Europe in World War I, socks were especially important because battles were being fought in cold, wet, wintry Europe and boots were not as waterproof as promised. This was a war fought predominantly by soldiers with boots on the muddy ground for months at a time. The American Red Cross took charge of the home front effort and promoted the idea that not only was it a patriotic duty, it was a way to reach across the miles to give endangered loved ones a piece of someone's heart from home, thus comforting and encouraging. Paula Becker wrote in a 2004 HistoryLink.org essay titled "Knitting for Victory—World War I" that "In the summer of 1917 the American Red Cross put out an urgent call for knitted goods and hospital supplies . . . their immediate need was for one and a half million each of knitted wristlets, mufflers, sweaters, and pairs of socks."

I doubt anyone could have avoided the ubiquitous Red Cross posters asking everyone to knit for the war effort. Had social media existed, everyone would have been sharing a meme that said "Knit for Sammie" (Uncle Sam). Men, women, and children were photographed knitting socks and scarves in public. Patterns and kits were created, and the response was so successful that wool yarn became scarce and led to more people learning to spin, even holding wool spinning competitions as big, patriotic events.

For those willing to knit but unable to afford yarn, the Red Cross organized donation efforts as a way for those who could afford it to provide the yarn for others to work up. Schoolchildren knitted simple washcloths, not only for soldiers but for residents of war-torn countries. Children were also encouraged to help with chores at home so their moms would have more time to knit, while men not involved in the fighting due to age or health issues picked up the needles as well, to do their patriotic duty.[10]

xxxxxx

Less than three decades later Pearl Harbor was bombed, and we were battling on two fronts in two vastly different parts of the world. During World War II, support from home became more complex, but knitting still played an important role. With posters declaring "Remember Pearl Harbor and purl harder," and the Red Cross again propelling the effort, this time in partnership with yarn manufacturers (a lucrative effort for the fiber industry), knitting again became a patriotic duty. Some crafters who'd learned to knit as part of the World War I support found themselves again answering the patriotic *Call to Needles*. The need for socks was still critical, as well as scarves, fingerless mittens (to allow access to triggers), toe and stump covers for the wounded, and miles of stretchy garter stitch bandages that were sterilized before being shipped to locations where they were most needed. Many used their needle skills to provide articles of clothing and comfort to citizens of our allies, like England and France.

By this time, we had become an industrialized economy with mass production in factories, and women stepped up and worked at the jobs all the healthy, able-bodied men had to abandon when they enlisted and were deployed to one of many fronts. This was a new way to support the war effort since many of these jobs involved the manufacturing of products necessary for the war, from Rosie the Riveter building planes and tanks to my mother working in a textile mill to provide nylon for parachutes or fabric for uniforms. That meant fewer knitters and less time for knitting, so those who could, and those who could be taught, tried to answer the new *Call to Needles*. The needed items could be, and were, manufactured for soldiers, but consider the psychological upside to the homemade versions. Many Americans had lived through the previous world war, so the request by the Red Cross was familiar—and there is always calm and comfort in the familiar. If everyone in their own way supported the effort, then that represented unity, patriotism, and hope. And a soldier receiving a hand-knit pair of socks might perceive them as much warmer and more comfortable than the manufactured version. Donated knitted items cost the military nothing and were more durable than machine-knit items. Even First Lady Eleanor Roosevelt was photographed knitting for the war effort.[11]

Crafting in Harm's Way

Closer to the action in times of war and turmoil (by choice or not), crafters, especially knitters, sometimes played courageous and dangerous roles.

The most iconic resistance crafter was fictional. In *A Tale of Two Cities*, by Charles Dickens, Madame Defarge is known for knitting through the French Revolution. She was the ringleader of the *tricoteuses* (French for "knitting woman"). In this Dickens tale, the term referred to the women who sat in witness to the public executions by guillotine, knitting as heads literally rolled. Banned from gathering together in public after a few too many protest marches, attending executions, needles in hand, was their work-around, as they still managed to publicly knit the red hats that became a symbol of the French Revolution. Readers in the late nineteenth century, when *A Tale of Two Cities* was published, were often shocked and offended by the portrayal of such radical women attempting to have a say in government matters, a reaction still often experienced by craftivists today. *(Think: conservative reaction to the Pussyhats.)*

Consider for a moment, the era Dickens was writing about. Opening the book with the line "It was the best of times, it was the worst of times" portrayed the disparity between the vast wealthy class and the even larger class of working poor, struggling daily to survive in the same city. In recent years in the United States, even before the election of Trump, we watched as the hard-earned progress of the middle class and unions slowly eroded, resulting in an under-protected working class, while the wealthy increased their wealth exponentially and the population of the working poor grew, becoming *a tale of two countries*.

Madame Defarge's anger, frustration, and drive for justice were fueled by the rape and death of her sister at the hands of the aristocratic Evrémonde brothers. She knitted a registry of those who should be executed for crimes against humanity. The names were "ingrained in the hippocampus" as well, but she was creating a fiber trail.* As part of the French resistance with her own

---

*When Christine Blasey Ford testified under oath at Supreme Court Justice Kavanaugh's Senate confirmation hearings about being sexually assaulted, that "ingrained in the hippocampus was the laughter" from her assailants, it had such profound resonance that I have chosen to honor her.

personal agenda of revenge and justice, "you might mistake her for just another well-behaved wife" knitting in silence (source unknown).

On the topic of well-behaved women in times of conflict, in an era when women's opinions were often not welcomed in any conversation, and men were making all the important decisions, colonial American women used the tools at hand as their voice. During the American Revolution women started weaving their own cloth rather than purchasing British-made clothing. Laura Sapelly wrote about this textile boycott in her dissertation *Pedagogies of Historical and Contemporary American Sewing Circles*.

In British occupied Philadelphia, in 1777, tavern owner Molly Rinker hid information about British troop movements inside balls of yarn. I can visualize her sitting on a rock overlooking a valley, pretending to knit, and—oops—dropping balls of yarn occasionally to General Washington's troops.[12] Even Betsy Ross, always pictured stitching our new country's new flag, could have been viewed as a craftivist.

Years later, answering another *Call to Needles*, sewing circles played an important role in abolition. William Lloyd Garrison wrote about their value in *The Liberator*, his abolitionist newspaper, on December 3, 1847:

> *Sewing circles are among the best means for agitating and keeping alive the question of anti-slavery . . . A friend in a neighboring town recently said to us, Our Sewing Circle . . . contributes very much to keeping up the agitation of the subject. Some one of the members generally reads an anti-slavery book to the others during the meeting, and thus some who don't get a great deal of anti-slavery at home have an opportunity of hearing it at the circle.*

If you paid attention in history class, you know that espionage played an important role in World War II, especially in Europe, but what may have been missing from the curriculum (one of many things!) was the lesson on how knitting was one of the more effective tools for spies of a certain gender. Some of it may be the stuff of legend, with no evidence to act as proof, but much is well documented. British secret agent Phyllis Latour Doyle used knitting as a cover to sneak information to the British after parachuting into occupied Normandy in 1944. Innocent chats with German soldiers harvested information that she then knitted into her work. As stated in Gyles Brandreth's *Writing Secret Codes and Sending Hidden Messages*, once Morse code was invented, it was observed that yarn or string worked well to transmit a message. "[A]n ordinary loop knot can make the equivalent of a dot and a knot in the figure-eight manner will give you the equivalent of a dash."[13]

Other codes were used, as well. Those to whom the mechanism of knitting was a mystery would never notice these hidden codes as anything other than part of the pattern, making knitting the perfect place to hide information in plain sight. Because so many people, predominantly women, were knitting for troop support, and since women were often marginalized and overlooked in wartime, they could often watch and listen unnoticed. Some counted trains while innocently knitting or sewing in a window, counting the cars into the stitches, tracking troop movements. Some listened in, unnoticed, to important conversations and reported what they heard to the Allies.[13] This type of activity was much more prevalent than stereotypical spy behavior and just as important. The concept of using the skills you possess to do what you could continued into modern times.

Suffragists and Feminists

There have been three rather distinct waves of feminism, beginning with the seventy-five-year-long suffrage movement demanding the right for women to vote as the primary issue. The main efforts were led by England and the United States. America kicked off its movement in 1848 at the first women's rights convention in Seneca Falls, New York. The Civil War saw a pause in this movement, but it resumed in 1876 and continued into the early twentieth century. Though the organizers were seeking a constitutional amendment, they also waged state-by-state campaigns. As a result, the first states to grant women the right to vote were Wyoming, Colorado, Utah, and Idaho, almost 30 years before it was eventually ratified by a total of 36 states, allowing for the Nineteenth Amendment to the Constitution to be adopted in 1920.

In England, the movement began in 1866, with fifteen hundred signatures on a petition delivered to Parliament requesting the right for women to vote. These efforts plodded along slowly until a more militant approach took hold in 1905. Much like American efforts, English suffragists won limited voting rights for women in 1918, and by 1928, most English women were able to vote. The two countries collaborated and shared ideas and approaches, but English women committed stronger acts of militancy than we saw in the United States.

One of the most effective and important tools for the suffragists was their needles. They weaponized their creativity and needlework skills. One of the common pushbacks from male lawmakers and private citizens was that women in the suffrage movement were trying to act like masculine men with their unreasonable demands. I admire the suffragists' decision not to feed that narrative, instead putting their careful, clever thought into their choices of clothing, colors, and the use of hand-sewn banners to be carried in marches. (See . . . *nothing masculine about these lovely women in their white dresses and wide-brimmed hats, adorned with flowers, carrying their colorful banners, made using traditional, acceptable female skills. Wink*!) Like so many efforts involving needlework through the ages, from sewing circles to quilting bees and arpilleras (chapter 10), these banners were typically made in group settings where the crafters shared common goals and a sense of community that unleashed their creativity and strengthened their resolve.

Clare Hunter of Sewing Matters, writing for *Processions* on the history of suffragists' banner making in

One of the most effective and important tools for the suffragists was their needles.

England, explains that women were always the banner makers, even when not the bearers, tracing these skills as far back as medieval dynasties. She discusses the thinking behind the banner efforts of the suffragists. Mary Lowndes, a stained glass artist supporting the women's movement, said: "Let us go and make banners as required, and let them all be beautiful." This quote echoes the lonely quiltmaker on the American prairie mentioned earlier in this book.

Mary Lowndes is also quoted as saying, with sensual overtones that reflected the very purpose of women's clothing at that moment in time:

> *A banner is a thing to float in the wind, to flicker in the breeze, to flirt its colours for your pleasure, to half show and half conceal a device you long to unravel.*[14]

New phrasing revealed the intent of the banners—"A new visual vocabulary," "deliberately made by hand," and "splendid, rich and beautiful." The banners carried through the streets by thousands of women were not purely requests to vote. That was the driving force, but the banners themselves and the statements made by the clothing that the banner bearers chose to wear described a narrative about their valuable contributions to culture and society. These creations attempted (quite effectively, I believe) to ask people to understand their hopes and dreams for their country and justified their desire to participate in their government in the most important way possible, with their vote.

For banners and "uniforms," suffragists chose a color scheme that encouraged the use of white for purity, purple and gold for loyalty and dignity, and green for long cherished hope. Women in both the UK and the US used their banners to speak their truths, with phrasing like "Deeds not Words," "Votes for Women," "Fortune Favors the Brave," "Blessed are the Peacemakers," and "Women Change the World." Their techniques included embroidery and appliqué, using fabric, paint, colorful threads, and even paper applied to fabric for emphasis.[14] Many of these banners live on in museums, taken care of like the treasured art that they are.

The year 2018 marked one hundred years since women won the right to vote in England with the passing of the Representation of People Act. Digital Drama, a multimedia company, working with museums, art organizations, and community groups in London, put out a call for interested crafters and artists to create one hundred banners to honor the suffragists' original banners. The request gave category suggestions that included heroines of suffrage, medieval style coats of arms, and associations that worked together for the right to vote. The modern tribute of one hundred hand-sewn banners was displayed at the March4Women in March 2018 and at other similar events that year. These banners can now be viewed in Royal Albert Hall, at the Women's Library, London School of Economics.[15]

xxxxxx

Before moving on, a reminder that the movement to obtain the right to vote for women was carried out mainly by white women of privilege. They persisted through the criticism, and worse, of family and friends, often facing arrest and torture at the hands of authorities. But in America, the ratification of the Nineteenth Amendment (which only addressed gender) did nothing to abolish state laws that kept Black Americans from voting, with only a few states standing as exceptions. That would not change until the Voting Rights Act was passed during the Johnson administration in 1965. And at the time of this writing . . . the fight continues for fairness in the American election process.

Post-War Crafting Intersects with Second and Third Waves of Feminism

My mother chose to leave her job at the textile mill when World War II ended to marry my father. But for many women, going back to the roles that women were expected to fill was not as easy, and as many as one-third remained in the workforce. That was especially true for war widows and women with older children, while young women focused on marriage and building a life around the family. After the horrors of war, people craved peace and normalcy, so during the remainder of the 1940s through the 1950s, suburbs evolved, soldiers pursued degrees with the GI Bill, businesses were created, and most of those factory jobs were reclaimed by our veterans. Unions grew their memberships and powered the emergence of the middle class.

Conformity may be the best word to describe the role of women in this new era, and they used their needle skills, in large part, not because they had to make clothing for their family or quilts to stay warm, but because it was deemed part of their role as housewives to create and maintain the nest, which sometimes meant knitting the matching argyle sweaters for father and son—an act of love and needle-worthiness.

The modern sewing machine became the new must-have, and companies like Simplicity and McCall's provided the motivation and creative input. Pattern companies expanded their line of products to include home decor, and with those versatile new sewing machines, a devoted homemaker could clothe the home in curtains, drapes, slipcovers, and tablecloths. Around the same time, needlepoint and crochet granny squares became very popular, now happily constructed in bright hues that did not involve military olive drab or navy blue. People still produced and donated warm items for those in need, but this was a time of gratitude and unity, not viewed as a time for activism, and most women understood that their role in the war effort had been essential but was now over. Nevertheless, no one could erase the feelings of empowerment so many women now possessed after keeping the American economy going during the war, and perhaps the seeds had been planted in the minds of many women that would put an expiration date on the role of a dutiful housewife.

If those seeds survived, they began to sprout during the 60s into a movement that represented the second wave of feminism. This was a time when women could not legally get a credit card *(I got my first one in 1974, but J.C. Penney required my husband's name on the account as well)*, serve on a jury, get birth control pills or make any reproductive decisions on their own *(my mother's obstetrician refused to tie her tubes after my younger sister's birth in 1963, even though that was her request)*, find equality in the workplace, or get an Ivy League education. And speaking openly about sex was taboo in most families and situations.

And then Betty Friedan wrote *The Feminine Mystique*, Gloria Steinem went undercover as a Playboy bunny, and Helen Gurley Brown wrote *Sex and the Single Girl*, helping launch the second wave of feminism, referred to as the women's liberation movement. The timing of the birth of this women's rights movement coincided with and blended in as a branch of the civil rights movement, with proximity to the antiwar movement, which likely brought women's issues more attention, respect, and credibility.

Needle arts, other than machine sewing, declined as they became associated with women who did not know their value as equals in the world of work or family life. Needlework was seen as the threads that bound rather than enlightened women. *("Ladies—you have more important things to do than sit there stitching.")* Those still wielding their needle of choice may have felt the need to be more discreet about the process or use it to make fashion statements, use it for charitable work, or relegate it to the proverbial grandma in the rocking chair.

The third wave of feminism began in the last decades of the twentieth century when modern feminists "sought to question, reclaim, and redefine the ideas, words, and media that have transmitted ideas about womanhood, gender, beauty, sexuality, femininity, and masculinity, among other things."[16]

Third wave feminists (typically Generation X, born in the 60s and 70s) stood on the shoulders of the women in the first two waves and in many cases were raised by them. Now the focus became more inclusive and focused on issues of gender, racial, economic, and social justice. If women were now able to be highly educated, successful, empowered badasses, that included the right to reclaim needlework, if that was their choice.

Women's liberation led to sexual liberation. The third wave of feminism also brought more attention to, and helped create a continuum of, gender definitions that tend to be more authentic and realistic. This most recent iteration of feminism also, rightfully, raised the bar in demanding the inclusion of people of color, Indigenous people, immigrants, and men as designers, makers, and teachers.

Many modern knitters credit Riot Grrrl, the 1990s feminist punk rock movement, for bringing knitting and other crafts out of the closet. Girl power meant girls choose and don't allow anyone's judgment to matter.

Needlework was seen as the threads that bound rather than enlightened women.

Modern knitters embraced the idea that one didn't need any particular artistic skills, or training, and encouraged the making of unique, one-of-a-kind objects. These personalized, clever, hand-crafted objects could be a message to reject mass production (creativity over commerce) and encourage engagement with small businesses, often woman or minority owned, that supplied fibers, patterns, and tools.[17]

In *Knitting for Good*, author Betsy Greer discusses how she reconciled her role as a feminist and activist with her love for knitting, when she learned the skill in 2000. At that time knitting was still "in the closet" it had been relegated to during the second wave of feminism. Greer wondered if she had found knitting or if knitting had found her. The book begins with a chapter titled "Reclaiming Craft" and includes vignettes by various and diverse artists with their views on the subject. Greer attests that as a Riot Grrrl fan, while the movement "opened my eyes enough to try new things and explore my creativity, it also rooted me even deeper in my feminist views." That helped her accept her own interest in knitting: "Knitting didn't make me a traitor to feminism; instead, I found myself able to connect with women of previous generations in a whole new way and celebrate their accomplishments" (p. 9).

Cathy de la Cruz, a filmmaker and podcaster featured in *Knitting for Good*, shares her thoughts on the subject. I strongly identified with this comment:

We can view our current continuance of knitting as something that keeps the creativity of our crafty relatives alive and thriving, because it not only allows us to better understand their lives (and society before machines ruled the earth), but also to honor "women's work." Our reclamation of the handmade is proof that these craft skills are valuable, worthwhile, and something to be proud of. (p. 15)

Stitch 'n Bitch: The Knitter's Handbook, published by Debbie Stoller in 2003, represented a more mainstream but feminist way of reclaiming the craft. With an opening chapter titled "Take Back the Knit," phrasing like "chicks with sticks" and "knitty-gritty," techniques and easy to understand patterns with names like "punk rock backpack," "big bad baby blanket," and "tank girl" quickly made it a bestseller. Another key to the success of this book was the inclusion of patterns by a diverse group of up-and-coming designers daring to veer away from the traditional four-ply standard yarn to have some fun with different types of fibers and colors. The success of Stoller's first book led to a series, with the publication of *Stitch 'n Bitch Nation* in 2004, *Stitch 'n Bitch Crochet: The Happy Hooker* in 2006, *Son of Stitch 'n Bitch: 45 Projects to Knit & Crochet for Men* in 2007, and *Stitch 'n Bitch Superstar Knitting: Go Beyond the Basics* in 2010.

If you are reading this, you may have answered your own *Call to Needles* for a cause you believe in or a need you wanted to help fill. My hope is that you will pause to consider your motivations, inspirations, and intentions, as I have. It is clarifying and empowering to do so. I have lived through the last two waves of feminism and have been using some form of needles and fiber through both. I have been knit-shamed, told I was too young to sit on the porch, knitting in a rocking chair. I have been referred to as "Needle and Thread" by colleagues rather than by my name when teaching high school home economics and told by people who mattered in my life that I was obsessed with that "hobby." So, personally, I am grateful to the most recent segment of the movement for being what Beth Ann Pentney, in an article called "Knitting and Feminism's Third Wave," written for *Third Space*, refers to as a continuum.[17] This is how I visualize that continuum: At one end are people using their craft in the way they choose, able to commit some of their time, income, and energy to the purchase of sticks and string or other craft materials. At the other end you can find the social justice warriors, using fiber art to build community, right a wrong, or as a more visual form of protest. Many of us can locate at several spots on this continuum, even at the extreme ends. For example, I was part of the Women's March in 2017, proudly wearing the Pussyhat I made. Since then, I have participated in several other craftivist projects, big and small. I can look for yarn bargains in a thrift store, or occasionally invest in a beautiful fingering weight wool for a project for myself. And all along the continuum you can find many of the people I write about in this book, committed to a cause and finding ways to improve someone's life. I'm finding that they all empower me to be proud of my choices and needle on.

My hope is that you will pause to consider your motivations, inspirations, and intentions. It is clarifying and empowering to do so.

Part II
5

MODERN CRAFTIVISM

Craft has the power to take down walls we may have spent generations building.

—Rachael Matthews, *The Mindfulness in Knitting*

Now that we have looked at a brief history of what is often called craftivism, if you aspire to be, or call yourself a craftivist, you should know that craftivism is now having a moment! I think the *Age of Trump* gets some of the credit for craftivism reaching a level of recognition and significance that has resulted in more people discussing, and sometimes disagreeing about, the definition. What craftwork qualifies as craftivism? What does not? Does it matter? Are these merely growing pains, or something more consequential? As an idea takes root and grows into a movement it should be open to a closer examination of the principles guiding it, the goals and desired outcomes, the process, and the people involved.

If these are growing pains, then, by definition, there will be pain, or at least discomfort, involved. As best practice, to keep the movement strong, united, and moving forward, we need to have conversations about whether particular acts of crafting qualify as craftivism. I participated in an online conversation in March 2021, hosted by the Fuller Craft Museum and moderated by Shannon Downey (**chapter 6**), called "Disrupting Craftivism: Reducing Harm and Creating Greater Impact." The driving force behind the panel of craftivists involved was the belief that the craftivism movement needs more exploration and vigor. You can watch the entire discussion on YouTube, and I believe you will find it thought-provoking. One of the panelists, Omkari Williams, writer, speaker, and host of the *Stepping Into Truth* podcast, believes we should be using craftivism to "advance a very specific social justice cause," and that means placing heavy emphasis on the activism component.[18]

The Pussyhat project was discussed as an example. If you made a Pussyhat, was that an act of craftivism? Probably not, unless you wore it to, and participated in, the Women's March. But, as you'll read in **chapter 6**, many people who could not physically attend the march made hats and donated them to those who could attend. These makers were encouraged to enclose a note for the hat's recipient, sharing the women's issue(s) that were most important to the maker. Craftivism assist?

A Wisconsin woman made Pussyhats and sold them online, donating the profits to Planned Parenthood. Now we're in craftivism territory! Pennsylvania yoga teacher Tracey di Paolo knitted herself a Pussyhat and decided that was only her first step. She then hosted a knitting circle after her yoga class for those who wished to make the hats. The classic "sewing circle" setting meant these crafters began discussing politics and community issues that concerned them. That group dynamic empowered them to start calling legislators and looking for other ways to participate and make a difference. They organized a community cleanup and raised funds for hurricane victims.[19] If the crafting inspires you to action and you then act, that seems like something that would qualify as craftivism.

A performance artist in Australia named Casey Jenkins sat in a gallery for twenty-eight days in 2013, wearing only a white sweater, knitting from a ball of white wool, which she had placed in her vagina, "to challenge the negative and fearful view of the femail [sic] genitalia."[20] An incredibly bold and fascinating act of protest art, and a way of amplifying a cause, but not craftivism.

A massive, crocheted banner, honoring Kamala Harris's memorable vice-presidential debate and made up of squares from 144 crafters around the country, was displayed in Washington, DC, in March 2021 as part of International Women's Day. The project was designed by self-styled yarn street artist London Kaye (www.londonkaye.com). This, too, was a form of protest art, or amplification, reminding us of the significance of the first female

Honoring the voice of *Madam* Vice President.

vice president, as well as the ongoing efforts of women to be heard. If a particular piece of statement art like this inspires someone to become active in women's rights efforts or run for public office, then can we call it craftivism? Maybe . . . It's complicated.

✕✕✕✕✕✕

I realize I have provided more questions than answers, so far. To move this conversation forward, it might help to think of craftivism as a continuum, similar to the third wave of feminism continuum (chapter 4). If we visualize craftivism this way, we provide space for a range in definition, with distinct extremes, as well as "softer," less intense, but important efforts. And let's try to distinguish craftivism from protest art, amplification of a cause, or acts of kindness, while acknowledging that there can be some overlap. I organized the chapters in this book, and created the subtitle, *Acts of Craftivism and Crafted Kindness*, in an attempt to do just that. But it is still complicated and, like so many other aspects of life, has so far resisted a generic, cookie-cutter approach to a specific definition beyond combining craft and activism.

We can think of one end of the craftivism continuum as the most targeted, direct acts, heavy on the activism, like wearing a Black Lives Matter hat that you made to a BLM march, or the Violet Protest squares in chapter 8 that were delivered to members of Congress, reminding them to do their jobs. At the other end of the continuum are the acts of *Crafted Kindness* related to a cause or issue the maker wants to draw attention to or support in some way. Between those extremes is the protest art—the work we put out in the world, in the hope we will inspire conversation or action when it resonates with someone's beliefs, causes them to reject a long-held paradigm, or creates a new activist. There may be a great distance between those points along the continuum, and that may be okay, as the discussion continues.

xxxxxx

One factor that can fuse our craft to our activism, or keep them separate, is our *intention*. Will our making change anything? Will it challenge people to reimagine their paradigms? Sara Trail, founder of the Social Justice Sewing Academy (chapter 8), believes in the power of upending the stereotypes of a traditional craft medium—quilting—to give disenfranchised youth a voice in the world. If we share our needle skills with those looking for a way to be heard, we empower them as craftivists and help them share their truth.

Sometimes subtle, sometimes obvious, people put their crafted work out in the open, on full display, with the intention of opening fact-based conversations, and by extension, minds and hearts, which can inspire action. The Welcome Blankets in chapter 8 might seem like merely an *Act of Kindness*, but the overarching intent of the project makes it craftivism, in my mind. The Yarn Mission in chapter 12 and the Knitting Nannas in chapter 6 draw curious people into their fiber "webs" and encourage discussions that they hope will lead to action for their respective causes.

It may seem that craftivism is populated only by those on the political left, but conservatives have participated in acts of craftivism. They often focus on the issue of most importance to them—abortion. In 2015, the Sisters of the Good Shepherd in St. Louis, Missouri, started a baby blanket ministry, ongoing as of 2021, collecting large numbers of blankets from crafters around the world, to be given to Birthright, an agency in St. Louis that gives the blankets to women receiving counseling from them about their pregnancies. The group's goal is to prevent abortions.[21] A similar effort was launched by a knitting group in Ottawa, Canada, in 2016. Its *Call to Needles* resulted in 6,978 baby booties, knitted, crocheted, and sewn, each representing fifteen abortions, displayed in front of Parliament on the eve of the March for Life in 2016. The booties were then distributed through anti-abortion pregnancy centers.[22]

You may have read about a number of designs created and posted at first on Ravelry, then on other sites, for Trump-supportive crafted hats and other items. However, today's craftivism seems to be predominantly carried out by more progressive-thinking crafters.

The *approach* used is another factor for craftivists. The Pussyhats sent an obvious, visual message, even if misinterpreted by some, but craftivists can, and often do, take a softer approach, which should not be interpreted as weaker or less effective. On the contrary, Sarah Corbett of the Craftivist Collective is a lifelong activist who discovered that "crafts, made in combination with a strategy that uses deliberate focus, principles of neuroscience, and positive psychology can be an effective collaboration" that she refers to as "gentle protest."[23] Intention becomes motive when Corbett encourages her craftivists-in-training to set aside ego in order to ensure pure and selfless motives, using nonviolent language and nonconfrontational methods. I believe the following statement from Corbett reinforces the idea that craftivism is a broad continuum and can have more than one definition:

> *I worry about whether what we do is making a difference but I know we contribute to long term change not short term solutions & others are doing other great work too that we try to complement rather than compete with (like charities and issue-led campaigning organisations). It's a good healthy concern.*[23]

Corbett's craftivist workshops "always start with our craftivism methodology (using craft as a *tool* to do slow, gentle and joyful activism), discussing what messages we are going to stitch and why, using instrumental music to help us silently meditate and then discuss our critical thinking."[23]

Among Corbett's successes was a campaign to compel one of the UK's most iconic department store chains, Marks & Spencer, to pay its employees a living wage. Fourteen board members became the target audience, each matched with a craftivist who researched their board member, looking for the most compelling approach. Handkerchiefs purchased from Marks & Spencer (now the craftivists were concerned customers) were embroidered with phrases carefully selected by each craftivist for their recipient. The finished hankies were enclosed in individual gift boxes, each with a personal letter, and an information sheet on the living wage. This effort was rewarded with slow, steady inroads, and finally, a commitment to raise the wages of employees. Getting to a sustainable living wage took further efforts, but this group of craftivists did not give up.[24] A marathon, not a sprint. You can learn more about Sarah Corbett and her Craftivist Manifesto on the Craftivist Collective website or from her books *A Little Book of Craftivism* and *How to Be a Craftivist: The Art of Gentle Protest.*

In the spirit of craftivism as gentle protest and an often painfully slow road to success, I share another example. When Hinda Mandell (*Crafting Dissent*) was conducting research and putting up yarn installations on statues of agitators and reformers in Rochester, New York, where she lives and works, she discovered that the home and Underground Railroad site belonging to abolitionists Frederick and Anna Douglass had become a parking lot. Installing her crafted "yarn-balmed" (see **chapter 6**) messages in various parts of the lot was not only her *Call to Needles*, but also her call to action, leading her to work with the city to get a proper historic marker installed on that site, making her an activist as well. After the plaque was installed she left "a crocheted North Star at the base of the pole to acknowledge Douglass's North Star antislavery newsletter and the fiber assist in getting the plaque installed" (p. 107).

xxxxx

An additional factor to consider, along with intent and approach, is the typical crafter persona. Many crafters are, by nature, introverts or highly sensitive people. Those of us who check those boxes may find it between difficult and impossible to challenge someone's fears or prejudices with facts and logic in a "let's talk about this" kind of way, but feel empowered letting our needles speak for us. Rachael Matthews wrote about this in *The Mindfulness of Knitting: Meditations on Craft and Calm*:

> *Caring deeply about the world, creatives do not always want to be caught up in the noise or violence that fighting for justice can generate. Craftivism can be a soft, quiet protest, where producing thoughtful designs helps deliver a deep message. (p. 83)*

That empowering voice can often encourage and nudge us to take the next step as an activist, working toward meaningful change and reform.

As a white woman who came of age in the 1970s, I can attest to the ways we were discouraged from appearing impolite or controversial or confrontational. A strong, assertive woman was often labeled a bitch, while those same qualities made a white man someone to admire. That conditioning began at home, was reinforced in school, then followed us into the workplace, where most authority figures were white men. We cannot be successful allies in the fight for equity for all if we can't overcome the lifelong gaslighting that taught us we were helpless.

As the examination of the term craftivism continues, I encourage you to think about what the term means to you and to participate in its evolution. Americans tend to expect quick fixes, immediate answers, promoting a "go big or go home" attitude. But small acts add up. Don't ever feel your efforts are too small to matter. Remember that one drop in a pond creates ripples than can expand outward for a long distance. It took decades to divide us so dramatically as Americans, and it will take a long time to fix what's broken. So, as you turn these pages, think about where you fit on the craftivism continuum, and how you can be part of the change you wish to see. What compels you to be an activist or a craftivist? Once you've examined that, it might help you find a way to get involved and, maybe, more importantly, sustain you through the process.

In the meantime, let the discussion and growth continue to move us forward and make sure we leave

Many crafters are, by nature, introverts or highly sensitive people.

no one behind on this journey. Sandra Markus interviewed Hinda Mandell for her dissertation *Through the Eye of the Needle: Craftivism as an Emerging Mode of Civic Engagement and Cultural Participation.* Mandell acknowledged that "Craftivism is re-emerging as a viable force within the political landscape . . . yet . . . needs to be problematized." She believes that the many ways crafters responded to their feelings about the Trump presidency gives us an "opportunity to learn how craft creates community as women stitch together a tapestry of politically engaged voices. Yet whose voices does it capture? Whose voices does it shut out?"[25] These are important questions, worth researching and answering.

And will white crafters be willing and able to set aside our privilege and look honestly at the issue of inclusion?

> Why are most modern craftivists left of center on the political spectrum? According to Hinda Mandell in *Crafting Dissent*, it "may be that women on the Left, who may possess baseline knowledge of the various waves of feminism dating back to the early twentieth century, may also be more comfortable using craft as a means for political expression—or to apply political ends to handicraft" (p. 5).

6

RESISTANCE CRAFTING

Going to a protest or calling your local politician is no longer the only way to raise your voice.
—Sayraphim Lothian, *Guerrilla Kindness*

THE CONCEPT OF RESISTANCE CRAFTING IS NOTHING NEW, but a growing movement has come out of the shadows of the more extreme and subversive elements, and today seems more mainstream. The Pussyhat project was the type of event that may have helped push craftivism into the spotlight in the *Age of Trump*. Suddenly, women from a wide range of demographics, who, like me, spent most of their lives attempting to fit in with societal norms, were creating and wearing pink Pussyhats to a protest march.

For now, there is no penalty for speaking our truth through our crafts. Freedom of speech covers all types of creative efforts, unlike the times that forced a slave to hide a message in a quilt, or a Chilean arpillerista to disguise her plea for help as a message embedded in a colorful wall hanging. We tend to put our messages in plain sight now because we can do so without fear of anything worse than being unfriended or attacked on social media.

Protest is Patriotic

The education division of the Smithsonian Institution created a tool for teachers on protest and patriotism that mentions in the introduction that "protest is often seen as dissent." It goes on, though, to say:

> *Many of the changes that were wrought by these movements have altered America for the better. In many ways, protest should be revered rather than feared. Struggling to improve America by protesting and reforming its flaws is often an act of conscience and love. In this light, protest should be seen as the highest form of patriotism.*[26]

Baby boomers, born between 1946 and 1964, came of age during the civil rights movement, the second wave of feminism, and the Vietnam War. I share part of my journey here, because again, I believe it was not unique and that many can identify with my experiences. I was in high school when Martin Luther King Jr. and Robert Kennedy were assassinated. Protest was going on all around me, but having been raised a "proper little miss" (according to a friend) and insulated in a home where discussing ideas, philosophy, or politics was not a common occurrence, my biggest struggles involved planning for college in a home where no one understood why I thought I needed college. *"Ok, if that's what you really want to do, but it will have to be a state school because that's all we can afford." Translated from parent-speak: That's all we're willing to allocate, because—girl.* We rarely traveled for vacations, and when we did it tended not to go well, because there was never any planning involved. So, I was quickly shut down when I wanted to go to England on a high school educational trip. My father always said he had seen the world during the war and had no desire to see any of it again. My world was intentionally kept very small and overprotected. That was how they loved me.

There was no specific event or moment of enlightenment. It was more like a file stored somewhere in my brain, full of shocking, concerning, or enlightening events, expanding over time. I would define myself as an apprentice to the social justice warriors in the late sixties. I remember feeling inspired by President Kennedy's speeches and wanting to join the Peace Corps after high school. But my parents never gave me the wings to fly that far from the nest. I don't remember if they talked me out of it or if I gave up that dream out of fear and a weak reserve of self-confidence.

Authoritarian parents can control where you are, your exposure to new ideas, and what you say in their presence, but they cannot keep outside influences from seeping through the cracks in the walls they built, and they cannot control a brain and a soul looking for more logical answers. Our high school literary publication, the *Plume and Parchment*, published our better efforts at writing assignments each year. A piece I wrote in English class was selected in 1970, when I was a high school senior.

Most of us involved in protest are attempting to bring attention to causes and issues that we strongly believe will improve the lives, livelihoods, health, and well-being of individuals, groups, or our democracy, generally. We are not anarchists, trying to overturn an election, destroy our government, or execute anyone, based on misinformation and intentionally placed disinformation. It was clear that many, many Americans were not happy with the results of the 2016 election. We didn't join in attempts to overturn the election results—we made pink hats, wore them to DC and walked around peacefully, chanting "This is what democracy looks like." Then we went back home and worked on the next election and the one after that, as the Founding Fathers intended. Just sayin'.

Once....
Her beauty surpassed that of all others.
She could be delicate and tender as a Kentucky hillside covered with spring flowers;
Or fierce and daring as a jagged cliff hanging over a raging river.
She was wild and free with a beauty that was almost frightening.
She had the ability to radiate a special feeling to everyone she met—
A feeling of hope and faith and an intense will to be as free as she.
 . . . . .
Now she is old.
There are traces of beauty left on her face;
But stronger are the lines of worry and strain.
 . . . . .
Problems brought about by greed and prejudice have slowly destroyed her.
The feelings of hope and faith and freedom she once inspired
Have changed to feelings of doubt.
Her arteries have grown hard and polluted with the wastes of years of hard work.
 . . . . .

Looking back at this now, in all its corniness, makes me proud. I spared you the entire piece and shared about half, and, of course, I reveal at the end that *her* name is America.

Ensconced in that paradigm after high school, my failure to join the Peace Corps was rechanneled into work with those committed to ending poverty and prejudice. Gandhi's directive to "be the change you wish to see in the world" became my mantra. The problem was . . . how? The inner city, a distinctively 70s term, became my focus, and my parents were stunned and worried when I took a teaching job in the Cleveland Public School District after college. They scraped and saved to get us out of what they perceived as the dirty, dangerous city. And there I was.

When reality collided with my inspiration from movies like *To Sir With Love* and *Up the Down Staircase*, I dug my high heels in and refused to give up. It quickly became apparent that no one wanted or needed me to rescue them. I began my teaching career in 1976 in an all-Black high school before desegregation, and my first non-teaching assignment each day began with another female teacher and me emptying a massive girl's restroom when it was time for homeroom. Humor and grit were our most effective tools. The best educational advice I ever received came from a principal who told me "your students won't care what you know until they know you care." I loved my job, I loved my classroom, and I loved my students, but it was a rocky start to my dream career—I was trying to fit into their world, quite different from mine, and my good intentions meant little to them.

The moment I knew I was where I was supposed to be? I always believed it was important to move around the classroom and not plant myself behind a desk. But one day, in my second year of teaching, attempting to appear taller than 5'2", my high heel slipped, and I went down, fast and hard, disappearing behind my desk. Total silence followed, until I popped back up, giggling in embarrassment. My students had waited to see if I was okay, and they looked for a clue that it was okay to laugh at what had happened. Then the laughter and comments poured out. That felt like acceptance and respect. Now I could teach! *And I remain eternally grateful this happened before smartphones and TikTok.*

Teaching gave me a sense of living and sharing my values. Now that I am retired, I realize there was so much more activism I could have taken part in outside the classroom. I didn't participate in any form of protest until January 2003 when a colleague and I rode a bus to Washington with a group from our area to protest the invasion of Iraq, with people from all over the country. One attendee at the 2003 protest against the Iraq War was Jo Freeman, an American feminist, political scientist, writer, and attorney. Her reflections on the anti-war effort encapsulates the sometimes maddeningly slow progress made with protest and dissent:

> *Protest by itself won't change policy . . .*
> *But protest, especially mass protest, cracks the facade of consensus.*[27]

Much like when a woman who ran for president made some serious cracks in a certain glass ceiling, creating a path for Madam Vice President Harris. As a craftivist, I was encouraged and inspired to see Freeman's comment that "the strength of American democracy is that there are many ways of making our voice heard."[27]

I repeated that overnight bus route on January 20, 2017, to participate in the Women's March the next day. Waking up for a potty and snack stop about 5:00 a.m., as we approached the Washington, DC, area, I looked out the window as our bus corkscrewed slowly around the exit ramp and all I could see in front of us or behind us was charter buses. That was the moment I realized what an amazing event this was going to be and how glad I was to be involved. Some of the coverage portrayed the participants as loud, mean, angry, and messy, leaving a stain on the capital. But I was there, and no one can take the truth from us. It was massive, it was peaceful, and it was powerful. The chants, so many pink hats, families and men supporting the effort, and lordy, the signs!—so clever, so inspired, so resolute, and so grammatically correct!

A favorite author of mine, Barbara Kingsolver, wrote an op-ed for the *Los Angeles Times* in the drive to war after 9/11, titled "And Our Flag Was Still There." It is included in her book of essays titled *Small Wonders*, and I found her words timeless. The op-ed was her attempt to remind people who felt it was dangerous and treasonous to question American leadership in challenging times that it was her flag as much as it was theirs and that it was dangerous to democracy *not* to ask questions.

> *It is precisely in critical times that our leaders need most to be influenced by the moderating force of dissent. That is the basis of democracy, especially when national choices are difficult and carry grave consequences. The flag was never meant to be a stand-in for information and good judgment. (p. 238)*

I encourage you to read the last sentence again and think of all the Trump flags you've seen—and all of the American flag-waving insurrectionists who invaded the Capitol in January 2021.

Those of us with needle and fiber skills have always found creative ways to participate in democracy, protest, and dissent by channeling our anger and frustration into our own, unique voice—what Betty M. Bayer referred to in *Crafting Democracy* as our "texturized voice" (p. 2).

The Pussyhat Project

It would be difficult to explain the concept of craftivism to anyone without bringing the Pussyhat phenomenon into the conversation. The pink hats with the little ears became so iconic after they debuted, like pink sprinkles on top of the massive Women's March in DC the day after Trump was inaugurated, that the hat itself made the cover of *Time* magazine.

The idea for a protest hat was conceived in the brain of Krista Suh, a new and passionate knitter, feminist, artist, and screenwriter with a background in film and event producing. She took her idea and built a team that included Kat Coyle, a Southern California designer and

The Women's March, January 21, 2017, Washington, DC.

owner of the Little Knittery, who created the pattern for the hat; Aurora Lady, the illustrator; and cofounder Jayna Zweiman, also featured in this book, who had the expertise needed to launch the project.

Why call it a *pussy* hat? It was a way to take back some of the power in Trump's comments on the *Access Hollywood* bus that should have been a deal breaker for America. Krista's own words in her book *DIY Rules for a WTF World*, make a more important point:

> *I also loved that using the word pussy was a reclamation of feminine intuition, something that has been much maligned in our culture, probably because it is so powerful. When women embrace intuition, they can change the world . . . The more we remove the patriarchal voices in our heads, the more we can hear our intuition speak its truth . . . the intuitive voice is never the one that speaks out of fear. (p. 19)*

In case you were wondering why a feminist on a mission would intentionally choose pink, it was all about reclaiming a color associated with women, and therefore weakness, turning it into something strong and resolute.

The pattern was kept simple enough that it could be made in a short amount of time by anyone with basic knit or crochet skills. Some adapted the idea to be sewn using fleece. The hat is simply a rectangle, folded in half and seamed, and when placed on our roundish noggins, the ears appear. Many people made more than one, and hats were made by people who could not physically be part of the march and given to others to wear, helping create that sense of community and networking so important in this type of effort. Over twelve thousand contributed hats arrived at the home of a volunteer family in Virginia to be distributed at the march. Others were collected by yarn shops throughout the United States and beyond, for local marches. And that's how you organize a movement!

Creating community, worldwide.

You were introduced to Hinda Mandell from the Rochester Institute of Technology in chapter 1. Mandell and Juilee Decker put out a call for what Mandell often refers to as "craft activism," looking for submissions created after 2015. They then curated an exhibition of thirty works (from over one hundred submitted), documented in their book *Crafting Democracy*. The Pussyhat was part of the exhibit. In her latest book, *Crafting Dissent*, Mandell has what I think is the perfect metaphor for the Pussyhat:

The image of tens of thousands of women busying their hands in protest to craft dissent contrasted with a different image: Trump's hands representing a symbol of misogynistic and abusive behavior, grabbing what he deemed was his without concern for the women whose bodies he believed were subject to his wants and whims; yet for women politically opposed to Trump's behavior and political agenda, their hands became the tools to craft (wearable) protest. (p. 4)

The Pussyhat project was definitely my *Call to Needles*. I managed to complete four hats (a modest act, compared to what many crafters accomplished), one of which I gave to a young girl on our bus to DC who was admiring them and wishing she had one. Participating in this bit of history introduced me to my inner craftivist and compelled me to look for more ways to participate, and I don't think I'm alone on that island. Mandell believes that the Pussyhat project "sparked an outpouring of politically motivated craft activism. It was if someone turned on the craftivism faucet full force" (*Crafting Dissent*, p. 4).

In case you missed it, there was a great deal of pushback as the Pussyhat project went public and gained momentum. Some, who took the name literally, found it vulgar. Some talking head conservatives, missing the point as usual, wondered publicly why any woman would want to wear a vagina on her head. Many yarn shops hosted group stitch-ups to make the hats, while other shops refused, one even refusing to sell pink yarn to anyone if making a Pussyhat was the plan.[28] *Did your eyeballs just roll? My eyeballs just rolled!*

This comment from Krista Suh on the value of the work that went into the making of so many of the hats validated our *Call to Needles*: "Creativity, craftivism and yes, knitting are the antidote to patriarchy because they prove to and remind people that there are many ways to do something. The way that you, as an individual, choose to do it is valid."[28]

Rather than resting on their laurels after the Women's March, the Pussyhat team found three ways to support the resistance by supporting similar fledgling efforts through their website, www.pussyhatproject.com:

- As a resource hub "for all aspects of women's rights"
- Using donations, they offer grants and scholarships to support ideas from people of all ages and education levels
- A design incubator—where ideas can be considered, enhanced, and encouraged. This is where the Welcome Blanket project from chapter 8 was born
- Early in the COVID-19 pandemic this incubator hatched a mask making effort called Masks for Humanity, discussed in chapter 11

Yarn Bombing

You may have seen a public yarn bombed object, perhaps a tree or a sign pole wrapped in knitted or crocheted colorful yarn. But what was the purpose and where did it begin? Why would anyone put that much effort into a garment to be worn by an inanimate object? Often compared to graffiti done with fiber instead of paint, it does

Yarn bombed examples spotted in Mississauga, Ontario, Canada.

tend to get your attention. I took these pictures when visiting friends in Mississauga, Ontario, near Toronto. These certainly don't seem like acts of resistance, so . . . ? Think of yarn bombing as a way to resist by reclaiming.

The yarn bombed bicycle seems like a great recycling idea, while adding contrasting colors and a softness to the concrete pier. Even its shadow is interesting.

Two reclaiming objectives seem to be at work in yarn bombing. Public places have predictably, and perhaps necessarily, become rather sterile and not as public as we would like. There is often little that allows us to feel that these public spaces really belong to us, so yarn bombing an immovable concrete or steel structure can bring about a softness and beauty that wasn't planned by the designers or builders, and at the same time acts as a reminder that *we are* the public. It is also a way to reclaim those skills that were relegated to the hobby realm to deliver a message in a new and clever way, whether a subversive motto, an act of loving kindness or simply artistic expression. The surprise of seeing a statue or public object covered in yarn, creating an unexpected burst of color and texture, is the desired effect.

It is often difficult to trace the origins of a technique or idea to a specific spot in time and place. But modern yarn bombing in the United States seems to have originated in Houston, Texas, in 2005 when Magda Sayeg covered the door handle of her boutique to soften the look of the stark metal. It received so much attention and interest that Magda began to consider other places that could use a little yarn treatment. She tried covering signposts and fire hydrants. As with so many discoveries and achievements, big and small, she didn't set out to create a movement, but there was soon a "global community of yarn bombers."

I recommend watching Magda's TED Talk on her role in, and thoughts on, the evolution of this technique. I especially enjoyed her thoughts on "the hidden power of the craft," and her realization that she may have started the concept but no longer owns it.[29]

Another pioneer in yarn bombing is Lauren O'Farrell, a.k.a. Deadly Knitshade, an English author, artist, and graffiti knitter. Her attempts began with installations of yarn that told stories, often using amigurumi (little knitted dolls). She coined the term "yarnstorming" in 2007 as a "softer, squishier term, created as an alternative to the more violent and destructive sounding 'yarnbombing.'"[30] One of her books, *Knit the City: A Whodunnknit Set in London*, penned under her Deadly Knitshade persona, tells the story of the crafty ninjas who stealthily covered many London landmarks in yarn. Two other books by O'Farrell, *Stitch New York* and *Stitch London*, both subtitled *20 Kooky Ways to Stitch the City and More*, provide patterns for iconic landmarks like the Empire State Building, along with strategies for displaying them.

While we're on that side of the pond, a yarn bombing group in southwestern England used to meet every two weeks to plan their yearly fiber display trail between the villages of High Littleton and Hallatrow, near Bristol. They had to meet virtually during their fourth year, 2020, due to the pandemic. And as we saw so often during this crisis, creativity rose to the occasion, making the display more child-oriented in a year when the model for education had been turned upside down. The theme was book titles; more specifically, twenty-five clues to (mainly) children's books. Try to imagine the number of stitches from various types of needles, the time and energy and creativity that went into this endeavor that had no patterns or templates. The display was open for three weeks and then taken down, hopefully to be moved into schools or libraries.

This creative group's 2021 protocol was similar to 2020 since the pandemic was still a factor. The theme was A–Z animals, which brightened the village (and its residents) for the time it was displayed.

The 2020 Fiber Trail between High Littleton and Hallatrow, UK.

Yarn bombing is usually done by knitting or crocheting, and books and sites online are full of ideas and inspiration, but it tends to be more of a custom, DIY technique. In her book *Guerrilla Kindness & Other Acts of Creative Resistance*, author Sayraphim Lothian includes detailed instructions for starting with an easy project to cover a pole, with an optional add-on that reads #METOO.[31]

A simple search of the internet will reveal yarn bombing ideas ranging from simple to complex, from art to directed messaging.

The Chinatown Yarn Circle Project STAND-SPEAK-SHAPE was created by a group of New York City crochet yarn circles, partnered with artist Naomi Lawrence and Chinatown organizations called Think!Chinatown and Creative Sanctum, to bring more awareness to issues that impact the Asian American and Pacific Islander (AAPI) community.[32] In the *Age of Trump*, unwarranted and disturbing levels of hate and violence were directed at these Americans over the origins of COVID-19. A yarn mural made of fifteen hundred crocheted flowers was installed at Columbus Park in New York City during the summer of 2021. You can see the mural at instagram.com/chinatown-yarncircle/. To my mind, these flowers will not convince the haters and purveyors of the emotional and physical violence against the AAPI community to see the errors in their thoughts and actions, or to change their behavior. But it reminds the rest of us—a much larger share of the population—to pay attention and act, whenever and wherever possible, in unity, and if necessary, in defense of those unfairly attacked, while acting as a proud statement on the beauty of diversity.

Philadelphia has strong street art energy that includes yarn bombing as one medium. City leaders decided to embrace these contributions to the cityscape as a tourist attraction. The Convention & Visitors Bureau's "Discover Philadelphia" blog describes an "active artist community that continually adds to its yarn art collection" (www.discoverphl.com/blog/philadelphias-street-art/). One of the main contributors is crochet installation artist Nicole Nikolich of Lace in the Moon (www.laceinthemoon.com/#/). Teaching herself to crochet and discovering the potential of that technique led Nikolich to begin installing modest, whimsical yarn bombs around Philadelphia, where she lives, eventually building a business around the concept. She "creates mural-sized installations for clients in the U.S. and abroad."[33] My personal favorite is the yarn bombing of an exact replica of the Liberty Bell in 2021 for the *Craftivism* exhibit at the National Liberty Museum.

Yarn bombed replica of the Liberty Bell, National Liberty Museum, Philadelphia.

You can watch a video of the installation on Instagram @lace_in_the_moon. Nikolich's artist statement for the exhibit includes the following:

> *Street art is the ultimate display of liberty and justice because it makes art accessible to all . . . My crochet-transformed Liberty Bell is a*

contemporary symbol of the fight for equality. By wrapping a historic artifact in a piece of public art, I am creating a reminder that everyone belongs in America. Using bright colors and textures, I'm calling on people to be bolder, louder, and more unapologetic when standing up for rights for all.[34]

×××××

Yarn bombing is featured in the award-winning documentary film *YARN*, highlighting artists using needle skills to "bring yarn out of the house and into the world" (www.yarnfilm.com).

Hinda Mandell, in *Crafting Dissent*, uses the term "yarn balming," suggested by Professor Sarah Kuhn from the University of Massachusetts. Balming is "a more soothing representation that sees yarn as providing remedy to social challenges, in contrast to the popularly phrased . . . 'yarn bombing'" (p. 96).

Everyone is a critic when it comes to art, and yarn bombing, yarnstorming, or yarn balming are not immune. Enthusiasm for an effort can so easily overcome logic and common sense that even with the best intentions, we sometimes cause unintended harm or cross ethical lines. Covering tree trunks in a knitted sleeve may not take trunk growth into account and can even cause changes in the natural habitat of the tree.[35] So, if you decide to use this technique for your activism, do your due diligence in terms of understanding the environment you are about to impact, because our motives are pure—let's be sure our actions are, as well.

The Kudzu Project

In 2018, the US Department of Arts and Culture invited artists and other interested parties to participate in A Week of Creative Action, with Dr. Martin Luther King Jr.'s words in mind.[36] Artist Dave Loewenstein created a series of sketches titled Defunct Monuments that included a tank (representing militarism), the Wall Street bull (materialism), and a Confederate monument (racism), all covered in kudzu vines, a particularly invasive type of weed found mainly in the American South. Kudzu is a quick-growing climbing vine that creates a thick carpet, eventually blocking out the sunlight. What an appropriate choice to choke the life out of a defunct monument.

×××××

The horrific Unite the Right two-day rally in Charlottesville, Virginia, in August 2017, organized and populated by the KKK, neo-Nazis, and other white supremacist groups, supposedly on a mission to defend Confederate monuments, resulted in the deaths of protester Heather Heyer and two state police officers and left the residents of Charlottesville reeling.

Charlottesville is a university town. The outsiders who showed up for that protest represent a mindset that sees higher education as indoctrination into things they fear, like free thought. Charlottesville had a proposal in the works to remove three prominent statues of Robert E. Lee, Stonewall Jackson, and an unknown Confederate soldier. Generally, these statues were not erected post–Civil War to honor the South's history, as so often

Loewenstein's Defunct Confederate monuments print; inspiration for the Kudzu Project.

Crafted kudzu leaves on mesh, ready to go.

claimed. They were put up during the Jim Crow era in the first few decades of the twentieth century. Then, more monuments were erected as a reaction to the civil rights movement. Where? In predominantly African American parts of Charlottesville, and more broadly, nationwide—not just in former Confederate states—often in front of institutions like city halls and statehouses.

A group of knitters in Charlottesville answered their *Call to Needles* and became resistance crafters when they saw an opportunity to let their needles speak their truth, based on Loewenstein's art. The mission statement is posted on the project's website: "The Kudzu Project was born out of a desire to realize Loewenstein's vision in yarn. More than thirty knitters from the mid-Atlantic region contributed to this guerrilla knitting installation."[37] Many of the knitters had put away the pink yarn they used to make Pussyhats and now brought out shades of green for the kudzu leaves.

Margo Smith, one of the founders of the Kudzu Project, is a museum director and curator at the University of Virginia in Charlottesville, and an avid knitter and activist. Smith wrote a detailed account of their attempts in a piece titled "The Kudzu Project: Vinebombing Virginia's Confederate Monuments" for the Decker and Mandell book *Crafting Democracy*. A healthy fear of backlash from white supremacists meant working completely in secret at the time, sharing nothing on social media or with anyone outside the group. Once the completed leaves were mailed to a post office box, a smaller group sewed the crafted leaves and vines onto fishing net, and an even smaller group attempted to cover the statue of the anonymous Confederate soldier outside the Albemarle County Courthouse, on November 19, 2017— early enough to not be noticed—on the day that the trial of one of the white supremacists from the rally was to begin. Three failed attempts, involving searching garbage cans to rescue the leaves after someone called the police, led the group to conduct "flash installations." Get in and out quickly, documenting the effort with a photo to be shared on the website, before removing the crafted leaves to prevent their destruction, leaving at least one vine behind as a statement.[38] *Seriously, are there Confederate ninja ghosts watching over these damn monuments, ready to catch anyone who would do them harm or bring unwanted attention?*

A CALL TO NEEDLES

Confederate soldier, Nelson County, Virginia, Courthouse.

There may be no way to measure the influence of these flash installations on attitudes toward the Confederate statues, but like so many other acts of craftivism and resistance, it makes people think (and hopefully, discuss), and "has given its participants a creative and public means of expressing their dissent through craft." Don't discount the healing, empowering effect on the creators either.

The project offered a form of therapeutic expression to those who had confronted violent white supremacists on the streets of Charlottesville and those who hadn't done so, but still felt violated. Participants stitched their trauma into three-lobed leaves in every shade of green.[38]

I watched the Unite the Right Rally on TV from a few states away, as many people did over those two days, stunned and appalled, feeling increasingly concerned about our country. Discovering the Kudzu Project provided a bit of comfort, hope, and inspiration.

Increasing public transparency of the all-too-prevalent killing of Black people by police, and mostly peaceful actions like the Black Lives Matter protests, awakened a powerful force that brought attention back to the Confederate flag, statues, and other visual representations of racism. If you would like to participate in a kudzu flash installation of your own making, it is easy to search for "Confederate monuments near me." The Kudzu Project website, no longer working in the shadows, will provide you with all the inspiration, tools, patterns, and advice you need to retain the element of surprise and then share your results (www.thekudzuproject.org).

Former Robert E. Lee High School (now Staunton High School), Staunton, Virginia, 2017.

Amherst County Courthouse, Amherst, Virginia, 2018.

On April 25, 2019, a judge in the Charlottesville circuit court ruled that Charlottesville cannot remove their Confederate statues because they are war memorials protected by state law. But in 2020, the Virginia legislature passed HB 1537, giving local governments in the state the right to choose the fate of these statues.[37] *Finally!*

Pears with A Purpose

Knit a pear so they can grow a pair or find the pair they possess.

As members of Congress (overwhelmingly older white men) failed to stand up to the developing authoritarian oligarch-in-chief, you may have found yourself wondering why so many members of the House and Senate appeared to be weak and spineless, so afraid of losing their jobs that they would defend anything the forty-fifth president said or did, as long as it served their own agenda.

Many of us have been involved for years in various efforts to remind local, state, and federal members of government that they work on behalf of we the people and were not elected to serve the president. We sent postcards, letters, and emails and made countless phone calls to let our representatives know what we expect of them. We know that they logged our calls and letters, but they no longer seemed to care why their constituents voted for them. And when we stepped up and attended town halls to let them know face-to-face, many stopped facing their electorate, cowardly closing this important communication channel.

It felt like it was time to get creative. I am a big fan of the double entendre. That may be one reason the Pussyhat project was so successful. It was a way to reclaim the word *pussy* from the man running for president who, on an open mic, said he could grab women by the pussy because he was famous and would therefore need no permission. But the Pussyhat was also perfect, because . . . pussycat ears!

If you would like to send a reminder to your representative or senator (in either political party) about finding the courage to do the critically important job of putting country ahead of party, consider sending them a pair of pears with a carefully considered message stating your request. (This could also be done at the state or local level.)

For all the examples of testicles used as a sign of strength, courage, and moxie, they certainly are delicate. To say that a woman has balls is an acknowledgment of *her* strength, courage, and moxie. Betty White once reminded us of the toughness and resiliency of the female vagina compared to the delicate external testicles of a man in its ability to take a pounding. Perhaps it would make more sense to tell a man he has brass breasts or a womb of steel instead of complimenting a women's courage by saying she has balls of steel. But, since we are currently in the Upside Down, I think I'll stay with a more familiar theme, gently disguised as fruit.

I am sharing my knitted pear pattern here. If you are not a knitter or are not comfortable using double-pointed needles, the pears can be crocheted, sewn from fabric, or even cut from felt. The message would be the same.

A template is also provided for a message you can attach to any pair of pears you send. If you choose to create your own message, let's remember to keep a respectful tone, which will more likely ensure we are heard. My hope is that our messages, although slightly tongue-in-cheek (or balls-in-sack), and a bit obnoxious, *(and don't forget, cute—who doesn't like a pear?)* will get the recipient's attention and stand as a unique approach to deliver a desperately important request to those who are supposed to be listening and have become quite adept at ignoring us.

After the House of Representatives impeached President Trump the first time in November 2019 and handed off to the Senate for the trial, which began in January 2020, I completed and boxed three pairs of pears to send to a few senators whose impeachment votes I considered key to the process. The first went to one of my senators, Ohio's Rob Portman, another to Senator Gardner of Colorado, and the last to Senator Romney from Utah. Romney was the sole Republican to vote to convict. *Coincidence?*

Boxed and ready to mail.

Senator/Congressman/Congresswoman:_____

I am: _____ A constituent in your district
_____ A concerned citizen, reaching out

You are receiving this hand-crafted pair of pears to remind you to:

_____ grow a pair
_____ remember the pair you have, and put them to good use

{Your message:}

With all due respect, this is my way of visually reminding you that it is time to take the most courageous stand of your political career, perhaps of your life, with an opportunity to be on the right side of history. I believe you are a good person who entered politics with the best intentions to help people. But right now, our democracy needs help and it's up to people in positions like yours, who will be responsible for saving our republic or letting it fail.

I'm respectfully asking you to put country ahead of party. Use this as a visual reminder that you work for us—"we the people."

Be a Bartlett, not a Bradford.

Made with hope and sent with great sincerity by:
{Your Name}
{Address and contact info}

Resistance Crafting

PEARS WITH A PURPOSE PATTERN

- Worsted-weight yarn in a pear-shade of green
- Brown worsted-weight yarn for stem
- Size 6 double-pointed needles
- Large handful of polyester fiberfill
- Tapestry needle

We can also let those who represent us well know they are appreciated by leaving a positive grateful message, working for their campaign, or sending a letter—or how about a letter and a pair of steel pears, recognizing their courage and grit. Works for men or women (female pears are carried higher).

Rather than working them up in pear green use a shade of gray, silver, or gold. There are yarns with metallic threads that would give the look of a strong metal.

Cast on 6 stitches and divide evenly between 3 double-pointed needles. Place stitch marker and join as you begin to knit in the round.

ROUND 1	knit
ROUND 2	kfb (knit in front & back) of each stitch (12 stitches)
ROUND 3	knit
ROUND 4	kfb of each stitch (24 stitches)
ROUND 5	knit
ROUND 6	*k2, kfb of next stitch, repeat from * (32 stitches)
ROUND 7	knit
ROUND 8	*k3, kfb of next stitch, repeat from * (40 stitches)
ROUNDS 9-15	knit
ROUND 16	*k8, k2tog, repeat from * (36 stitches)
ROUND 17	knit

Insert some fiberfill into bottom of pear and continue to knit. (This is easier than stuffing the entire pear at the end.)

ROUND 18	*k1, k2tog, repeat from * (24 stitches)
ROUND 19	knit

Add a little more fiberfill

ROUND 20	*k2, k2tog, repeat from * (18 stitches)
ROUNDS 21-26	knit

Insert a little more fiberfill

ROUND 27	*k2tog, k1, repeat from * (12 stitches)
ROUND 28	knit
ROUND 29	*k2tog, k1, repeat from * (8 stitches)

Add any fiberfill necessary for a plump pear.

Cut yarn, leaving a tail long enough to thread through a tapestry needle. Thread through the remaining 8 stitches as you remove from needles. Pull tight and secure the yarn end.

Stem (connector): Using brown worsted weight yarn, cast on 3 stitches and create a 5–6" long I-cord. Attach one end to each pear.

Be a Bartlett, Not a Bradford

Bartlett pears are the most popular type in America and carry a true pear shape . . . with abundant juice.

Bradford pears are often preferred for the big show of spring flowers and colorful fall leaves. *We've seen and heard enough of the showy displays and glittering generalities in Washington chambers.* Bradford pear trees are considered in some areas to be an invasive species and as damaging to environmental balance as the kudzu vine. *So, let's stop falling for those who try to dazzle us with alternative facts (the Bradfords) and pay more attention to those with strong character and moral substance, capable of putting country ahead of party, even at risk of personal threat (the Bartletts).*

If you'd like to print or save the pattern and message template, both are available on Ravelry as a free download. (www.ravelry.com/patterns/library/pears-with-a-purpose)

Cross Stitch and Other Acts of Embroidery

Full disclosure: I am a recovering counted cross stitch addict. A good friend and I latched on to the process in the late 1980s and were instantly obsessed. We were both high school teachers approximately ten years into our careers and frustrated with the demands of our jobs (not the students—they were never the problem). When we saw a local shop was for sale that specialized in counted cross stitch and framing, we dived in hearts first, with heads cautiously following. It allowed us to justify and share our craft obsession and escape some of our work problems. We had experience with various types of embroidery over the years, but here was something different. Counted cross stitch involves following a pattern, but the stitches are done on a particular fabric that has subtle squares to coordinate with the pattern. I always found it fascinating to watch an intricate picture evolve on a blank canvas simply by making Xs with needle and thread. This technique is more sophisticated and detailed than the stamped cross stitch pillowcases and table runners that my mother's generation made, popular in their time, like a paint-by-numbers project. Counted cross stitch patterns range from simple to intricate, and designers put out patterns, kits, books, and specialty fabrics for the technique. There was no stamped design to follow, just a chart. The counted cross stitch phenomenon eventually faded a bit in popularity and now joins the many other techniques and options for embroidery that have taken a back seat in the craft car for a while now.

But could there be a renaissance in the works? Late in 2019, as we slogged our way through the third year of the revolving door of the Trump administration, I began noticing more *Acts of Craftivism* and protest art using embroidery techniques, first on social media sites like Craftivist, but then it went mainstream.

Subversive Cross Stitch designed and stitched this in response to the Rachel Maddow Show segment.

Resistance Crafting

Rachel Maddow got all of my attention on November 13, 2019, when her coverage of the House Judiciary Committee's hearings on impeachment included a jaw-dropping statement made by State Department official George Kent. Maddow's graphics department created a wallpaper for the segment that looked like cross stitch.

Nine days later, near the end of her popular weeknight cable news show, Maddow announced the Best New Thing Today was *impeachment embroidery*, holding up gifts sent by viewers who found Mr. Kent's statement very stitch-worthy. You can watch the segment at www.youtube.com/watch?v=uh3ZA4mAAvs. Fans don't watch Maddow because they think of her as a craftivist, but she did shine a bright light on the subject that night.

Patterns were rapidly graphed and made available on sites like Etsy for those feeling the need to participate in stitching a piece of history. Maddow stated her love and respect for these efforts emphatically that night, but begged that no more be sent, as she had received enough embroidered pieces on this subject to start her own gallery in her office, which she intended to do, and suggested that those who felt called to stitch more share them with others around the country, maybe even with someone you disagree with, to start a conversation.[39]

SUBVERSIVE CROSS STITCH

One source of the pattern for Maddow's wallpaper quote from George Kent is Subversive Cross Stitch, at www.shop.subversivecrossstitch.com/products/pdf-george-kent-quote. Julie Jackson began this site in 2003 as a form of self-prescribed anger management.  It wasn't Trump, but a bully of a boss making her want to stab something. Her weapon of choice was an embroidery needle. In the *Age of Trump*, however, it is not just the therapeutic effect of working with fiber and needles that helps us cope, but a way to express and share in the collective anger, frustration, fear, (name your emotion) that these times are causing us to feel.

The women's lifestyle magazine *Bust* gave this assessment of Julie Jackson's creations: "What makes Subversive Cross Stitch so amusing is that Jackson doesn't shun the traditional bunnies, birds, hearts and flowers our grandmothers used to stitch. And nestled amid a garland of pink lilies, the word 'fuck' has never looked more polite and genteel."[40]

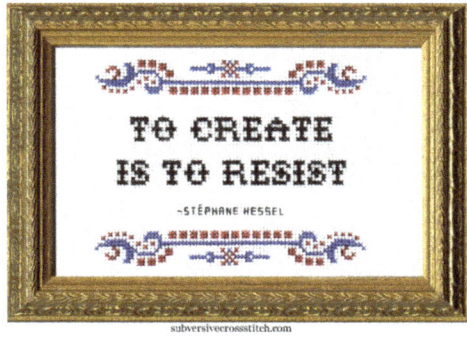

Her latest book, published in 2015, is titled *Subversive Cross Stitch: 50 F*cking Clever Designs for Your Sassy Side*. More recent designs are focused on voting and issues of social justice.

As is often the case, her website tells a more complete story, so I recommend you pay Jackson an online visit or follow her on social media for inspiration and community, even instructions, should you feel like stabbing something and haven't tried cross stitch yet (www.subversivecrossstitch.com).

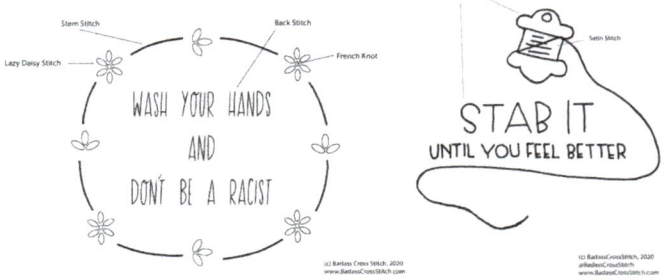

Two of the many patterns available from Badass Cross Stitch.

Badass Cross Stitch

Shannon Downey describes herself as an artist, educator, feminist, activist, craftivist, community builder, general instigator, queer, anti-racist, anti-capitalist, highly political, committed to growth, learning, honesty, and doing whatever she can to make this an equitable world. "My art generally tackles what I call "the big three" systems of oppression: white supremacy, patriarchy, and capitalism. I am nomadic, living in my R.V. and traveling the U.S." You can read more about that two-year adventure on her website, where you will find many craftivism patterns she has designed and stitched (including pandemic craftivism), some offered free, some for sale, as well as excellent tutorials and other forms of inspiration. "I want everything I do to inspire action, movement, community, and civic engagement. I love teaching others how to create and my goal is to teach 1 million people to embroider before I die."[41]

Badass Cross Stitch

One of Shannon's early acts of craftivism brought her some notoriety and was inspired by the *Access Hollywood* tape that most people of conscience thought would end Trump's 2016 bid for the presidency. It is one of the patterns she offers free on her site.

In an interview conducted by *No Kill Magazine*, Downey mentioned that she kept thinking as she stitched this piece that Trump "will never be president." *(Many of us had that moment, stitching or not.)* The article highlights a kerfuffle regarding this piece that came after the Harvey Weinstein scandal broke. A male celebrity shared the piece on social media without mentioning its creator. When it went viral, Shannon had a message for him: "You're a white man and you just erased me from my work that you're using to talk about holding a white man accountable, I mean what the . . ." He quickly apologized, corrected the injustice, citing the artist and encouraging people to follow her.[42]

Trump-inspired.

The phrase "you erased me from my work" is what I hope you take away from this part of Downey's story, since women, BIPOC, LGBTQ, the poor, immigrants, and too many others have so often experienced the sentiment in those words. It matters to hear someone say them publicly, and there is a lesson for many of us to learn in the way Downey handled this.

And of course, as is common in the experience of women, it did not end there. An apparel company put the "Boys will be . . ." statement on the back pocket of a line of their women's jeans without Downey's permission. Working on her own behalf, as well as with counsel, Downey's communications with the company continued, and while the outcome was unresolved at the time this was written, they removed the product from their line. But a badass doesn't stop there! She stitched a few messages on the back pockets of her own jeans, posted them for her massive social media following, and added a do-it-yourself tutorial on her site. To see the overwhelming response, visit that page on the Badass website at www.badasscrossstitch.com/communityprojects/rebuttal for messages like "still not asking for it" and "no does not mean convince me" stitched on participants' jean pockets.

If you are not a practicing craftivist but Shannon Downey's name sounds familiar, you may have seen the story of Rita's Quilt on the news or on Kelly Clarkson's show in December 2019. According to Shannon, there are two types of crafters: "People who start projects but don't finish them, and people who don't move on until they've finished what they're working on." She describes herself as the latter type of crafter, and, I humbly admit, I do not.

Fortunately, there are some who walk among us, taking on one project at a time, and not allowing any distraction until it is completed, like Downey. She developed a penchant for finding unfinished embroidery projects at estate sales and feeling compelled to purchase and finish them. Is there a needleworker among us who is not aware that we will die with unfinished projects lurking in our homes? Downey strongly feels "There's no way that soul is resting with an unfinished project left behind."[43]

In 2019 Downey paid five dollars for a box of one hundred hexagons of fabric that were intended to become a representation of each state with its state bird and flower, accompanied by fifty stars. At that same sale, Downey purchased a framed piece hanging on a nearby wall with an embroidered map of the United States surrounded by

---

I'm going to have to declare a third type of crafter here, which I believe will fit most of the crafters out there. Category three would be those of us with multiple works in progress. The average crafter has five WIPs going at any given time. Some projects are long and tedious to complete, but so worth the effort. Sometimes we just need a break and a less detailed or even mindless project to work on in order to keep our crafting mojo energy strong. Do some projects become forgotten and neglected and never completed? Sure. But sometimes, we return to a stashed project, refreshed and renewed, and proudly take it to completion. Many an abandoned project was retrieved from storage and completed during the pandemic when stay-at-home directives were in place. A complicating factor is that some of us are so passionate about the endless possibilities that can result from the multitude of patterns, threads, colors, and techniques available, that a new creation calls our name, and we must answer. *(Or . . . Squirrel!)*

the state flowers. It seemed like a companion piece to the unfinished project.

A little digging found that a woman named Rita Smith had taken on the hexagon project at the age of ninety-nine because she was a "ferocious crafter" and, I would add, an optimist. What may have bonded Shannon to Rita was discovering that Rita had completed two state squares before she died, giving Downey insight into Rita's plan for colors, threads, and techniques.

As an avid embroiderer, Downey realized the magnitude of this undertaking and sent out a *Call to Needles* on her social media platforms. Within twenty-four hours she had one thousand volunteers, and, after creating detailed spreadsheets of volunteers and their contact information, Shannon sent fifty volunteers a state square and one star to stitch and return.

This entire journey is moving and profound, but let's zoom in on these volunteers. They each had a personal reason for volunteering, whether it was pride in a particular state, a memory of a loved one who crafted, or understanding what it would mean to one of them to have someone care enough to complete a project they were unable to finish. For at least one volunteer, it became part of her recovery story. It was definitely personal, and many volunteers shared their thoughts in video diaries. You can read more about the volunteers' experience on the Badass website.

Some of the stitchers researched Rita and found more details about her life, including a high school yearbook picture and the fact that she was a school nurse. Her family was contacted to share this journey, which helped the volunteers feel a little closer to a woman they didn't know, and her family was able to share their love for Rita with new fans. These efforts created a legacy piece of art. Random comments from volunteers on Downey's website describe their feelings about the project:

> "Humans are amazing."
> "Community can be built anywhere."
> "A loving practice in a dark time."

After the finished, embroidered state squares and stars were sent back to Downey, who admittedly is not a quilter *(yet!)*, a team of thirty-five volunteer quilters, including two master quilters, completed the quilt top in Chicago in one day, placing the already completed state map in the center. When finished and put on display, there was a great deal of media coverage that often, predictably, managed to minimize the story into a standard

Rita's Quilt, now completed.

sound bite: "Nice ladies on the internet finished an American quilt for a dead lady." *("Awwwww," says viewer, "such a feel-good story.")* But the volunteers involved in this project made a quilt "about their lived experience in the United States—their version of a patriotic quilt . . . This is a political and feminist act."[42] It is Rita's legacy, but Downey and her team of volunteers are all part of that legacy now.

Continuing the adventure that had become Rita's Quilt, Downey tours with and talks about the quilt, which included a display of honor at the National Quilt Museum in Paducah, Kentucky.

xxxxxx

Once Rita's crafty soul found peace, Downey was able to return to her main mission, to teach as many people as possible the embroidery skills they can love and use to change the world. The plan was for Downey to give up her job and home, purchase an RV to live in, and take craftivism and Rita's Quilt on the road. She would meet the makers, especially the volunteers who made Rita's Quilt possible, giving them a chance to see their work in person, when along came a pandemic. It was too late to scrap the plan, so adjust the plan to meet pandemic protocol, it was. Downey still met as many people as she possibly could traveling around the country, holding socially distanced stitch-ups and Zoom classes, and displaying Rita's Quilt and Downey's own stitched collection in as many locations as possible along the way.

I signed up for a Zoom class that Downey teaches regularly, Embroidery 101, to refresh my hand stitching skills, which led me to join an online stitching group that she hosts. It turned out to be critically important to my stay-at-home pandemic survival, making new friends here and abroad, and making me a Badass fan for life!

xxxxxx

The cross stitch and embroidery patterns Downey designs and Rita's Quilt are only a fraction of what this busy human has going on. She created the country's first Craftivist-in-Residence program, with the Fuller Craft Museum becoming the first to participate. The plan is laid out in detail on the website. And, because badasses rarely rest, Downey started the "How to Be a Good Human" series of online radical skill-share classes that include Bystander Intervention Training and How to Be an Activist, among many others, with badge patterns for completers to stitch. But wait . . . there's more. Downey's Badass *Herstory* is a global craftivism project that asks women and nonbinary people to tell their story on a 12" x 12" piece of fiber art, because:

> *Most of us are never taught that we are the heroes of their own story. We are, at best, supporting characters. There is great value in exploring, centering, and sharing your story. There is great value in making art about yourself.*[41]

The herstories and other Downey works were part of the "Craftivism, Activism through Craft Exhibit" at the National Liberty Museum in Philadelphia that opened in November 2021.

As the pandemic continued so did Downey's RV life. She began a second trek around the country as 2021 ended. By the time this book is published, I have no doubt Downey will have created more adventures in craftivism, so check the Badass website occasionally, order her book, and try to keep up. And if you've been meaning to learn embroidery, you can sign up for that online Embroidery 101 class.

THE TINY PRICKS PROJECT

Could there be a more apt branding name for an act of embroidery in the *Age of Trump*? With every prick of the needle, feelings are acknowledged, released, and recorded for history.

Diana Weymar, an artist and activist (channeling her inner Madame Defarge) decided it was important to create a "material record of Trump's presidency." In January 2017, as I was finishing my final Pussyhat, Diana was stitching "I am a very stable genius" on an unfinished, decades-old piece of her grandmother's needlework.

Samplers and other types of embroidery were discussed earlier in this book as the training ground for women of means to learn a skill worthy of their place in the world, likely managing a household and creating heirlooms and decorative touches for a proper home. Many now reside in museums and private homes, like the art that they are. But consider how fitting it is to take an unfinished or neglected piece of needlework that represents a past most of us don't identify with, even those of us who are passionate about needlework, and give it new life, documenting the odd phrasings of a man promising to bring back a way of life to which most of us do *not* wish to return. EVER!

The first of many!

In Weymar's words from the Tiny Pricks Project website, "The collection counterbalances the impermanence of Twitter and other social media, and Trump's statements as president, through the use of textiles that embody warmth, craft, permanence, civility, and a shared history. The daintiness and integrity of each piece stand in stark contrast to his presidency." It has also been referred to as "a subversive series of antique textiles."[44]

Weymar's original, personal goal was to stitch one Trump quote a week. *(I know you see where this is going.)* The weekly quotes became daily word salad and she completed hundreds of hoop-framed quotes. It did not take long for others to become enthralled, inspired, and involved. Workshops evolved and the Tiny Pricks project became "the largest textile Trump protest ever, with over 1,100 pieces completed" early on, by hundreds of *global* participants.

It wasn't long before Weymar found a willing partner and co-curator in Rachelle Hruska MacPherson and her Lingua Franca Boutique on Bleecker Street in New York

"Official presidential tweet."

City. The TPP fit nicely with the mission of her shop, to "bring people together in a common language." It held a street show in June 2019 to unveil and share all of the contributions to the effort. By then, Weymar had stitched about three hundred quotes herself and received at least four hundred pieces from strangers. They covered the walls of Lingua Franca and filled the window as well. You can get a closer look at the contributed pieces on the TPP website, Twitter, and Instagram.

The goal was to collect 2,020 embroidered quotes by the time of the 2020 election. A reelected Trump would provide another four years of material, while a rejected Trump would no doubt still have much to say, providing an endless supply of word art.

The TPP website includes information on ways to participate. If you feel inspired and called to your embroidery needles, even after the 2020 deadline, to create a piece, and believe it would ensure you never forget the words that resonated most for you, go for it. (www.tinypricksproject.com)

Weymar keeps a database of all the quotes that have been used so far, but she welcomes repeat submissions, saying "the more they're repeated, the more it shows how that quote resonated. And everyone does them in a different way."[45]

During my cross stitch obsession, many patterns were created replicating the samplers made in the late nineteenth century, often modernized using colors and phrasing. I was fascinated by antique stitched samplers, and I was determined to find one. I scoured antique stores, vintage art shows, and flea markets. The only one I found and purchased was deemed to have no monetary value (not my motivation anyway) because the frayed edges were too close to the stitching to allow framing and no identifying information was stitched into the piece—no lineage, you see. I deemed it the perfect choice to hold a serving of Trump word salad, especially since he always seemed a little frayed at the edges. It was sent off to be added to the display and I was able to consider myself part of another community of craftivists.

Trump's tweeted threat to Kim Jong-un stitched on an unraveling sampler.

Knitting Nannas Against Gas (Australia)

As a grandmother myself, quite accustomed to being underestimated and overlooked, I found kindred spirits among Knitting Nannas Against Gas, a group of Australian craftivists who have turned the stereotype of the docile knitting grandma completely upside down while at the same time modernizing and using it to their advantage. *Well played, Nannas, well played.*

This "disorganization" was formed in 2012 by Clare Twomey and Lindy Scott as a place "where people come together to ensure that our land, air and water are preserved for our children and grandchildren." The approach is to "peacefully and productively protest against the destruction of our land, air, and water by exploration and mining of unconventional gas and other non-renewable energy sources."[46]

In the early days, the plan was to be a presence and bear witness to what was happening to the environment around them. Members were determined to sit and knit, while quietly observing injustice, inspired by the tricoteuses of French history. In Defarge mode, "small groups went out into the countryside, parked by roadsides with their knitting, folding chairs, and thermoses to 'scope out the works,'" bearing witness to the corporation's largely ignored activities.[46]

It turned out, though, that just observing was boring and unproductive, except for whatever was being worked on those needles while observing, so the group expanded its focus and found willing and able participants all over Australia. Participants began holding "knit-ins" and created their Nannafesto:

We peacefully and productively protest against the destruction of our land, air, and water by corporations and/or individuals who seek profit and personal gain from the short-sighted and greedy plunder of our natural resources.

And my favorite part:

We sit, knit, plot, have a yarn and a cuppa, and bear witness to the war against those who try to rape our land and divide our communities.[46]

The Nannas' mission includes protecting lands they thought would always be off-limits, much of it populated by the Indigenous people of Australia. The Nannas are not affiliated with any political party, and participants often

2019 International Women's Day Rally outside Parliament in Sydney.

KNAG 2017 Conference in Narrabri's Bohena Creek where Santos planned to dump tons of toxic salt.

No Water No Life rally in Sydney.

include conservative and liberal women. "We annoy all politicians equally." *Makes me love them even more.*

They choose to work with bright yellow and black yarn as they sit and knit, because yellow is a color associated with danger and warnings. They make yellow berets trimmed in black (the pattern is posted on their website) to create a unifying identity. The words "Lock the Gate" are often incorporated into knitted or crocheted triangles to associate with the Australian Lock the Gate Alliance, which attempts to raise awareness of the dangers of coal and gas mining.[47] They also craft yellow danger tapes and still manage to craft for charity.

Imagine a group of grandmothers, knitting passively outside of the parliament, courthouses, or at community events, happy to let observers bask in their stereotypes as they are drawn into conversations with these craftivists, perhaps even offered a cup of tea, only to discover that while these are polite, nonviolent, mild-mannered women, many with college degrees, they also have talking points, data, and an educational approach, with no intention of negotiating on important points. They use evidence-based research and follow Australia's nonviolent direct action guidelines. "The iron fist in the soft yellow glove."[46]

Other locations for knit-ins, information tabling, or marches include selected politicians' offices, the corporate offices and work sites of the offending companies, community events, flash mobs, and as they put it, "whatever else works."

I am truly jealous that we don't have a group of Knitting Nannas here in the United States, especially since a certain president pulled us out of the Paris climate accord and started opening sacred, protected land for plunder by the same types of corporate energy companies, including land that has been designated as national parklands or belonging to America's Indigenous people. America's water is not safe either, and fracking has invaded farmland throughout the United States. Even if our future presidents reinstate environmental protection policies, how much damage will not be reversible? So, allow the Knitting Nannas to inspire you to act, wherever you call home on this planet. You can learn more at www.knitting-nannas.com.

One truth being noticed in every developed democracy on the planet is that we seem to be at a tipping point, and democracy as a form of governing is endangered. When the KNAG say "Protest and satire are not yet completely illegal," we hear them. *"Viva la Nannalution!"*[48]

DIY Techniques

In a previous life, I discovered Igolochkoy, a Russian punchneedle, with the smallest size using only one strand of embroidery floss, with a result that looks similar to French knots. After I inherited my mother's dollhouse, a solidly built structure unlike most made today (it was going to be her retirement project until my dad introduced her to golf), I attended several miniature shows, picking up furniture and decor for what is now, apparently, *my* retirement project. I found that many of the soft products, like bedspreads and rugs, were a bit rigid and difficult to translate to scale. I started experimenting with the smallest punchneedle and found it made the perfect pile and texture for miniature rugs. I created an inventory of various size miniature rugs and started setting up at miniature shows within a day's drive of home.

The point of this ramble: As I tried to sell my rugs at miniature shows, I discovered there were very few attendees looking to spend the amount of money I was asking as compensation for the amount of work that went into these rugs. Most miniaturists attend these shows looking for ideas and prefer to do it themselves. That inner drive to make things ourselves is what keeps the craft stores in business. I adapted and turned to selling the needles and DIY kits.

Miniature punchneedle rugs.

Punchneedle is worked from the back.

This principle is no less true for the craftivists among us. Sometimes you have a vision, idea, or concept so timely, clever, or unique that you cannot find a pattern for it, and if you have the right skills (none too complicated), you can design and make it yourself.

Design and Create— Say What You Need to Say

If you have ever knit or crocheted from a chart or graph, and you understand how that process works, all you really need is a piece of graph paper or the ability to graph as you work in your head and spell out what you want to say. Many crafters just pick out a yarn and compatible needles or crochet hook and chain or cast on, waiting to see where their ideas take them, making notes and creating a pattern later, if it results in something they want to share. You can say whatever you want in any color or medium; several examples are offered in the Talking Heads section of chapter 8. I found the "exasperation hat," summing up our sentiments on the year 2020 and beyond, for when one F-bomb just won't do. The pattern is available as a free download on Ravelry by creator Pam Gabriel (for the common good—and cheaper than therapy) at www.ravelry.com/patterns/library/fuck-the-exasperation-hat.

xxxxxx

Any item knitted in a stockinette stitch can have words or images worked into the pattern. You can use a generic hat pattern and graph out the lettering yourself. If you have no experience with Fair Isle, a.k.a. stranded colorwork, which is often used for adding words to a knitted piece, there any many instructional videos available online. For larger objects, like a heart, intarsia, which gives a more inlaid look, may be the better technique choice and can also be learned online. A simpler process when knitting in one solid color would be to knit where you would ordinarily purl in your stockinette stitch in a way that spells out what you want to say. This dishcloth was my Christmas gift for friends in 2020, using April Collins's free Ravelry design (www.ravelry.com/patterns/library/fuck-2020-dishcloth).

If crochet is your preference, you can still stitch words into the piece, using a variety of techniques that include surface slip stitch crochet, cross stitch, or chain stitch embroidery. There are many online videos that will show you these processes step by step.

If you get more involved and want to share or publish your design, there are many free apps and programs that can assist you in graphing your pattern or even designing a pattern from a picture. Like many apps these days, there are free usable versions such as Chart Minder or Stitch Fiddle that can be upgraded, if necessary, for a price.

If you decide to go pro, you can produce more professional looking patterns with programs like Knit Foundry for under two hundred dollars. There are others only a search away. You can learn more about the entire design process at www.sistermountain.com/blog/design-knitting-patterns.

Duplicate Stitch— Fast Track Your Message

Duplicate stitch works best on pieces already knit in stockinette stitch. Using a separate strand of yarn and a tapestry needle, you create a "duplicate" V stitch over one of the upright V's on the right side of a knitted piece. When completed with the same weight yarn it imitates the look of the more complicated Fair Isle technique, as if it were knitted into the piece. (This is also the fix for a missed stitch in Fair Isle knitting.) You can get ideas from cross stitch patterns or Fair Isle charts—or just speak your mind.

When I say "fast track" your message, I mean that you don't have to knit a hat or sweater first, you can duplicate

Exasperation hat. When one F-bomb just won't do.

Knitted dishcloth.

Duplicate stitch.

stitch onto any garment knitted in stockinette stitch, even a store-bought garment. For visual learners like me, the Spruce Crafts has an excellent tutorial on how to do the duplicate stitch, which you can view at www.thesprucecrafts.com/how-to-duplicate-stitch-2116380.

ILLUSION KNITTING— NOW YOU SEE IT!

In 2019, I made a scarf with a hidden message using the illusion knitting technique, also called shadow knitting. The message embedded in this scarf involved two words, one verb and a certain person's name. When you look at the scarf directly it looks like simple knitted stripes, but at an angle the words appear as intended. I discovered this pattern online and made it for my husband, so when he walks the dog in cold weather in our rather conservative neighborhood, only he will hear what the scarf is saying and he won't offend anyone.

In January 2020, I attended a Vogue Knitting LIVE event in my state. I was fortunate enough to get a spot in Franklin Habit's shadow knitting class. Habit is a professional knitter, designer, teacher (a good one), and illustrator. One of his books is titled *It Itches: A Stash of Knitting Cartoons*, which I mention here to give you some insight into Habit's engaging persona. You can find Habit on Ravelry or on his website, www.franklinhabit.com.

I had already finished the illusion knit scarf for my husband, but after taking Habit's class on the subject, I felt I understood the process enough to design my own shadow knitting pattern. So, I created the Nasty Woman scarf pattern, which is available on Ravelry. The proceeds from the sale of this pattern are donated to Chef José Andrés's World Central Kitchen.

Habit credits Vivian Hoxbro as the first American to write about and design patterns for shadow knitting. Her 2004 book, *Shadow Knitting*, contains patterns for clothing and items that have hidden designs, not messages, and offers good training on the process. Hoxbro was inspired by a Japanese knitting book on hidden patterns.

Shadow, or illusion, knitting is always worked in alternating stripes of two colors. One of those colors will always show the intended illusion, only when observed from an angle. To create the illusion, a basic 4-row repeat is required. Rows 1 & 2 are worked in

Nasty Woman illusion-knit scarf.

the base color. Rows 3 & 4 are worked in the contrasting color and that is where the hidden message emerges when the pattern is followed.

The basic pattern (without illusion):

- Row 1 is knit using Color A
- Row 2 is knit using Color A
- Row 3 is knit using Color B
- Row 4 is purled using Color B

Rows 1 & 2 form a garter stripe. Rows 3 & 4 form a stockinette stripe. The illusion appears when rows 2 and 4 reverse certain stitches, following a pattern, flattening the surface in row 2 (which helps reveal the illusion) and creating a visible garter bump in row 4.

xxxxxx

A pattern may include hundreds of rows but will follow this four-row sequence. Another way to consider the process is that since you will always knit the first row of each color stripe, the pattern only matters in the even numbered rows. Once the first few rows, usually just plain stripes, are completed, most illusion knitting patterns only chart the even-numbered rows, because that is where all the action is happening. Rows 1 and 3 are always knitted, although in different colors, on the right side of the piece, while rows 2 and 4 are worked on the wrong side.

If this seems confusing, I can attest that the best way to understand the process can be to jump in and try it out. If you want to try a simple word or phrase, visit the Woolly Thoughts website. You were introduced to Pat Ashford and Steve Plummer, the "mathekniticians," in chapter 1. A subdomain of the Woolly Thoughts website, called the "World of Illusion Knitting, Where Nothing is Quite as it Seems," is an excellent resource on illusion knitting. When they discovered this interesting technique, even they found much of the available information on the process confusing and cumbersome, and they decided to approach it with their trusted math and logic. They created their own way of charting that allowed them to create very elaborate, detailed patterns, to portray great works of art like the Mona Lisa or less intense baby blankets and fandom items. You will find their basic instructions on this technique, and you can download ten free illusion alphabets to create your own scarf, wall hanging, sweater, shawl, afghan, or whatever idea you conceive. You will find tutorials, charts, and many patterns.[49] It is worth a virtual visit to their jaw-dropping gallery even if this is not a technique you see yourself doing.

A Stitch in Time

My mother had a large repertoire of memorable Appalachian adages, but I have strong memories of hearing *a stitch in time saves nine*. It may have been her way of getting me to put down a book or getting my father off the couch to get to other important jobs that needed our attention—a procrastinator buster.

From a craftivist's point of view, I ask you to consider the phrase in another way. A stitch in time might save nine *dollars*, or more, and can act as a form of resistance to the planned obsolescence that is today's clothing industry, with its emphasis on overconsumption and the appalling exploitation of workers worldwide. With roots in the 90s feminist punk rock movement Riot Grrrl's message of "creativity over commerce" (chapter 4), a movement is growing to recycle, reuse, mend, and upcycle, using techniques like embroidery, appliqué, or "visible mending," which repairs and embellishes at the same time. Visible mending is based on sashiko embroidery, which relies on a simple running stitch, as well as the lost art of darning.

In spite of the fact that I recycle plastic and paper, I admit I have existed too long in uninformed privilege, quite self-satisfied when donating clothing that has gone out of style or no longer fits to any number of local agencies, confident they would be resold or given to those in need. *(How many will admit to parting with never-worn items that still had the tags on them?)* And I had an annual tax deduction for those donations. Reality, however, informs us that the massive amount of clothing donated each year is impossible to manage and distribute, and many of our well-intended donations become textile waste in landfills. Keeping in mind that not all of those articles of clothing are made from organic, sustainable substances, most using chemicals in the fibers and finishes, we may wish to reimagine our habits, from defining our "needs" and rationale for our clothing purchases to how we part with such items, maybe learning to mend or upcycle more.

Visible mending.

Jane Milburn, author of *Slow Clothing*, says in an article for *The Conversation*: "We don't need to throw our clothes away, and we're wearing our mends as a badge of honour." The article describes visible mending as "a quiet, global protest movement that's happening at a grassroots level, challenging the way we consume clothing."[50]

Sarah Kuhn writes about this trend in a chapter titled "Mending Our Clothing, Mending the World" in the book *Crafting Dissent*. Kuhn points out the many benefits of visible mending, including agency (*remember the Betsy Greer quote "craftivism does not expect you to come with skills but with willingness"?*), sustainability, anti-consumption, and community-building. It also tends to grant the mender the soothing benefit that comes with so many forms of needlework, and it is gender-neutral, challenging the image of "women's work." Kuhn organized mending workshops after the 2016 election, not only for the practicality of the technique, but in the spirit of the Hebrew phrase "tikkun olam" or mending the world.[51]

You can find a thriving visible mending and upcycling community on social media, websites, Pinterest, YouTube, and blogs. Up-Cycled Cloth Collective on Facebook, "My Make Do and Mend Year (blog)" and GreenAmerica.org are a few examples. Clever teens and young adults are posting tutorials for upscaling unwanted clothing, especially T-shirts and men's dress shirts, converting them into bags, skirts, and fitted tops. There are groups that crochet plastic sleeping mats for homeless people from strips of "yarn" cut by volunteers from plastic bags.

You will find ample "mendspiration" at Visible Mending, www.visiblemending.com/, with profiles, techniques, tutorials, a blog, and a list of the top ten reasons to mend.

Looking to the past, we often realize that many "new" ideas have a history, dusted off and reimagined for today's needs. Much like the American Red Cross's efforts during World War II (described in chapter 4), the British Ministry of Information provided a pamphlet with tips for housewives to be both frugal and stylish. Women were encouraged to cover holes in clothing with decorative patches, unravel sweaters to reknit more modern pieces, alter men's clothing to be worn by women, protect clothing against moths, and darn as needed.

xxxxxx

I often see examples on social media of knitters who have unraveled an old sweater, for example, and made something completely different with the yarn. I tried it myself with a sweater I made and never wore because I didn't like the way it sat on my body, but I loved the yarn, a light, fingering, slightly fuzzy purple with occasional, embedded, tiny sequins. Full disclosure, taking that sweater apart was a challenge, on the scale of unraveling a yarn mess made by small two- or four-leggeds, but tolerable, since it didn't require much concentration. Then I used the yarn to make myself a scarf and hat, with enough yarn left to make a pair of fingerless gloves.

Look and you will find a large, supportive community doing this work. I can attest that it feels good to find alternatives to throwing something out while protecting the environment in the process.

The Protest Banner Lending Library

One thing we know for sure about using our needles to support our activism is that it consumes a large amount of time, by hand or by machine. The benefits of using our time in that way are varied and significant, but not always practical. I discovered the Pussyhat project near the end of 2016 and I was already a little late to the party at that point, preparing for the January 21st march. I engaged with several of the projects described in this book. In some cases, like the Welcome Blankets in chapter 8, I used a bulky yarn and large needles to quick knit a 40" x 40" blanket in order to help meet the need. The Violet Protest (also in chapter 8) moved its deadlines further down the calendar due to COVID-19, which allowed me to spend more time, stitching in more detail, to make my point more clearly.

But sometimes a march or a protest evolves quickly and organically, in response to an event that requires urgent action. And sometimes, a paper posterboard just won't speak loudly enough for those with needle skills! Artist Aram Han Sifuentes, "an immigrant womxn of color, and a daughter of a seamstress," answered her *Call to Needles* when she began making banners in her Chicago apartment the day after Trump was declared the winner of the 2016 presidential election. Like so many of us at the time, she also felt the need to draw in a community of like

Look and you will find a large, supportive community doing this work.

minds and skills. She invited friends to participate, which led to creating workshops for the public.⁵²

Sifuentes saw the added, and possibly more significant, benefit of giving voice to disenfranchised people, specifically women of color working in the garment industry for little pay. For a variety of mostly socioeconomic reasons, most of these makers did not feel they were in a position to safely take to the streets with protest banners, reminding me of the arpilleristas in chapter 10. But they could make the banners, and others could "check them out and carry our words for us, with an understanding that they come from this community."⁵²

Like seeds planted in rich soil, good ideas sprout into strong, healthy vines that spread, and the Protest Banner Lending Library workshops have made more than three thousand banners. The lending libraries are housed all over the US and Canada. "The banners carry the histories of the hands that made and hold them, and the places to which they have and will travel."⁵³ Some are radical, some inspire and lift up, some demand justice, and they are as varied in their messages as the people who made them and those who choose to carry or display them.

Aram Han Sifuentes, "sharing skills as a point of connection."

A different kind of library.

7

CRAFTED COMPASSION

The key to working toward the greater good is knowing what to give and when to give it.

—Betsy Greer, *Knitting for Good*

OUR COMPASSION has often been a *Call to Needles*, but in the *Age of Trump*, hearing and answering that call may also come from a place of concern, frustration, anger, fear, despair, or a combination of these emotions, served up with a large side of hope and determination.

Ellen Gadberry, a career educator and resident of Atlanta, conducts classes that use art and creativity in diverse locations such as libraries, churches, the county jail, and refugee family literacy programs. A statement she wrote for Compassionate Atlanta fits well with this introduction to compassionate crafting:

> *What happens to your thinking when you settle into a hands-on creative process? How can simple, repetitive actions of making, drawing, knitting, or building clear your mind from distractions and allow you to access deeper levels of attention, awareness, and compassion for yourself and the world around you? How does the work of your hands create space for the work of your mind when you are listening to a speaker, participating in a conversation, meditating, or praying?*[54]

Gadberry's podcast and her other endeavors can be found at www.contemplativecrafting.com.

Science supports the concept that compassion for others is good for us. Dr. James Doty,[55] the director of the Center for Compassion and Altruism Research and Education at the Stanford University School of Medicine, sums up what science has told us about compassion:

- To flourish and thrive one must be compassionate
- Being compassionate increases longevity up to twofold
- Being compassionate decreases your stress and decreases markers of inflammation

- Being compassionate is what we were fundamentally designed for

As discussed in the chapter on resistance crafting, and reinforced in Dr. Doty's list, *Crafted Acts of Kindness* bring the maker a needed release in the form of action that, hopefully, benefits the recipient as well. That release can be a coping mechanism—a critical tool in sustaining the maker, important in any act of protest or resistance. That is not to say that compassion is not still the driving force, but those other emotions enable us to find the courage and the techniques to resist effectively. I have only scratched the surface here of some of the compassionate crafting in our world. People are amazing in their capacity to find ways to help others. As Jayna Zweiman said of the response to her Welcome Blanket project, "the love is palpable" (www.welcomeblanket.org).

Little Sweaters for Little Penguins

You have probably seen one of the ads that show volunteers using Dawn dish soap to remove thick coatings of oil from ducks and other animals who became endangered victims of oil spills. And you may remember the 2017 story of 109-year-old Alfie Date, an Australian man who knitted little sweaters for Little Penguins injured in oil spills. In 2001, a spill near Phillip Island in Australia resulted in a crisis for the little blue penguins that are found only in Australia and New Zealand.[56] This miniature version of the penguin typically weighs less than three pounds and stands about one foot tall. Phillip Island Nature Park has approximately thirty-two thousand breeding adults, and

Well-dressed Little Penguins display at Phillip Island Nature Park.

the oil spill resulted in 483 Little Penguins taken into the rehabilitation center, because a coating of oil affects their buoyancy in the water and their ability to regulate their body temperature. They also tend to ingest too much oil as they preen themselves in an attempt to clean it off.[56]

In what was probably the cutest global *Call to Needles* ever, a request went out to knitters for tiny sweaters using a specific "jumper" pattern posted on the Penguin Foundation website. The sweaters were helpful for some of the life-threatening issues created by the spill. The response was predictably overwhelming and may have received a publicity boost because of Date's efforts. But knitters gotta knit, and many sweaters were delivered that seemed to be trying to create penguin couture, embellished with buttons, ribbons, and other extras. The foundation received thousands of little knitted jumpers. The excess jumpers and those that could not be used for the penguins became clothing for toy penguins at the gift shop or were used in school education programs to teach about the impacts of oil spills on seabirds. Both these efforts helped raise funds for the Penguin Foundation.

So many people sent sweaters that the foundation released this statement:

> *We are pleased that a large percentage of the penguin jumpers have been suitable for rehabilitation purposes, and we therefore have ample supply for future oil spills—should one occur. Please send in any completed penguin jumpers, but please do not start anymore for the time being. If you would still like to support the Little Penguins of Phillip Island (Millowl), you may adopt a penguin or make a donation via the website shown in the picture.*

Mission accomplished, as 96 percent of the little penguins in the rehabilitation center were able to be released back into the wild.[57] I hope they are never needed, but they have enough sweaters. So, *to be clear*, this is not a current *Call to Needles*, just a worthy example that may inspire you. But it perfectly describes the type of response we get from crafters and how they step up when called to help in a crisis.

This happened before the *Age of Trump* but represents an important need that can emerge when environmental changes put people or other living things in danger. Environmental concerns were not high on Trump's agenda, resulting in increased concern from those who work to protect our planet's resources. You will read about a more current crafted response in chapter 8.

Warm Up America! and Made with Love

The national nonprofit Warm Up America is celebrating thirty years and looking to the future. It began when founder Evie Rosen (1926–2012) enlisted volunteers to make blankets for people in need. Those interested had options: You could knit or crochet a 7" x 9" square or an entire blanket, donate money to cover materials, or share the mission on social media or by word of mouth. Warm Up America teamed up with local yarn shops and big chain craft stores to promote the project and provide drop-off bins or donations of yarn for other makers.

This effort has expanded well beyond the original concept as times and needs have changed and grown. More than one million blankets have been donated to those

7" x 9" squares, ready to be assembled into blankets.

Combined efforts of the Dallas Yarn Bombers and the first Made with Love drive, 2015.

in need, crafted by more than twenty-five thousand volunteers. The new model is to post specific needs with addresses where finished items can be mailed directly to designated organizers, who then forward them to locations in need. You can look at the current needs on the website under the "Make" tab and find instructions and inspiration as well.[58] And if your needles are otherwise occupied, consider making a donation to support their efforts, through their website (www.warmupamerica.org).

xxxxxx

My personal favorite branch of this original tree is what happens when a compassionate crafter meets a yarn bomber. The result is the annual Made with Love drive. In January 2015, the staff of Warm Up America collaborated with the Dallas Yarn Bombers for the first Made with Love drive in Dallas. Donations of colorful handmade hats, gloves, mittens, scarves, and blankets were made available by decorating trees with them or hanging items on fences or playground equipment, each wearing a tag that said, "Take me, I'm yours."

Instructions are provided on how to plan a Made with Love event in your city, with details on selecting the best location, display ideas, getting the word out, and ways to assure people that it's okay to take what you need. Media coverage is encouraged because it promotes success and more events.[59]

Like so many organizations, the Warm Up America offices in Dallas closed for a time in March 2020 due to the pandemic, and makers were encouraged to keep making but not to send in finished pieces until notified to do so. But the need only increased, and the organization soon found ways to move forward with its mission, sharing COVID-19 updates regularly on its website and Facebook page. Made with Love events were easy to continue during the pandemic, since personal contact was limited.

Crafted Compassion

The Giving Doll

The Giving Doll is one profound example of how a single act of *Crafted Kindness* can become a movement that grows and endures through the years, having a positive impact on tens of thousands of children, with collateral benefits for large numbers of crafters as well. In March 2006, family and consumer sciences teacher Jan Householder of Ohio made the first doll for the daughter of a friend, to comfort her as she was treated for cancer at St. Jude Children's Hospital in Memphis. The child asked if Householder could make twelve more for the other children being treated in the same research program, which she did.

More requests led Householder to recruit a group of volunteers to help fill the need. She created and copyrighted the pattern. One group quickly became six groups, and a small grassroots nonprofit organization was born. There are now groups all over the United States. Their mission is "to give faith, love, joy, hope, and comfort to children worldwide, at times of special need, through the construction and distribution of handmade cloth dolls." The joke is that they are "a bunch of ladies playing with dolls."[60]

Hospitalized children are still at the top of the recipient list, but dolls are also given to children:

- with serious illnesses,
- who are experiencing homelessness,
- who have been through natural disasters,
- who have had a death in the family, or
- with a deployed military parent

The mission continues to expand:

- The Cleveland police department's sex crimes and child abuse unit uses the Giving Doll as an important aid in the communities they serve.
- In December 2012, sixty-five dolls were donated to siblings of children killed in the Newtown school shooting.
- Dolls going to hospitals now include a coloring book, with an apron or pants pockets full of crayons. Some dolls travel to their recipients in a tote bag with a 24" x 24" blanket.
- Dolls with red feet were donated to each Ronald McDonald House around the United States.
- During the pandemic, efforts turned to making masks for the Cleveland Food Bank.

Since the first Giving Doll was sent to St. Jude's, more than sixty thousand have been made and distributed in every US state and sixty-four countries, to children experiencing difficult situations for which they are in no way responsible. Each numerical milestone is rightfully celebrated.

There is a statement on the Giving Doll website from a woman returning from a mission trip to Haiti, where dolls always travel with her to be distributed as needed:

> *To me these dolls are more than dolls. They are love. These children have been touched by these dolls. Even though there is a language barrier here, there is no barrier when it comes to love. They have been made to feel special. They are no longer feeling alone. They have something to hold and love.*[60]

People interested in participating have many options since each doll takes eight hours to make and involves at least fourteen people. You can volunteer as a doll maker, even specializing on one aspect, like faces, in a group near you, or you can help start a group. The closest group to me meets twice a month at a fabric store, but groups also meet in churches, in homes, or as part of quilt and sewing guilds. If sewing is not in your skill set, you can donate supplies or make a tax deductible donation through the website, www.thegivingdoll.org.

Sharing Our Heart(s)

Knitted, crocheted, or sewn hearts are a quick make and a great way to use up those bits of leftover yarn or fabric. Their impact, when donated, is beyond heartwarming.

One example is the *Call to Needles* that followed the Tree of Life synagogue shooting in Pittsburgh in October 2018 that killed eleven congregants and left four police officers wounded. Pittsburgh resident and founder of the Pittsburgh Creative Arts Festival, Barbara Grossman, created HandMade Hearts, in the hope that "people will keep making and sharing hearts long after the initial shock begins to fade."[61] The idea was based on the successful

Masks for all.

Doll platoon.

Kindness Rocks movement that emerged in 2017 with its activity of leaving small painted rocks in public places.

By early 2019, fourteen hundred hearts had been made and most of those distributed. They "appeared" in places like coffee shop counters, library shelves, and bus stops. The hearts are intended to be left anonymously but may have tags attached that read "If you find this it's yours to keep, or you can pass it on. #ShareAHeartPgh." Other taglines included PittsburghStrong and LoveIsGreaterThanHate.[61] Grossman conducts public and private workshops on how to make the hearts and encourages makers all over the country to distribute hearts where they are needed.

I think the randomness of the availability of these hearts could be very helpful in the aftermath of a tragedy like Pittsburgh's, because once the media attention fades and people return to their daily lives, the grieving continues. Grievers are often caught off guard when the impact of a mass shooting, for example, sneaks its way into their day, breaking their hearts all over again. Finding one of those hearts is a reminder that there are people who understand and want to support their healing. It doesn't take the place of tangible actions, reforms, and legislation that could prevent these shootings from happening, but don't underestimate the impact of kindness just because it's a small random act.

The pandemic resulted in a similar *Call to Needles* in the UK for handmade hearts. There was a call for crafters to make *pairs* of hearts, with patterns provided, to

Crocheted hearts.

spread some love and comfort to COVID-19 patients. One heart was to be given to a patient on admission and the other to a family member, partner, or friend. People could hold the hearts close during calls or video chats and feel a little more connected to each other when they could not be together. Hospitals began requesting the hearts because they understood how isolated and afraid their patients were and the important benefit of any small acts of kindness.[62]

And since we have necessarily become more observant of sanitation and safety, as we go forward, post pandemic, we need to do our research before we act, making sure to meet the requirements of the facility to which we wish to donate. It may have guidelines that must be met such as quarantining or sanitizing the items first.

Knitted Knockers

People diagnosed with cancer are on a very specific, terrifying, individual journey. Our hope and intention  is that they never *feel* alone. Research continues, new treatments bring more cures and longer lives, and more people living with various forms of cancer, but it continues to be a brutal and exhausting process and does not always result in the hoped-for outcome. Many crafters have heeded their *Call to Needles* to help family, dear friends, and complete strangers who are on that journey, in a variety of ways.

This *Crafted Act of Kindness* began with Barbara Demorest's breast cancer diagnosis in 2011. As she recovered from a double mastectomy, thinking she was on the path to some normalcy, she was devastated again after learning that she could not use a traditional prosthesis for at least six weeks. Her doctor gave her a flyer about a knitted prosthesis, which she showed a friend, who knitted a pair for her.[63]

It all began with a young woman in Maine named Beryl Tsang, who then owned a yarn shop and was also diagnosed with breast cancer. Tsang and a group of knitters created the pattern for Knitted Knockers (originally called "Tit Bits") and made them for those in need. You can read more about Tsang and her journey at www.knitty.com/ISSUEfall05/PATTbits.html.

Demorest's experiences convinced her that she wanted and needed to share, so she contacted Tsang, who was thrilled to have someone take up this effort. Demorest created the Knitted Knockers Support Foundation (www.knittedknockers.org) to connect knitters in the effort to provide the softer, kinder prostheses to those who preferred them, at no cost. Like so many other endeavors I've written about in this book, it takes a vision, a passion, and a team to turn these acorns of ideas into mighty oaks. As we have seen with so many other acts of crafted compassion, one group of knitters became a website reaching out into the world, and as of March 2022 there were over 4,400 groups around the world, with more than 384,000 Knitted Knockers provided to women worldwide.[64]

One result of the work of the foundation is that many doctors and breast centers are now aware that there are handcrafted alternatives that are much more comfortable than the typical silicone prostheses, which are terribly expensive, heavy, sweaty, and irritating to the skin—in other words, extremely uncomfortable. They may recommend the knitted version to people frustrated with or unable to use the medically manufactured silicone devices.

Knitted breast prostheses are inexpensive to make, come in sizes A to DD, and can be placed inside most regular bras. No special fittings are required, and no insurance approval is needed. In addition to women who have had mastectomies, they also work well for those who have had lumpectomies followed by radiation, which can cause a lopsided look to the breast, and those undergoing tissue expansion reconstruction, since the fiberfill stuffing can be easily reduced or increased, and the shape adjusted.

The only requirements for the makers of Knitted Knockers is that they use approved patterns and yarn. Knitters or crocheters can choose from several patterns adapted to different skill levels. Yarn that guarantees the needed comfort level is typically soft, nonwool, and washable.

Soft, comfortable Knitted Knockers.

> **Why is a *Call to Needles* necessary for a comfortable, tolerable breast prosthesis?** We have the technology—it shouldn't be that difficult, leading me to the conclusion that even in the twenty-first century, if it would make sense for women, or ease their journey in some way, someone decided it just isn't worth the effort. In a similar way, symptoms of a pending heart attack have too often been dismissed in women because their symptoms are atypical and different from men's, often diagnosed as stress or fatigue. So the emotional and physical aftermath of removing a woman's breasts may not be deemed important enough to find a comforting alternative to silicone. OK, we got this, but we deserve better.

The Knitted Knockers website also gives advice on how to set up a volunteer group and recruit makers; how to approach doctors and clinics so they can share information with their patients; how to request Knitted Knockers if needed, along with how-to videos and tutorials and a directory by state of groups if you would like to participate in the making. And, as with so many other groups involved in providing help at no cost to the recipient, your monetary gifts are needed and welcomed, since postage alone is a challenge for the organization.

Et Cetera, Et Cetera

If a random *Call to Needles* ever compels you to look for a way to contribute, you will surely find a niche that can be met by your needle(s) of choice. What follows is a brief sampling of agencies and organizations not mentioned elsewhere in this book that are always in need of handcrafted items. The details are a just an online search away. The list is endless and always evolving, because the need is endless and always evolving.

- Lap blankets or shawls for your local hospice, skilled care facility, nursing home, or VA facility
- Blankets, hats, gloves, or scarves for shelters for the homeless or victims of domestic violence
- Hats and mittens for your local Head Start
- Octo Project—crochet octopuses for babies in the NICU. The tentacles of the octopus resemble the umbilical cord and remind babies of the womb and comfort. www.facebook.com/octoforapreemieus/
- Clothing, blankets, and toys for premature babies (check with your local NICU) www.bliss.org.uk/support-bliss/volunteer/knit-for-premature-babies, www.warmbabyproject.com/
- World Vision's Knit for Kids www.knitforkids.org/our-story
- WildCare's Baby Bird Nest Campaign wc.convio.net/site/PageServer?pagename=babybirdnest_howcanIhelp_nest_patterns
- Twiddlemuffs for people with Alzheimer's, dementia, autism, and sensory disorders www.facebook.com/groups/514961262039457/, www.goldencarers.com/how-to-make-twiddlemuffs/5015/
- Bereavement burial gowns for stillborn infants, often sewn from old wedding gowns, but many making options are available. There is a free knitting pattern available on Ravelry. Search for "Simple Tiny Angel" pattern by Christine M. Wooley. www.ravelry.com/patterns/library/simple-tiny-angel

A CALL TO NEEDLES

8

BeCAUSE CRAFTING

There are scores of people waiting for someone just like us to come along; people who will appreciate our compassion, our encouragement, who will need our unique talents. Someone who will live a happier life because we took the time to share what we had to give.

—Leo Buscaglia, author and professor

MOST HUMANS HAVE A CAUSE THEY HOLD CLOSE—something for which they are willing to give their time, passion, energy, skill, or money to promote, defend, or try to improve. We often refer to it as fighting for a cause and it seems to be baked into our DNA. Finding our cause(s) may be based on personal experience—our own, or someone we love—but it can also be about people we don't know in places we've never been. I mentioned previously in this book that we may be inspired by observed or experienced injustices—wrongs we hope to right. Our causes may be rooted in patriotism, spirituality, or social justice. We often have more than one cause we feel strongly about, but limited time, energy, and funds may curtail our efforts to support all of them.

In a 2017 Medium article titled "5 Reasons We Should Stop 'Fighting for a Cause,'" writer and entrepreneur Swati Jena suggests there are better terms to use when supporting our causes. She focuses on the bigger picture in a sprint versus marathon way. Swati also suggests rethinking the use of the word *fighting*, which implies all-out effort for a short period of time, not sustainable for what most causes require, like "patience, persistence and long-term commitment."

The term fighting has overtones of violence as well, and we have seen in the *Age of Trump* how risky that can be to manage. Following principles of non-violence seems at odds with the word fighting. Swati says, "No change that is significant and long lasting can come from a few days of slogan shouting, breaking shop windows and jamming traffic." So, what is the alternative? She suggests, among other things, to commit to one or two causes and don't "fight against"—instead, "work for."

The projects in this chapter originated in the type of energy and commitment to a cause that Swati described and is the reason I chose the title "BeCAUSE Crafting."

The Welcome Blanket Project

What a perfect picture to represent the concept of the Welcome Blanket, reminding us why we have always embraced cultural diversity. I discovered the Welcome Blanket project and started working on one early in the Trump administration, after the president made it clear that the United States would not be accepting refugees from Syria, and after he placed a travel ban on Muslims entering the United States. It was a *Call to Needles* for those who believe our strength is our diversity. Even before these two decisions, Trump the candidate made it clear that there would be a "great wall" in America to stop illegal immigration at our southern border, to be paid for by Mexico.

"Crafting our Country with our Head, Heart, Hands, and Histories."

Like so many other acts of craftivism, it was always more than a blanket. Jayna Zweiman, the award-winning multidisciplinary artist and designer who also cocreated and cofounded the Pussyhat project, created the Welcome Blanket project "to connect US residents with our newest immigrants through stories and handmade blankets, providing both symbolic and literal comfort and warmth," prompting us to be reminded, in the process, of our own family's immigration story. An added impact was that displaying the blankets publicly was a way to open a dialogue about immigration, in the hopes of reminding us that we are an inclusive, welcoming people.

Jayna also saw an opportunity to create a visual means of measuring the nearly two thousand miles of our southern border in yarn yardage. The goal was to have participants make 40" x 40" throw blankets, about the size of a receiving blanket, traditionally used to welcome a newborn to the world, which would average about twelve hundred yards of fiber each. If 3,200 blankets could be made and donated, that would represent the two thousand miles.[65]

There are patterns and recommendations provided on the Welcome Blanket website for knit, crochet, and quilt blankets (www.welcomeblanket.org). If you look at pictures in the website's gallery you will notice the simple beauty and practicality of some, while others were made with intricate, sophisticated, detailed designs, as if they were attempting to make an important point in every stitch and color choice. People have even sent woven and knotted fleece blankets; all are appreciated. In the interest of finishing in a timely way, I chose the "Come Together Blanket" pattern, designed by Kat Coyle from the Pussyhat team. It is made up of sixteen knitted squares, each divided diagonally into two triangles, with many options for arranging the squares in a variety of ways. I used a chunky yarn in navy, maroon, and ivory for the one I made.

When it was finished, I realized making the blanket was the easy part. The process included letting immigrants know your story and why you feel a connection to them as you imagine yourself in their situation, so makers were asked to share their own or their family's immigration story on a tag, with the option of using the template provided on the website.

Writing my message on the tag proved to be the more formidable task, bringing emotions to the surface I wasn't even aware existed and making me feel part of a community committed to keeping the words at the base of the Statue of Liberty alive. This is what I wrote on the tag I attached to my finished blanket, which I share, confident it was a common theme, knowing I would have loved reading all of them:

Dear receiver of this blanket: Here's a story meaningful to my family's history about immigration, and/or relocation:

As far as I know, most of my family immigrated from Germany and Scotland, a few generations ago. They were farmers and coal miners. When my father returned home after serving in the Pacific in World War II, he tried to make a living as a watchmaker in a small town in West Virginia. It became too difficult to support his wife and child that way, so he and my uncle moved their families north to Ohio where the steel and auto industries were booming. They agonized over moving only one state away because they were leaving "home." Both worked for the railroads until they retired.

My words of welcome and advice about living in the United States:

I cannot imagine being forced to leave your homeland because of war, crime or violence, and my heart hurts for you and all you have gone through. I understand you are trying to do what is best for the survival of your family. The bad attitudes of some of my fellow Americans is embarrassing to most of us.

I hope you find a welcoming, nurturing neighborhood somewhere in our country, because there are more of those than you can imagine. The angry and intolerant make the most noise, so please don't judge all of us by their words and actions. Let this blanket be my welcoming hug to you.

This first phase of the project (with the goal of 3,200 blankets) involved sending finished blankets to the Smart Museum of Art at the University of Chicago, where they were displayed between July and December 2017. Goal achieved, the tagged blankets were deservedly treated like art, organized, and catalogued before being distributed to refugees and immigrants via partner resettlement organizations.

But the blankets kept coming. The Museum of Design Atlanta was the next to curate an exhibit of the blankets in 2018 as part of Betsy Greer's exhibit *Making Change: The Art and Craft of Activism*. I encourage you to read MODA's blog post about the exhibit at www.museumofdesign.org/making-change. It is quite extraordinary and includes a couple of other craftivists covered in this book.

Welcome blankets displayed at the Fuller Craft Museum, 2018.

Another display was featured at the Fuller Craft Museum in Brockton, Massachusetts, in 2018.[66]

Throughout the four years of the Trump presidency, a disaster unfolded along the Texas and Arizona borders when immigrants seeking asylum in the United States were held in detention, with conditions that often separated parents from children and sent many back without due process and often alone. The Welcome Blanket project rededicated its efforts. The name changed slightly to Welcome Blankets ON CALL, and a partnership was formed with the International Rescue Committee's refugee resettlement efforts. The blankets, which kept arriving, were delivered to an address in Arizona, where they continued to be distributed to refugees and asylum seekers. The organization also requested more cot-sized blankets.

IRC supply chain supervisor Madelynn Paz is quoted on the website, saying:

These blankets provide a warm, handmade welcome to asylum seekers recently released from detention, who have been through so much already on their journey. The knowledge that someone cares enough to send handmade blankets makes a huge impact, especially when many families with children are released at bus stations or churches with few or no belongings. These blankets provide both comfort and warmth to what has been a difficult journey for many.[65]

Building a powerful engine driven by social media platforms and encouraging each blanket maker to share the idea with their circle of friends and makers on social media is a big part of the reason the results have been so impressive—although if I think about it too long, it saddens me to realize we needed to do this, and that the need may continue, indefinitely.

In 2021, as President Biden ended US involvement in Afghanistan, thousands of refugees were evacuated from Afghanistan and welcomed to several countries, including the United States. A new request for Welcome Blankets went out, specifically for Afghan immigrants. This resulted in another display by Museum of Design Atlanta in early 2022.

Accepting the phenomenon that the Welcome Blanket Project has become, Zweiman decided to take it global, with a new initiative called "A New Hope: Wrapping the

World in Welcome. The new goal is to blanket the circumference of the earth that connects us all (24,901 miles) with 36,521 blankets and notes."[65] And so it goes . . .

The Mourning Project: United Against Infant Mortality

Mary Vaneecke is an artist, author, and the founder of the Mourning Project. When I look at this graphic, which is the logo and a placeholder for the project, I see a heart broken over the loss of a child. Imagine you are looking at it from a drone. Then imagine zooming in close enough to see that the pixels are twenty-three thousand pairs of baby booties in white, black, and gray, representing the twenty-three thousand little souls lost in their first year of life, in one year, in the United States. This idea was inspired by the success of the AIDS quilt. Mary describes her motivation and devotion to this project:

> As a visual artist, I believe in the power of art to change hearts, minds, behavior, and the world . . . By 'drawing' a picture of a problem, we can see and feel the enormity of it. Our country, our leaders, and lawmakers need to see exactly what infant mortality looks like in America. My vision for the Mourning Project is that each of the infants lost in a given year will be remembered with a unique, handmade, heartfelt little elegy. I am asking the fiber art community to come together to create an image of infant mortality with 23,000 pairs of baby booties. This is the number of American infants who die every year.[67]

It is a disturbing reality that the United States leads the developed world in infant mortality rates.[68] This measure is determined by the number of infants who die in the first year of life per one thousand live births. This fact should be a national embarrassment. But I wonder how many Americans are even aware of this distinction. A few other facts may help us understand:

- An infant born in the United States is three times more likely to die in the first year than one born in Finland or Japan.

- Our infant mortality rates are twice as high among African Americans and are also higher in Hispanic and Native American populations than in white demographics.

- The rates are highest in southern states and a few midwestern states.

- CDC data show 6.1 infant deaths/1,000 infants in the United States in 2010; if you look at state rates, it was 8.7/1,000 in Alabama and 9.6/1,000 in Mississippi. In 2017 our rate was 5.8/1,000 births.[69]

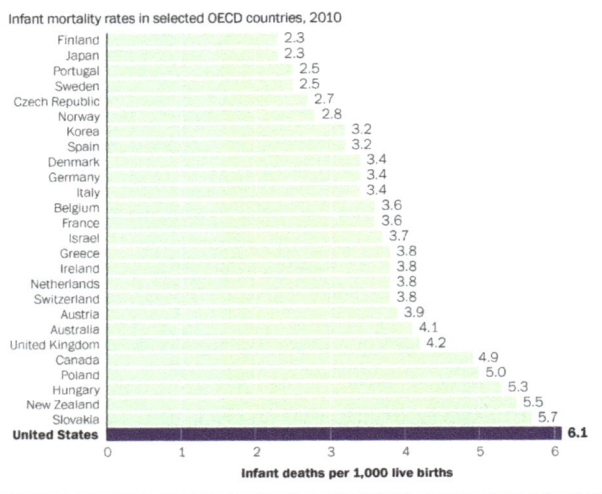

U.S. lags behind other wealthy nations on infant mortality

Infant mortality rates in selected OECD countries, 2010

Country	Infant deaths per 1,000 live births
Finland	2.3
Japan	2.3
Portugal	2.5
Sweden	2.5
Czech Republic	2.7
Norway	2.8
Korea	3.2
Spain	3.2
Denmark	3.4
Germany	3.4
Italy	3.4
Belgium	3.6
France	3.6
Israel	3.7
Greece	3.8
Ireland	3.8
Netherlands	3.8
Switzerland	3.8
Austria	3.9
Australia	4.1
United Kingdom	4.2
Canada	4.9
Poland	5.0
Hungary	5.3
New Zealand	5.5
Slovakia	5.7
United States	6.1

WASHINGTONPOST.COM/WONKBLOG   Source: CDC
Note: Canada data from 2009

The reason we lead the world in this sad statistic is not well understood, especially since we spend more on health care than any other country. The causes of infant mortality include birth defects, low birth weight, pregnancy complications, Sudden Infant Death Syndrome, and injuries. The numbers may be somewhat skewed because we have phenomenal success with infants born prematurely, while in some countries, the death of a preemie would be recorded as a miscarriage or stillbirth. That may be a factor but doesn't take into account the gigantic disparities within the borders of the United States.

Looking at state numbers reveals the disturbing reality that people of color and people living in poverty experience the highest rates of infant mortality. It is no coincidence that the states with the highest numbers are the states with the highest poverty rates and the least access to health care, especially lack of access to Medicaid. The CDC tracks and posts the data, and organizations like the March of Dimes make valiant efforts to educate and support mothers at risk.[69]

Vaneecke was inspired to create a visual way to get people to pay attention with a massive *Call to Needles*. The goal was to inspire knitters, needlework guilds, and groups around the country to make baby booties and send them in for a planned April 2020 display of the finished 38' x 38' grid of the logo filled with booties. Larger groups of craftivists completed entire square panels for the project, each holding one hundred pairs of booties.

Makers, often loss parents and grandparents, were given several options with patterns for various skill levels posted on the website, and were encouraged to embellish them as they wished. Some were knitted, others crocheted, and many sewn from fleece.

One panel, 6-O on the grid, was to be displayed at Tucson Quilt Show (cancelled during pandemic).

Booties made for the cause by Jill Holbrook.

Display representing one day in the US, 63 pairs of booties.

COVID-19 affected so many aspects of our lives, and the Mourning Project was not spared. But people on a mission will find a way. The Facebook page detailed progress and changes in plans. One adjustment was to create a traveling display, first shown at a Chicago gallery, representing one day of US infant mortality numbers, with sixty-three pairs of booties on an American flag.[70]

The website (www.maryvaneecke.com) and Facebook page also have a virtual display showing the logo pieces coming together, and it was the best place to check on the progress of this effort. Several other virtual displays were planned, and booties were still being made at the time this was written, eventually finding their place in the mosaic. As of February 2022, 14,000 pairs of booties had been placed into the display grid, with a few hundred held in reserve for mobile displays. I think Vaneecke has other ideas in the works, and I predict this will not be her only act of craftivism.

This particular project struck me as existing at an intersection of systemic racism, Black Lives Matter, poverty, and the inequities of the American health care system, making it a classic act of craftivism in addition to commitment to a specific cause and possibly, more relevant than originally imagined.

The Tempestry Project

When Trump announced his run for president, concerns rose among those representing specific causes, like the environment. You did not have to be Greta Thunberg to understand that a Trump administration would not support policies intended to protect the environment. As a candidate, Trump made it clear he would roll back environmental rules and restrictions that put any costs on businesses, even as he stated his commitment to clean air and water as a political talking point. As president, he followed through on those campaign threats, making decisions that, according to the *New York Times* "over four years . . . dismantled major climate policies and rolled back many more rules governing clean air, water, wildlife, and toxic chemicals."[71]

Trump, as president, wasted no time announcing that the United States would pull out of the Paris climate agreement, followed by executive orders opening public lands for business with no accountability and, more quietly, hoping to go unnoticed, ordering fewer prosecutions for EPA violations, enabled by a proposed thirty-one percent budget cut for the agency.[71]

What would a *Call to Needles* on behalf of the environment look like? There have been many, but the Tempestry Project stands out as a shining example of amplifying a cause that makes people look closer and think. A Tempestry is a temperature tapestry.

I am about to describe three people who created, nurtured, and continue to sustain the Tempestry Project. When they first read about climatologists so concerned about the impact of a Trump presidency that they were scrambling to preserve climate research data because they thought the data might be removed from government websites by the new administration, it resonated.

Take a breath and read that last sentence again. Pause . . . and imagine how many other government agencies, from all realms of science, must have had similar, justified concerns.

Marissa and Asy Connelly and Emily McNeil thought they were joking when their reaction to climatologists' worries was "we should return to more concrete forms of data storage."[72] But that joke became their *Call to Needles*, and the Tempestry Project was conceived.

Emily, with a background in library science, managed the local yarn shop in Anacortes, Washington. She designs, she knits, and she is part of the Tempestry team. Marissa made her living as a certified nursing assistant and senior care specialist in the same city, but in her precious spare time, she knits and works on Tempestry. And, as we have seen in other successful craftivism efforts, every team needs an Asy who can take a common concept like temperature knitting and craft it "into a meaningful, powerful, collaborative visualization of our changing climate." She's a knitter-in-training and even created the clever needle wranglers sold on their website.

The first Tempestry was knit by Emily in May of 2017, using daily high temperature data from the Naval Air Station on nearby Whidbey Island. It was exhibited that June at the Pacific Northwest Quilt & Fiber Arts Museum in La Conner, Washington. In the months that followed, they shared their idea with the local fiber community, and while many were interested in participating, the team found that few wanted to do the behind-the-scenes work of data gathering and spreadsheet curating. The Tempestry Project as a business was created in response to the community requesting kits that would let them get yarn on the needles without all the headaches. Since then, the team has processed and sold nearly 2,000 custom Tempestry kits, including for every state, over thirty different countries, and all seven continents.[72]

xxxxxx

An original Tempestry banner can be knitted or crocheted as a way to visualize climate data by documenting with needles and yarn a year of daily high temperatures in a specific location. For uniformity, the yarn originally required for the project was Wool of the Andes by Knit Picks, but the Tempestry Project has since developed its own line of domestically sourced high-quality yarn that stands up well to the pull of gravity, since these banners were meant to be hung for display. Every five degrees of temperature experienced in our weather was assigned a specific color. For example, 57°F calls for dawn, while 47°F is represented by moss. The hotter temperatures use more reds, oranges, and yellows, while the colder temperatures are represented by blues and greens.

The banner is designed to be approximately eight to twelve inches wide and four to five feet long, depending on needle size and technique used. Garter stitch or linen stitch are recommended when knitting, to make a stable banner. The maker begins with January, which becomes the bottom of the banner, knitting the high temperature for each day as one row of knitting, all the way to the end of December at the top of the banner. Instructions include the option of adding beads to represent precipitation.

×××××

The inspiration for the New Normal Tempestries, introduced in June 2019, came from the warming stripes climate data visualization work of climatologist Ed Hawkins, which represents annual deviations from average temperature from the 1800s to the present.[73] These offer a macro perspective on the climate, showing more than a century's worth of data in a single piece. Five dollars from each New Normal Tempestry Kit sold goes to nonprofits, most related to climate or environmental concerns. Over two thousand dollars has been donated to date.

Educators know that people learn in a variety of ways, usually a blend of more than one. I am a verbal and visual learner. I have always been an avid reader, but if you show me a picture, or draw me a map, I will absorb and retain it better. If large numbers of people are paying attention to the talking heads on the twenty-four-hour news cycle, that means they are seeing and hearing short, succinct sound bites that really do little to support a well-informed electorate. And we know from every disaster movie, they are *not* listening to the scientists. Sometimes, you need to get their attention with a visual image.

Pikes Peak.

Making your own Tempestry banner creates a personal connection between your life and the environment in which you exist. If you'd like to participate, you have decisions to make and options for obtaining the materials and data needed. I'm considering making two banners, one from the year I graduated from high school and another for 2020, several decades later, in the same city. I can have the Tempestry team gather the weather data for those two years and compile a chart for me of all the daily highs with optional precipitation data, related color chart, and detailed instructions that will tell me which color yarn to use in each row. I have other options. I can have them send me only the data, in a worksheet, and a color chart for reference, or a kit that includes everything I need to make my banners. You provide them with the location, year(s), and Fahrenheit or Celsius, and they do the research. One advantage I see to doing it this way is that I would not have as much investment in yarn, and little left over, because they custom make each kit to include only the yarn you will need, but you would be paying for their labor. Individual decision.

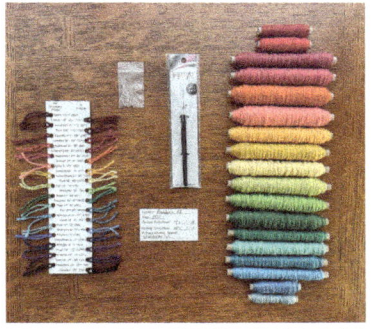

Providence, Rhode Island, 1977 kit.

If you prefer to research and gather the data yourself, the Tempestry website provides all the links you need, including access to the National Oceanic and Atmospheric Administration and Weather Underground. (www.tempestryproject.com) Ravelry and Etsy are also good places to start your process: www.ravelry.com/patterns/library/tempestry-project or www.etsy.com/shop/TempestryProject. Many online tutorials are available for help along the journey. You can also take the concept and create scarves, blankets, quilts, and other items.

Tempestry banners can mark special occasions as gifts or become larger projects with bigger goals, carrying a bigger message. Philadelphia used data to create banners representing temperatures in every fifth year from 1875 to 2018. The results are on permanent display at the Schuylkill Center for Environmental Education in Philadelphia. Other cities have created similar displays specific to them. Well-deserved recognition came for the Tempestry Project and its team when their work was displayed and honored at the Creative Climate Awards in New York City in 2018.

Permanent display at the Schuylkill Center for Environmental Education, Philadelphia.

Using craft to draw attention to a subject that doesn't get enough legitimate news coverage, a Tempestry maker may be thinking about climate change as the banner grows in their hands, and they will have created a visual for someone else to appreciate and ponder, as well, spreading the message in a unique but compelling way. And, as we have seen documented with other acts of craftivism, the making is soothing and therapeutic for the maker, helping to lower anxiety, not only because they feel they are opening eyes and bringing some enlightenment to a concerning topic, but the repetitive, rhythmic motion in the process works its magic on the maker. "Physical data objects can help people come to terms with the interlocking environmental crises we face. And they may even make us more likely to do something about them"[74] *(Craft inspiring action.).*

Talking Heads

Baseball caps have always served as mobile advertisements, promoters of logos, and declarations of team loyalty or political preference, proudly perched on people's heads. The most obvious, and to some, most obnoxious example, would be the well-marketed made in China MAGA hat, bright red and inscribed with Trump's motto Make America Great Again. Joe Biden chose a more subtle hat promotion during his 2020 presidential campaign, with his iconic aviator glasses embroidered in red, white, and blue on a blue cap. *'nuff said.*

Equally popular in head couture is the beanie (an American term), a.k.a. skull cap, tuque, slouchie, stocking cap, etc. Commercial machine-knitted hats lend themselves well to professionally embroidered logos and messages of all types, but words and illustrations can also, rather handily, be incorporated into a knitting pattern or a finished hat enhanced with hand embroidery, including duplicate stitch, described in chapter 6. Crocheted beanies are another option but usually result in less precisely formed packed lines of wording.

Your favorite search engine will reveal any number of patterns for hats and headbands with craftivist messages that might resonate with you. I've included a few of my favorites here. Etsy, Pinterest, and Ravelry are also good resources.

The Women's March in January 2017, with its common hat theme, was followed by the March for Science on Earth Day around the world in April of the same year. Trump's dismissal of science and multiple executive orders dismantling environmental protections drove people to the streets on behalf of the planet, many wearing hand-knitted "brain" hats, proudly showing their gray matter, and declaring they were not afraid to use it. Alana Noritake designed a basic beanie with a lengthy I-cord attached to resemble the human brain. It is available as a free download on Ravelry if you search the pattern database for "brain hat for science."

✕✕✕✕✕✕

Rahel Wachs's *Call to Needles* resulted in her first attempt at designing and posting a pattern for a patriotic Pussyhat, also available as a free download on Ravelry. I'd like to see more of these in the world for the same reasons she designed it: "I made this hat in order to promote

Patriotic Pussyhat.

the idea that freedom, equality, human and civil rights, woman's rights, diversity, and tolerance are all patriotic values!"[75]

✕✕✕✕✕✕

Exploring message hats led me to designer Donna Druchunas. Like many of us, Druchunas learned needle skills from her mother and grandmothers, and after taking years off from crafting, she returned to knitting when she was ready, with genuine passion. She also spins and dyes yarns, and you can see her beautiful work on her website, www.sheeptoshawl.com.

Watching the news with the rest of us became Druchunas's new *Call to Needles*, using her skills as a response to the "disturbance deep in the soul" that so many of us felt. The project on my needles as I write this is her "history has its eyes on you" hat, because I continue to be amazed at the way people justified voting once, let alone twice, for a narcissistic madman and his many enablers, and I'm confident the message will resonate long after Trump has left the Oval Office.

A CALL TO NEEDLES

Designs by Donna Druchunas on Ravelry.

I am highlighting three other hat designs by Druchunas here, all inspired by disturbing events in the *Age of Trump*. The "Blue Wave" trended in 2018 during the lead-up to the mid-term elections, two years into Trump's first term, and the blue wave memes, hats, and such proved to be predictive, as Democrats took control of the House of Representatives, electing many young, energetic, passionate, and more importantly, diverse people to Congress.

On another front, when the Trump administration directed actions to be taken at our southern border that would terrify asylum seekers and immigrants with the goal of discouraging any attempts to enter the United States, responses ranged from "Well, if they would do it legally there wouldn't be a problem" to "How can I help . . . What can I do?" Druchunas questioned whether she was complicit as she went about her daily routines, unaffected, except for the lurch in her stomach.[76] Many of us did. We watched parents separated from their children by ICE, with *(dare I say, intentionally)* poor documentation and no due process, mothers given yellow wristbands as some type of visual identification *(or branding)*. In response, Druchunas designed the No Human Is Illegal yellow armband.

The "Enough Is Enough. We Call BS!" headband was designed to support the Parkland students who organized the March for Our Lives, highlighting Emma González's speech that day with the repeated mantra "We call BS." Orange is the identifying color for Everytown for Gun Safety, founded after the Sandy Hook shootings.

All of the hats shown here, and others supporting Black Lives Matter and the Resistance, are available as free downloads on Donna Druchunas's Ravelry page (www.ravelry.com/designers/donna-druchunas). She is a prolific designer, and I encourage you to look at her other patterns for scarves, hats, shawls, socks, and more. We need to support the designers we love by purchasing patterns, in gratitude for the ones provided at no cost.

xxxxxx

Finally, since great heads think alike, Lynne Sosnowski created a pattern in 2021 she named "Talking Heads" that provides a place for you to stitch your own message in a speech bubble. The pattern is available on Ravelry (www.ravelry.com/patterns/library/talking-heads). You could use embroidery or duplicate stitch. Sosnowski describes the hat as "a cosy slouchy hat with something to say." And don't we just have so much to say!

Read.My.Head.

Menstrual Craftivism

There are two ways to think of menstrual craftivism, the first as an environmental issue and the second as a social justice and human rights (health) issue.

I am embarrassed to admit, I have lived way too many of my years unaware or in denial of my personal, monthly contributions to the everlasting waste dumped on our planet. According to the link below, I, alone, may have used 16,800 disposable pads and tampons in my life. I was completely unaware of the concept of reusable pads and cannot honestly say I would have used them, had I known, living as I did in my bubble of convenience and privilege. Not only are cloth pads better for the environment, and less expensive, but they may be less irritating to skin and healthier to use if made with 100 percent organic cotton. They would not be everyone's preference, but these links explain many of the pros and cons.

- www.greenchildmagazine.com/making-the-switch-the-benefits-of-cloth-menstrual-pads/
- www.conserve-energy-future.com/strong-reasons-switch-reusable-menstrual-products.php
- www.theecofriendlyfamily.com/mama-cloth-plus-free-patterns/

xxxxxx

Those fortunate to have a steady income take so many things for granted, like knowing that the purchase of those monthly hygiene products will not be a financial problem. But the United Way's Period Promise campaign uses the term "period poverty" to describe the struggle some women have, to afford or have access to enough products for their monthly cycles so that it does not interfere with work or school.

Menstrual products, as a human rights issue, also require us to think more globally—to consider, for example, the struggle of young girls throughout the world to attend school. It is a well-established truth that educating girls dramatically changes the dynamics of a developing country. Oprah, the Gates Foundation, and many other philanthropists have brought attention to the powerful drive of young women in various developing countries who long for and are willing to go to great lengths for an education, even at the risk of personal harm.

xxxxxx

A former colleague of mine in education, Malawi native Yakoob Badat, created the international nonprofit Nanze Children's Services (www.Nanze.org) in 2013. Its goal is to "create endless opportunities and provide education so that the children of Malawi and Sub-Saharan Africa can soar" through "grassroots initiatives in education, water, and poverty reduction." In the United States, Badat is a principal at a high school in an inner-ring suburb of Cleveland, raising a family of his own. But with the help of family and a dedicated team, Nanze raises funds year-round for Malawi, one of the poorest countries in the world, where people survive on $1.25 a day and only 35 percent of children complete elementary school. The core efforts of Nanze include education, health and wellness, and livelihood. In just a few years, Nanze built a school

A CALL TO NEEDLES

Nanze Primary School in Linthipe, Chickwasa Village, Malawi.

Yakoob Badat (standing) at the 2019 menstrual health workshop in Dedza, Malawi, where participants made reusable pads.

serving grades one through eight in Dedza, Malawi, and a supportive compound that includes additional school buildings, teacher housing, staff workrooms, and volunteer housing. It means students in the area don't have to walk seven miles to what had been the nearest school, missing most of the rainy season because mud made the walk impossible.

Many girls in Malawi are unable to go to school when they are menstruating not only because they lack access to sanitary pads—but also because of a patriarchal society with strict cultural beliefs about the role of women in society, including the monthly female cycle. Therefore, building the physical schools and staffing them with teachers was only part of the process. As they tracked attendance, a pattern emerged of female students not in attendance for several days each month. Nanze purchased sewing machines and made plans to teach locals how to make reusable menstrual pads, school uniforms, and in 2020, masks during the pandemic.

xxxxx

In July 2019, students, teachers, parents, and village chiefs attended a workshop put on by Nanze that taught participants how to make the pads and also educated families, especially the decision-makers, about female health and hygiene, with the goal of enabling girls to attend school, uninterrupted. I encourage you to visit the Nanze website for inspiration and more information and consider making a donation.

Days for Girls, mentioned in the following list, has also made great progress in Malawi on two menstrual issues—shattering menstrual stigma by delivering accurate health education to students *and* adults, and building connections with policymakers, tribal chiefs, and organizations who amplify the importance of menstrual health in Malawi.[77]

Badat and Nanze Children's Services are my personal connection to the need for menstrual craftivism, but it's a big world, and there are many other groups attempting to address the needs in different ways in different locations. A few are included here:

- **Period Aisle** (www.periodaisle.com) *(formerly Lunapads)*
  Aisle has several dignity projects, in the belief that "access to reliable menstrual products is a health and safety issue that affects millions of people with periods globally." By this third decade of the twenty-first century, Aisle has supplied reusable pads and period underwear to more than seventeen thousand menstruating women in eighteen different nations. Its founders also serve as mentors and support for similar organizations including financial help.

- **Days for Girls International** (www.daysforgirls.org)
  "Turning Periods into Pathways . . . Every girl. Everywhere. Period." This is one of the largest pad sewing groups worldwide and has chapters in many different towns in several countries. Using the proven techniques of health education, income generating opportunities, and quality menstrual care solutions, the goal is to "give back days of opportunity and health to young women." Reach has extended into 140 countries with no plans to slow down. For quality control, the organization only accepts sewn pads made with its pattern and from approved fabrics.

- **I Support the Girls** (www.isupportthegirls.org/)
  This international network collects and distributes bras, underwear, and menstrual products. "Around the globe we're helping girls and women experiencing homelessness, victims of domestic violence, victims of sex trafficking, refugees, and evacuees of natural disasters . . . breast cancer survivors, inmates in correctional facilities, transgender teens and adults, veterans, native Americans and many more." The network's philosophy is based on the idea of collecting and distributing locally whenever possible. The pandemic resulted in a 35 percent increase in requests for these products, and this organization has worked hard to meet that demand, ramping up efforts, collecting and distributing over two million products to individuals and organizations, because "periods don't stop for pandemics."

- **AFRIpads** (www.AFRIpads.com)
  This effort includes a small factory in Uganda that employs 150 local women making reusable pads to be provided to women and girls who need them. In 2010, AFRIpads reached 3.5 million women and kept more than seven hundred million pads from ending up in the environment. In 2016 AFRIpads collaborated on a graphic novel style book titled *Girl Talk* that teaches the facts about puberty. It has been translated into many languages and revised for the Muslim culture.

- **Sew in Peace** (www.sewinpeace.blogspot.com/2013/08/feminine-cloth-pad-tutorial.html) Sew in Peace serves Haiti as part of a church mission. In 2018, the organization distributed over six thousand cloth menstrual pads to women of all ages. Similar to the efforts in Malawi and through AFRIpads, educating young women is one of the main goals, and that means removing as many obstacles as possible to consistent school attendance. Sew in Peace distributes kits to young female students containing basic hygiene information, two bars of soap, three pairs of underwear, one hundred ibuprofen tablets, five safety pins, and ten reusable cloth feminine pads.

If making menstrual pads becomes a *Call to Needles* for you or you want to help, there are many options. You can make reusable pads to donate, sew or buy underwear to send to organizations for their pad kits, buy reusable pads from businesses that will send them directly to aid organizations, or donate to the organization of your choice. And spread the word!

There are many reusable pad patterns available as free downloads:

- Luna Wolf (www.lunawolf.co.uk/wordpress/)
- The Eco Friendly Family (www.theecofriendlyfamily.com/2011/06/mama-cloth-plus-free-patterns/)
- Cloth Menstrual Pad Database (www.clothpads.wikidot.com/patterns)

Before donating reusable pads to any organization, be sure to check its website for any specific requirements.

Consider as well, that in the *Age of Trump* detainees seeking asylum at our southern border were reportedly denied simple hygiene products like toothpaste, soap, diapers, and menstrual products. I did not find an organization that collected only menstrual products for those immigrants. There were organizations collecting a variety of necessities to meet simple human needs. The generosity of Americans was, as always, overwhelming, but the Trump administration made it so ridiculously difficult to distribute those products that there was a great turnover

---

Those of us who received "the talk" from Mom in the sixties can attest that it was as difficult a subject to broach in that era as it probably is today in developing countries. Many, like my mom, handed us a book, and trust me, it wasn't a graphic novel, although there were illustrations (very medical). I was told to read the book and then we would "talk" if I had any questions. (Her fingers crossed as she left the room hoping there would be no questions and that I would become enlightened regarding the "burden" of being a woman.) This is why I cannot comprehend and barely tolerate fellow boomers who blah-blah-on-and-on about the good old days when we were kids. Because . . . ignorance is bliss? We are so much better at so many things now. Let's just keep moving forward, please!

in agencies attempting to do this work. So, assume your best internet sleuth persona if you would like to help a specific population not already served by the organizations mentioned here.

The Violet Protest

In previous chapters, I have written about protest art, craftivism, and *Crafted Acts of Kindness*, some as a direct result of the Trump era and some continuing a long-standing endeavor because the need still exists. I turn now to a different type of *Call to Needles* with the intention of focusing on healing and unity, the Violet Protest. It managed to be political but not partisan.

As the 2020 presidential election approached, Phoenix artist Ann Morton conceived an idea for a way to remind those who represent us in DC that the intended model is to *work together*. "A physical message of friendly protest." Her intention became a movement, with plans that called for her to receive 26,750 squares from crafters around the United States, Puerto Rico, and DC by November 15, 2020, using their needles of choice, or even no needles in some cases. These squares could be knit, crocheted, sewn, quilted, embroidered, woven, screen-printed, appliquéd, or felted. The unifying concept was that the squares must measure 8" x 8" and contain equal parts red and blue, creating an illusion of violet, the color resulting from the mix of those two patriotic colors.[78] Of course, the pandemic caused delays and revisions to the calendar.

And why such a specific number of squares? This was the result of artistic vision and creativity. After the 535 members of the 117th Congress were sworn in in 2021, each member would receive a package of fifty crafted violet protest squares, with a letter explaining the intent of the gift and asking recipients to support these core American values:

- Respect for others
- Citizenship
- Compromise
- Country over party and corporate interests
- Courage
- Candor
- Compassion
- Creativity

One paragraph of the letter said the following:

We as makers—knitters, quilters, stitchers—carry the tradition of American hands that have crafted ideas into productive objects for centuries. Through our hands, we have made for you a physical symbol of our collective voices, a tangible expression of our diversity and our common hope for unity.[78]

One line in this quote resonated strongly in me: "The tradition of American hands that have crafted ideas into productive objects for centuries." *That is the common thread holding this book together.* The entire letter can be read on the Violet Protest website (www.violetprotest.com).

A CALL TO NEEDLES

Makers (top to bottom, left to right):

Heather Kirschner, Mesa, AZ; Cheryl Hopper, Washington, PA; Azra Kearns, Phoenix, AZ; Doerte Weber, San Antonio, TX; Carol Sanger, Phoenix, AZ; Mary Logue, Golden Valley, MN; Katie Leinweber, Scottsdale, AZ; Candace Wilkinson, Phoenix, AZ; Hannah Allen, State College, PA; Tané Clark, Tempe, AZ; Wendy Raisanen, Phoenix, AZ; Bonnie Scott, Salem, VA; Maxene Harlow, Clarksdale, MS; Tara Ritacco, Carlsbad, CA; Nancy Nakamoto, Torrance, CA; Kitty Spangler, Pittsburgh, PA; Cheryl Goodberg, Marana, AZ; Maureen Craddock, N. Massapequa, NY; Audrey Good, Mesa, AZ; Sarah Fabbri, McKinney, TX; Kathy Arello, Golden Valley, AZ; Debra Everett, Mesa, AZ; Carol Garland, Perris, CA; Kelly Waterman, Blue Ash, OH; Kelly Reo, Columbus, OH.

Deadlines were adjusted due to the pandemic. Part of the new plan involved creating a public display of the finished squares in spring 2021 at the Phoenix Art Museum, before they were to be mailed to Washington late in 2021. The museum exhibited the squares on the walls but also in a compact, unique way, in 116 stacks of squares spelling out US in that double entendre I so love—for the United States, but also for all of *us* speaking through our creations to our Congress.

Participants in the Violet Protest were asked to commit to making a number of squares (in multiples of five). I committed to making five squares. After registering as a volunteer, I received tags to attach to my squares, providing maker's name, address, and optionally, a personal message of unity. The tags also became part of the display at the museum and ensured each member of Congress would know who made the squares they received. Like an unrolling spool of thread, this project covered a long span of time, and the donated squares reflected changes, events, and experiences along the way.

By October 2021, the Violet Protest team had collected 13,127 squares, enough to send each member of the 117th Congress twenty-four to twenty-five squares each, several of which would come from their own states. Volunteers not only sorted and packed squares but also conducted the time-intensive task of recording who would receive whose squares.

Movements this large require a team that includes tech support, allowing visitors to the site to click on various stacks of squares, by grid, and learn more about the people who made the squares, by name and what part of the country they are from, long after completion of the

Phoenix Art Museum display.

project. This gives makers a sense of belonging to a community. Displaying the work in an art museum reminds us that we *are* creating art and gives it deserved respect while, hopefully, inspiring and uplifting others in solidarity. And try to imagine being a member of Congress receiving from makers all over the country these squares containing their urgent pleas in every stitch and written message. *(Remember chapter 3 . . . It's always personal.)*

The Social Justice Sewing Academy

The research for this book has been enlightening and fascinating. But, somehow, this effort touched me at a much deeper level. I think it's because I feel like I know the young people involved in this project. I taught them every year of my thirty-five-year teaching career. I recognize and remember the stories of those willing to entrust me with their truths. It was always my goal to help them speak that truth, whenever possible. To see a dedicated team helping students find and use their voices, enabling them to speak to a wider audience is very moving for me. There are so many imposed limits on classroom teachers to meet standardized curriculum goals and prepare for the relentless testing that these limits cannot help but stifle creativity and individualized instruction. And rarely are there any rational limits on class size, which allows some students to go unnoticed.

The Social Justice Sewing Academy does not use the word craftivism, but the combination of art, education, and activism is the very definition of craftivism. Founder Sara Trail and her team have created and are sustaining an "intergenerational collective of textile artists and activists" to create a "21st century sewing circle" with a timely mission. Trail is the executive director and brings a graduate degree in education from Harvard, in addition to her crafting bona fides, to this position, having learned to sew at age four. She is an author (since the age of thirteen), sewing teacher, and designer of patterns and fabrics.

Her personal *Call to Needles* came in 2012 at age seventeen. Not allowed to attend a protest over the killing of Trayvon Martin, she turned to the tools she trusted most and made a quilt in his memory, the Rest in Peace, Trayvon quilt, which she was able to give to Martin's mother at a Black Lives Matter event.[79] The power of this project awakened the craftivist inside.

Trail launched the Social Justice Sewing Academy in 2016 as an undergrad at Berkeley. Her vision was to empower middle and high school students, mostly in low-income areas, another population of typically unheard, marginalized people in this country, to understand the concept of social justice using an educational component, in a workshop format, followed by a discussion of the subject. Participants were then encouraged to find their voice and use the workshop to send that voice out into the world.

The ultimate goal of these workshops is to create quilts to display at quilt shows, art shows, art exhibits, art museums, and event openings. The idea is to have the maximum exposure and impact and share the message with a public not always familiar with the feelings, experiences, and insights of these teens.

Consider the average quilter (predominantly white and female) navigating her way through a typical quilt show, awed by the skills on display, when she turns a corner and sees something unique: quilts that speak to social justice issues and stitched personal experiences.

I can only imagine the reactions, and I am sure some observers felt uncomfortable and quickly moved on. I like to think most people would stop and admire the creative ways the students found to speak about their reality, and a

Your Voice Matters.

QuiltCon 2020.

few may even be changed or willing to consider ideas that don't fit their worldview. *(That is always the hope.)* One woman, shown in a video on the SJSA website attending a quilt show, said that seeing a quilt that read "build movements, not walls" led her on a personal journey to research the issues related to the Trump-proposed wall, which resulted in her own personal paradigm shift.[80]

In Trail's words, "Politics, equity, and social justice themes are not typically found in traditional or even modern quilt techniques."[80] But quilts, through their makers (and crafts, generally) speak to each other in a language of their own. The woman in the video may have previously had few, if any, conversations with teenagers of color, but here was a visual conversation in a language they both understood.

In my experience teaching job-hunting skills to teens, they communicate well with each other but, for those not raised in a communication-rich household, they often feel inadequate trying to have a conversation with an adult they have just met, or with adults, generally. So, when given other ways to communicate, they will have much to say to those willing to hear (or see).

These social justice sewing circles begin each journey to a finished quilt by discussing the concept of social justice and asking teen participants to consider how their lives fit into that discussion. They ask them to consider "who has the power: to craft their own story; to tell their stories from a first-person narrative; to create an accurate sense of self; to define their community; to see themselves and people like them portrayed positively?"[80] Workshop leaders ask them to consider how their stories could be shared and used as tools to create change and bring what has been missing in conversations for so long into clear view.

The volunteers, who include college students and skilled quilters, then have students formulate an idea

QuiltCon 2020.

SJSA Remembrance Quilt by Diane Owen.

and create it on paper, after which they are introduced to the array of available fabrics to turn the idea into art. If they wish to learn the necessary embroidery skills, they will be encouraged and taught. The more common process, though, is to select colors and fabrics for maximum impact, cut out the lettering and pictures depicted in the drawing, lay it out, stand back, and take a look before using fabric glue to anchor everything in place. These young social justice warriors then write an artist statement in which they identify themselves to the next part of the team, the volunteer embroiderers, scattered around the country, who will stitch the temporarily glued pieces into place with a variety of embroidery stitches. The creators can give instructions as specific as they like but also usually allow some creative license for the embroiderers to enhance or embellish if so inspired. The creators may want features on a face or a phrase to be stitched in and can request that in their artist statement.

The typical community quilt will have 20 squares made by 20 students embroidered by 20 volunteer stitchers. A quilt may have a specific theme like Black Lives Matter or may represent a range of social justice issues. The finished squares are turned over to the volunteer quilters, who make decisions about the arrangement of the blocks and the fabrics and colors to connect them together. The layered pieces are quilted together using long-arm quilting machines and the edges are bound for the finished product.

I love the intergenerational aspect of this project. Collaborative efforts mean we teach each other, and everyone comes away better for it. And consider the fact that these fabric statements, while under construction, move around the country, touched by many hands, which itself is uniting. This idea is addressed on the SJSA website as the components of a quilt reflecting the mission, "layers of community that come together to create":

- the quilt top—the students and workshop leaders;
- the quilt back—the support team of organizers, sponsors, and volunteers that hold it all together;
- the batting—the donations and materials from artists and vendors; and
- the stitching—the intergenerational community of volunteers that embroider, embellish, and quilt, increasing the volume of the message from the student artists' voices.[80]

Like most successful endeavors, it doesn't end there for the SJSA. The mission continues, with fresh ideas and approaches like the portrait art quilts made for the Remembrance Project, which tells the stories of people who have died due to social injustices, now shared in the book *Stitching Stolen Lives: Amplifying Voices, Empowering Youth, & Building Empathy Through Quilts* by Sara Trail and Teresa Duryea Wong.

Collaborative efforts mean we teach each other, and everyone comes away better for it.

Other adventures for the SJSA include the following:

- Banners representing solidarity and remembrance, available for display at events, when requested by local and national activist organizations
- Students from two high schools creating an Obama portrait quilt to be displayed at the Barack Obama Presidential Center in Chicago
- Quilts of remembrance for families who have lost a loved one to violence, using textiles donated by the family
- 2020 Block of the Month Club series to create your own community quilt, based on student art

If you'd like to be involved in the SJSA, you can volunteer as an embroiderer or quilter, be trained to use the soon-to-be-standardized curriculum as a workshop leader, or support them financially with a donation. Behind the scenes, organizations like this are often looking for grant writers, marketing specialists, and bookkeeping experts as well. You can find more information on the website, www.sjsacademy.org.

One more thought on this organization that I hope touches you as it did me. I watched the videos on the website and found myself thinking of the abolitionist sewing circles and the arpilleristas of Chile I have written about in chapter 10 and all that they have in common—the sense of finding a community of like minds and the comfort that brings, as they so resolutely find ways to be heard. I have no doubt these statement quilts, produced by SJSA, the Mother's Dream quilts, the AIDS quilts, the Gone But Not Forgotten quilts, the COVID Memorial quilts (all in chapter 9), and others, will speak for decades to come, documenting history and what mattered most to us. They will rightfully hang in museums and be sought by collectors as treasures like early American samplers or Gee's Bend quilts.

Or . . . You Can Just Show Up and KiP (Knit in Public)!

World Wide Knit in Public Day (www.wwkipday.com) has been held on the second Saturday in June since 2005. The US typically has the most groups participating each year, hosted by local yarn shops as well as individuals, but the KIP groups can be found in more than fifty countries. All forms of needlework are welcome and there was, traditionally, *no* political or activist motivation. The intention was to promote knitting with the motto "better living through stitching together." However, this is just the origin story. There are several examples in this book of craftivists who take their knitting into public places as important conversation starters.

Have you ever found yourself knitting alone (or wielding your needles of choice) in a public setting outside of an organized KIP? I have found that stitching in public can sometimes turn out to be an unintended study in anthropology or sociology. "Raise Your Needles: In Defence of Public Knitting," a 2021 article in the online magazine Public Books, by Aleesha Paz, describes "two kinds of public knitting: incidental and intentional. The former refers to the kind of public knitting that is to do with passing time. The latter is when the act of knitting in public *is* the point, for example, as a mindfulness exercise, a piece of performance art or protest, or as a social activity."⁸¹

×××××

Paz clarifies the concept of public versus private, important to this discussion:

*The line between public and private is a curious thing. Most of us cross this divide multiple times a day, moving between home and work or from one private space to another, passing through public areas to get there. By definition, the public and private are opposed—each space has its own distinct purposes and designated sets of behavior. Performing what is considered a private act in a public place can have consequences.*⁸¹

Paz goes on to say that knitting, while not always accepted in public settings, has made this transition, even if non-knitters missed the memo. "To them, it was still something old-fashioned and embarrassing that firmly belonged within the privacy of the home." Consider some of the activities you have observed in public spaces that are not necessarily public activities, like an individual or small group working out or practicing yoga or tai chi in a park, street performers in the city, marches or protests, or photographers posing a wedding party, and, perhaps, realize that knitting in public could be allowed, without concern. "Public spaces should be platforms for human expression and interaction . . . where we can be inspired by each other's creativity and individuality. There's power in the way we inhabit public space. The way we move through it, make use of it—fill it with our selves, our objects, our activities."⁸¹

Knitting on a bus or train, commuting to work or school, it would not be unusual for someone to start a conversation about what you're making, a unique sight in a world of people relentlessly facing their phones. In a business meeting, however, a needleworker might be perceived as rude and inattentive, bored, or even a distraction to others, but when not intrusive, the process may help the knitter better focus on what is being said without zoning out.

Rozsika Parker wrote in her classic *The Subversive Stitch: Embroidery and the Making of the Feminine* that "there is something disturbing in the image of the embroiderer deep in her work . . . her autonomy is suspected by some men to be a control mechanism" (p. 11). Hinda Mandell, in *Crafting Dissent*, takes Parker's statement further:

Bringing the production of traditional "women's work" out of domestic space and into public places has been used to both cast suspicion on women and to belittle them . . . Both reactions emerge from men in power unsettled by the actions of seemingly subordinate women. (p. 3)

Mandell shares an example in the story of her knitting instructor, attending a local city council meeting, knitting as she listened to the lawyers for a developer state their case. During the public comment portion of the meeting, she set down her needlework, went to the microphone and shared her concerns, receiving "supportive applause." On the way back to her seat, the attorney for the developer said, "Why don't you stick to your knitting, lady!" (p. 3)

Knitting or crafting in public can be used as a craftivism technique, when done in public or at selected sites, to start a conversation, when onlookers (especially women, less likely to find crafters threatening) become curious and begin to ask questions. It becomes an opportunity, as demonstrated by the Knitting Nannas Against Gas (chapter 6) or the Yarn Mission (chapter 12), to engage people in a dialogue they were not expecting, in a way that does not make them feel challenged, disrespected, or mocked.

Knitting or crafting in public can also act as a silent form of protest. Sixty-eight-year-old Mary Holden showed up to participate in a planned action in Louisville, Kentucky, in August 2020 that was covered by local news outlets. Grannies for Justice for Breonna planned to sit in the front yard of Louisville Attorney General Daniel Cameron to protest the lack of any act of justice for Breonna Taylor from ten to eleven a.m. (one hour). Mary chose to use her time knitting. With four minutes left in the hour, the grannies were told they had to leave. Mary told the police she was staying for the remaining four minutes to finish what she started. *(Is there any doubt she would have packed up and left quietly after those four minutes?)* But alas, I refer you back to the Rozsika Parker quote earlier in this section. The Louisville Metro Police decided to arrest her and charge her with third degree criminal trespassing.[82] *Getting into "good trouble," Mary!*

Knitting or crafting in public can also act as a silent form of protest.

A CALL TO NEEDLES

9

METAPHORIC QUILTS

Making a quilt is actively committing to life, one small, breath-like stitch at a time. Wounds, it appears, can be patched. Torn hearts can be sewn.

—Bonnie Lee Black, *The WOW Factor*

9/11 Quilt at John Marshall High School, Cleveland, Ohio.

In the year following the terrorist attacks of September 2001, large numbers of memorial quilts were lovingly sent to New York City from all over the country. They arrived at fire stations, police precincts, schools, churches, and other institutions, in an attempt to let the people of NYC know they were being held closely in our hearts. My high school students made one as a class project and decided they wanted to send it to Stuyvesant High School, which they saw in the news was the high school closest to the Twin Towers and all the souls lost that day. When a friend of mine ran into an acquaintance at the grocery store who had a son attending Stuyvesant, she asked for contact information on behalf of my students and was told "please . . . no more quilts!" They don't know what to do with the ones already received. So many quilts! We found a home for this one in one of our school's showcases.

We had better quilting success a little closer to home, on a smaller scale. My students had the biggest hearts, in spite of, or perhaps, because of, their personal experiences.

In the late 1990s, as one of my classes was about to begin a brief, basic sewing unit in a comprehensive family and consumer sciences class, I told my students that they would each be making a small, simple block quilt, which they would then layer and knot to finish. I suggested that they each make their quilt with someone in mind to give it to when completed. After class, one of my students told me about her sister's premature infant spending months in the NICU at Metro Hospital in Cleveland and how the nurses draped donated lap quilts over each incubator to warm up a necessarily sterile environment. When the preemie was able to go home, the donated quilt went too, now part of the family. We decided, together, to make this a service learning project to document for our FCCLA (Family, Career and Community Leaders of America) chapter. Everyone in the class seemed fully committed and thrilled with this project—a rarity. From piles of donated fabric scraps, these young women, most using a sewing machine for the first time, created small, colorful, fun, well-made quilts and matching pillows. We took pictures of everyone with their finished quilts and were able to take a field trip to see the NICU and deliver them in person. I still see those pictures occasionally and the smiling faces remind me how proud they were of their accomplishments.

At the beginning of the next school year, one of the students from that class stopped in to tell me that while in the park for a family picnic that summer she noticed a family with a baby on *the* quilt she had made and donated to the NICU. She introduced herself and identified herself as the quiltmaker. They told her how much the quilt still meant to them and were able to thank her, and she was able to meet her quilt's former preemie. At least one student was able to realize the impact of her gift and hopefully understand her ability to make an impact.

Our classroom was not exactly the traditional sewing bee working to complete a single quilt, but it still created a more social, shared environment, where everyone could talk freely about anything as they worked, individually, which is rare in a classroom setting. And for all of us, collectively, it created a moment of community in a large, often impersonal environment, as well as individual feelings of accomplishment, and empowerment to fill a need in the larger community.

xxxxxx

Perhaps one reason the appeal of quilts is so universal is because they have played so many roles in our history. Repeating a quote used earlier in this book, credited to a pioneer woman on the prairies of early America, "I make my quilts as fast as I can to keep my family warm, / and as beautiful as I can to keep my heart from breaking." Necessity (protection from the elements), practicality (reusing and recycling), our need for aesthetics and expression, and satisfying the need for tactile stimulation (for reasons

Quilts for our local NICU.

that range from a need to be busy to the satisfaction that comes from creating) have all influenced quilt making.

But quilts are also, often, metaphors for our lives. Bonnie Black, who writes and maintains the blog *The WOW Factor, Words of Wisdom from Wise Older Women*,[83] describes the metaphor of the quilt beautifully:

> *There's nothing like patchwork quilting to make a girl (I use the term advisedly) feel as if she's sewing the worn, torn pieces of her life back together. It's quilting as metaphor, quilting as medicine, quilting as magic.*

It may also be true that quilts as metaphors are sometimes less about the personal journey of an individual and more about contributing to the greater good. When history and events leave us feeling, individually, quite helpless, quilting and other crafts can tell the stories of the unheard, while bringing the makers something they need as well, whether comfort, empowerment, community, or a complex combination of psychological rewards.

Americans today tend to think that quilts and quilting are somehow a uniquely American experience. I can both deny and defend that thinking.

The creation and use of quilted fabric can be traced back to ancient Egypt and Asia in late BC and early AD. Relics uncovered and now residing in museums include a quilted linen carpet found in a Siberian cave tomb from the first century, and pieces of quilted garments worn by crusaders under their chain mail.[84] *(The mystery is, did they leave home wearing them or discover them on their journeys and bring the concept back home?)*

Pieces of the Tristan Quilt, believed to be "one of the oldest decorative surviving quilts," possibly made for a wedding in the 1390s, are shared by the V&A Museum in London and the Bargello Palace in Florence. Quilting came to America with the arrival of immigrants from England, Wales, and Holland who brought with them needle skills and intimate knowledge of cloth production.[84]

While the "invention" of quilting is obviously not something for which Americans can take credit, I can state with confidence and conviction that we have given quilting a unique American flavor. We are a nation of immigrants, and our struggles to determine the nation we would become included a blend of good, bad, and ugly. But the result, a republic *(if we can keep it)* with a diverse, driven population has been tracked and documented by people with needles and sewing machines in ways as diverse as its citizenry.

Like so many other craft related topics discussed in this book, the history of quilts in America evolved with and reflected the role of women in each era. Sometimes personal, sometimes political, but always, also, a form of art.

From the Puritans experiencing difficult winters on the East Coast, to the prairies of the Midwest as immigrants

I can state with confidence and conviction that we have given quilting a unique American flavor.

pushed deeper into this continent, quilts were necessary for survival. For those makers, functionality trumped beauty. New fabric was not usually available, and time and circumstances did not allow much creativity. Every scrap of every worn or outgrown article of clothing would become part of a quilt. These fabric sandwiches were usually knotted together, rather than quilted, since winter days were short, lighting was bad, and space was often inadequate for setting up a quilt frame. Any pleasing enhancements were usually in the surface stitching and knotting.

Much like the embroidered samplers discussed earlier, quilt-making looked far different in the homes of the wealthy. Whole cloth quilts were created with intricate designs, using colorful fabrics and threads, and complex techniques like appliqué and trapunto.

Quilts Made by Enslaved People—Legend, Folklore, Art

Hidden in Plain View: A Secret Story of Quilts and the Underground Railroad, by Jacqueline L. Tobin and Raymond G. Dobard, tells the oral history of African American quilter Ozella Williams, after the authors learned about her and her beautiful work in the Old Market Building of Charleston, South Carolina. *(So much beautiful, crafted art to discover there.)* Williams shared the stories, handed down through generations of her family, about slave-made quilts that contained hidden codes to help slaves escape, then find the Underground Railroad, and ultimately, freedom. According to Williams, many traditional quilt patterns had specific meanings and were first made into sampler quilts to teach slaves the codes, since most slaves were denied the right to learn to read or write. For example, the Flying Geese pattern was code for *follow the migration of geese north toward Canada and freedom*, while the Crossroads pattern meant *once through the mountains travel to a crossroads in Cleveland, Ohio, code-named "hope."*[85]

I live in a suburb of Cleveland, which includes as its motto "crossroads of the nation." A landmark home on the square, now housing an upscale restaurant, was used as a waystation for the Underground Railroad, one of eight such landmarks in Northeast Ohio. Runaway slaves were often hidden in cellars before being transported, hidden in loads of hay, to a boat headed to Canada.[86]

Ozella Williams's recorded oral history was embraced by the public and written into children's books and lesson plans for teachers.[87] From this teacher's viewpoint, I can say those lesson plans are quite well done and could be used in math, history, or art classes. The authors and the book have taken a great deal of criticism, though, from experts in American history, as well as quilt historians, who point out that folklore is not the same as history.

Unfortunately, no evidence or documentation has ever been discovered that backs up the idea that enslaved people constructed quilts with patterns that had meanings ranging from when to attempt escape to how to find the route to freedom and safe houses along the way.[88] One argument against the folklore is that many of the quilt patterns mentioned did not exist until well after the Civil War. The concept of coded quilts was also never mentioned when slave narratives and oral testimonies were recorded and, not surprisingly, no original proof in the form of quilts have survived this long. Another argument is how unrealistic it is to assume that on a large scale, slaves could have obtained enough fabric, tools, and time (in secret) to create so many sampler quilts and also create additional blocks and pieces to post on trees, in windows, etc.

Women who were part of the Northern abolitionist movement, however, including freed slaves, felt a strong enough *Call to Needles* to state their opposition to slavery visually, in their quilts. One documented example contained this inscription:

> I'd sooner spend my days within
> Some dark and dismal cave
> Than to be guilty of the sin
> of holding one poor slave.[88]

These northern craftivists hosted antislavery craft fairs in Ohio, Pennsylvania, and New England to raise money for their cause.

I understand the logic and depths of research of historians on this topic, and I look to science and research for most of my answers in life, but folklore often has at least a "thread" that connects to real experiences and even science, whether a cure for an ailment, a farming technique, or a *Call to Needles*. And there are books and a lot of documentation supporting the existence of many an African slave as seamstress and quilter extraordinaire. If slaves were not creating codes in quilts, that does not dismiss the concept that slaves with needle skills dedicated some of their efforts to resistance and acts of defiance, or what we now call craftivism.

In general, the enslaved people who made quilts were often following the design and color wishes of the mistress of the house and working under constant supervision, just as they did when constructing clothing. Keep in mind that most of the slaves in the Southern states were forcefully brought there from West Africa, where they had their own crafting culture rich in the use of bold, bright colors and stitching techniques like appliqué. Since it was illegal for slave owners to allow enslaved people to learn to read and write, a quilting slave might tap into her cultural heritage to let her needlework speak her truth, sometimes even "under her eye," slipping an African symbol into a quilt that the mistress would never notice for any reason other than its beauty and workmanship.

× × × × × ×

For more on this subject, I recommend the book *The Invention of Wings* by Sue Monk Kidd. This gem of historical fiction covers the childhood and life of Sarah Grimke, a famous abolitionist and women's rights advocate, born and raised in Charleston, South Carolina. There are many intricate, strong threads woven into this story. I am going to pull on one of those threads for this discussion of quilts.

The life of a slave in a large city varied a bit from plantation life. In a city like Charleston, slave owners were more aware of the abolitionist movement and may have given their slaves slightly less supervision than on the plantations, sending them out on shopping errands, referring to them as maids, and (in the telling of this story) allowing them to make small amounts of personal earnings selling their homemade wares at a local market.

None of these examples actually improved the life of an enslaved person in any meaningful way.

Miss Grimke and her family are not the only important characters in *The Invention of Wings*. Charlotte is the house slave and seamstress who makes all the clothing for the entire household, including the slaves. The detailed, fitted, ornate dresses worn by the women and their elaborate hats and accessories were works of craftsmanship while the clothes for enslaved people were, of course, more practical. Charlotte also quilts and teaches all her needlework skills to her daughter Handful. The character of Handful was based on Sarah Grimke's personal slave, Hetty:

> *Nights she teach me everything she knows 'bout quilts. I tore up old pants legs and dress tails and pieced 'em. Mauma say in Africa they sew charms in their quilts. I put pieces of my hair down inside mine.*[89]

As a needleworker reading the book, I was fascinated with the quilt frame Charlotte constructed in the small quarters that housed her and her daughter. It had a hoist mechanism, so her *story quilt*, another important character, could be worked on top of the bed, and then pulled up out of the way, as if to become part of the ceiling when not in use. No one in the big house paid much attention to the scraps of fabric left over in the construction process, so those precious waste pieces often found their way back to Charlotte's private stash. These small, high-risk acts of defiance and craftivism were micro-acts of control in a life where control was neither granted nor tolerated. Important documents or keepsakes were sewn into hidden pockets in the quilt. Charlotte was a strong woman, determined to resist the system that denied her freedom in whatever ways she could.

When the finished story quilt is revealed in the book, each block, set in chronological order, tells a part of her story, in all its moments of beauty and ugliness, joy and sadness, set in the fabric, detailed in the colors, using needle and thread as her voice. I have discussed the power of using needlework of any type, in difficult times, to empower, comfort, and heal, so I am including the author's thoughts here on that subject:

> *The quilt in the novel is meant to be more than a warm blanket or a nice piece of handiwork. It is Charlotte's story ... Above all, I wanted Charlotte's story quilt to speak about the deep need we have to make meaning out of what befalls us. I wanted it to suggest how important it is to take the broken, painful, and discarded fragments of our lives and piece them into something whole. There can be healing, and power, too, in giving expression to what's inside of us, in having our voices heard and our pain witnessed.*[90]

Charlotte's story quilt in *The Invention of Wings* was based on the famous quilts of African American quilter Harriet Powers, whose extraordinary work can be found at www.mfa.org/collections/object/pictorial-quilt-116166.

World War and Post-War Quilting

Earlier in this book I discussed the home front knitting efforts during World Wars I and II, endorsed and promoted by the Red Cross. Quilts were also part of these patriotic support efforts. During World War I, Americans were urged to make more quilts for their homes, sparing blankets for soldiers. By the time we were involved in World War II, the Red Cross saw an opportunity to raise money for their efforts, encouraging the creation of "signature quilts." Sponsors paid a small fee to have their names embroidered on individual quilt blocks. The finished quilts were then raffled off with the proceeds going to the Red Cross.[91] Many home front efforts also included donating handmade quilts to war-torn areas of Europe, benefitting, as always, the recipients as well as the makers.

In the post-Depression, post-War era, quilting faded in popularity for a time, somewhat doomed by its association with making do in lean times. People wanted to move forward, and quilts were considered old-fashioned. They made a strong comeback in the 1970s, as sewing machines, quilting tools, and techniques became more sophisticated and fabric stores provided so many options in colors and prints. There was a small explosion in quilting in 1976 during America's bicentennial. I was one of many who made a patriotic quilt in the ubiquitously merchandised red, white, and blue patriotic-themed fabrics.

At that point, quilting moved into the realm of a leisure art. Patterns, tools, magazines, clubs, classes, and specialty shops created a large following of loyal fans and customers, before technology and social media spread access and enthusiasm exponentially. It is now a $4.5 billion-dollar industry. Activists with needle skills saw the possibilities.

Narrative Quilts—The Modern Storytellers and Craftivists

Once quilting evolved from a necessity to a leisure art, creativity won out over practicality, and makers began to see the power of quilts as art, to speak one's truth, much like the story quilts made by enslaved people, described earlier. These quilts are not made for warmth or as home decor but are intended to tell a story of importance to the maker, in every fabric, color choice, and stitch. Like the Social Justice Sewing Academy and the Women of Color Quilters Network and so many other examples in this book have demonstrated, public-facing crafts can be so subtly subversive that they draw people in and act as a starting point for conversations that people would typically avoid, complacent in their comfort zones.

THE AIDS MEMORIAL QUILT

The first quilt that could be considered an act of modern craftivism and was definitely a *Call to Needles* was the AIDS Memorial Quilt.

HIV/AIDS was the first pandemic known to most Americans, with a limited number still alive who experienced the 1918 influenza pandemic and many who were not yet born, or quite young, when polio was rampant. Much like COVID-19, AIDS was new and took time

National Mall, Washington, DC, 1987.

to identify. Our first AIDS case was diagnosed in 1981, before the disease was named, and in the twenty years that followed, 450,000 Americans died of AIDS and over one million became infected.[92]

No cure or vaccine has yet been rolled out for HIV/AIDS, but research eventually developed best practices for preventing, treating, and managing the virus in the HIV stage, dramatically reducing the number of cases and deaths. In 2018, 37,968 people were diagnosed with HIV in the United States. The CDC estimates 1.2 million people were living with (managing) HIV at that time. For more information, amfAR, the Foundation for AIDS Research, has a detailed timeline.[92]

The AIDS Memorial Quilt became a phenomenal hands-on reaction to the grief and shock felt by families and friends of those who died of AIDS, and a visual reminder to those who may not have realized the momentous impact of this disease. It did not begin as a quilt, but as a series of posters developed in 1985 by Cleve Jones, a gay rights activist who wanted to make sure victims were remembered. The posters were displayed on the outside walls of the San Francisco Federal Building during a candlelight vigil.

The sight of so many posters on a wall resembled a quilt and led to a plan that would allow anyone who wanted to memorialize someone lost to AIDS to create and contribute a quilt block. It was decided that each quilt block should measure 3' x 6' (the size of a grave) and would tell a story about the person lost to this disease. Individual panels were then joined into manageable 12' x 12' blocks that could be stored or displayed. The response was overwhelming. In October 1987, nearly two thousand panels were laid out on the National Mall in Washington, DC, where half a million people visited the quilt in one weekend. More collaborations led to the creation of the NAMES Project Foundation to act as custodian, protector, and curator of the AIDS quilt. "Weighing an estimated 54 tons, it is the largest piece of community folk art in the world as of 2020."[93] Quilt panels are still coming in from all over the world.

One thousand blocks at a time, rotated from the collection, are displayed each year in a variety of venues.

Every square has been identified and assigned a tracking number in the database. If laid out end-to-end the entire quilt would be over fifty miles long.

If you would like to view the quilt panels or create a panel in memory of a friend or loved one lost to AIDS, visit www.aidsmemorial.org/custom-templates/quilt.

I have no doubt that every panel, created by sewists and non-sewists alike, was an act of love as well as an *Act of Craftivism*, and a way of coping with grief and healing, so it is good to know all of that love and light is being cared for and given the respect it deserves. The AIDS Memorial Quilt Project set the standard for future memorial quilts.

The COVID Memorial Quilt

One woman who worked on the AIDS Quilt to honor a friend now has a teen daughter *(with mad sewing skills)* who picked up the mantle and found a way to honor victims of COVID-19 during the pandemic. During the universally convoluted 2020 school year, Madeleine Fugate needed an idea for her seventh grade community action project with the theme "Young Changemakers in a COVID-19 World," just as she was noticing that the media was referring to numbers of cases and deaths, and she felt it was important to remember that each number was a human being. Madeleine and her mother agreed it was time for another memorial quilt. Word went out for donations of fabric squares representing loved ones lost to COVID-19. The decision was made that the squares would be 8" x 8", because 8 is the infinity symbol and would represent that life goes on. Each panel would have twenty-five squares to form a larger square. Fugate hoped to display the quilts in public places like churches, museums, and hospitals. By early 2021, Fugate had received seventy squares from all over the US, the UK, and New Zealand. Placing someone's name on a square in a quilt "means they existed."[94]

February 2021 was the month we reached the grim and hard to grasp milestone of half a million deaths from this novel virus, just as the equally novel vaccines were finding us, giving us hope. This committed crafty teen is

Youth craftivist Madeleine Fugate, panel 1, panel 20.

not the first to begin making quilts for victims of COVID-19 and she won't be the last, but I do see Fugate's effort as a unique *Call to Needles*, for a couple of reasons, that could match the success of the AIDS Memorial Quilt and require a similar coordination of efforts. One reason for my belief in the power of this project is that Fugate has a powerful team working with her on this collaboration, at home and at school. She reached out to Cleve Jones, the founder of the NAMES Project AIDS Memorial Quilt, as well as its board of directors for advice on making and caring for such treasured remembrances.

You can learn more about this project at www.covidquilt2020.com, including how to donate squares and where you can see public displays of the panels, numbering in the twenties as of fall 2021. Squares were still being accepted, with instructions given on the site, and I cannot imagine that will end anytime soon. *Maybe a college thesis, Madeleine?*

And in the best spirit of craftivism, summer 2021 saw Fugate join efforts with Kristin Urquiza, who founded Marked by COVID (www.markedbycovid.com) after her father died of COVID-19. Urquiza began sharing people's stories of lost friends and family after gaining recognition for the "honest obituary" she wrote about her father's death, which she attributed to his known trust in Arizona Governor Doug Ducey, who told Arizona residents that it was safe to resume normal activities in June 2020.

Fugate, Urquiza, and many allies lobbied in Washington, DC, in late July 2021, talking to lawmakers about the need for a COVID Memorial Day to be held each year on the first Monday in March. One of Fugate's quilts was displayed at a candlelight vigil at the White House, but now wearing the mantle of *craftivist*, she also wrote a letter to First Lady Jill Biden, respectfully reminding her that as we push to move on with our lives, let's please remember and honor those lost, as well.

Their visit to the U.S. Capitol brought fresh and increased attention to HR-174, memorializing those impacted by and lost to the COVID-19 virus. This bill was sponsored by Representative Greg Stanton, in February 2021, with 52 sponsors at the time of this writing. On July 8, 2021, Senators Elizabeth Warren, Ed Markey, and Martin Heinrich introduced a resolution on the Senate side to create a COVID Memorial Day.

I am sure of two things, that quilt squares will keep arriving and that Fugate, Urquiza, and all who participated in the lobbying efforts will not rest until this bill is passed and signed, so go ahead and mark your calendars for the first Monday of March each year.

The Mother's Dream Quilt Project

I have always felt a powerful frustration with gun violence, which I think partially stems from teaching in a large, urban school district and being aware of the gun culture in which many of my students were enmeshed. In that environment, it wasn't about deer hunting or learning responsible gun ownership from a young age. This was about power and control in neighborhoods where residents often felt the absence of both. I attended more than one funeral for a student killed by someone with a gun.

Having taught in that environment for so many years, I was increasingly alarmed at the commonplace event that came to be known as "another school shooting." Not because I spent each day in fear on the job. On the contrary, I was aware that a student's backpack or locker might contain a gun, but I knew it was for protection from something or someone they feared coming to and going from school, not to shoot up the school.

From Columbine on, even as observers with no personal stake, each school shooting left a bruise on many of our souls. But the Sandy Hook shooting was the one that broke many of us. Young children, their teachers and the principal who tried to protect them, killed. I joined Moms Demand Action for Gun Sense in America (www.momsdemandaction.org), founded by Shannon Watts, a mother of five. The organization is based on the model used by Mothers Against Drunk Driving (MADD), which changed drunk driving laws in this country dramatically. This group partnered with Everytown for Gun Safety and Mayors Against Illegal Guns. The coalition continues to grow, with chapters in every state and Students Demand Action chapters in high schools and colleges. They have put extreme pressure on the NRA and have helped elect gun sense candidates like Congresswoman Lucy McBath to legislative positions at local, state, and federal levels.

When our local chapter of Moms Demand Action held a Day of Action in 2019 at our state capitol in Columbus, I was an eager participant. Talking face-to-face with the people elected to represent you is vitally important, and it was a very productive effort, given that Ohio, at the time, had several pieces of legislation pending that supported gun rights over the safety of children, citizens, and even police officers. The day began with a meeting near the capitol to explain the agenda and while listening to the speakers my eye caught a glimpse of a quilt displayed in the front of the church. At this point you know me well enough to know I couldn't look away and had to take a closer look ASAP. That was my introduction to the Mother's Dream Quilt Project. The one on display had been made by a group in Cincinnati, but I learned this was a nationwide effort launched in February 2014. The following quote serves as a mission statement:

Every mother dreams that her child will grow up safe, healthy and happy. Unfortunately, too many American mothers see their dreams for their children shattered by gun violence. Moms Demand Action has created the Mother's Dream Quilt Project to symbolize the human toll of gun violence in America, as well as mothers' shared commitment to making our country safer for our children.[95]

Much like the AIDS quilt, people are encouraged to share something from a loved one lost to gun violence. That is not a requirement for participation, but in those cases, participants are encouraged to use or donate an article of clothing from the deceased to be used in the

The Sandy Hook shooting was the one that broke many of us.

quilt. Each square represents a victim or survivor of gun violence, or someone with profound concern about gun violence and the impact on their own children. Much like we try to wrap these survivors in our love, their quilt squares are surrounded by quilt blocks from people who, like me, make up the collective sadness and grief over too many lives lost. Each participant submits a statement of the Mother's Dream for her children, or the story of the victim or survivor, whose story is told in that block.

The Mother's Dream quilt block was an existing tool available to quilters and was deemed the perfect choice for this project.

This quilt project uses the time-tested concept of the quilting bee and recommends that anyone interested in participating put together a team that would include expert quilters to work side by side with people passionate about their cause, sewists as well as non-sewists. The team then schedules and promotes their quilting bee and brings participants together, first to plan the quilt blocks, then piece and quilt, the quilting often completed by machine rather than by hand. Imagine the support and validation felt by someone showing up at such an event with a fallen son or daughter's favorite shirt to become a part of one of these quilts.

On the group's website, www.mothersdreamquilt.org, you can view more than a dozen completed quilts with names like the Peace Quilt, the Tennessee Quilt, the Butterfly Quilt, and the Georgia Peach Quilt, reflecting the state of origin or a meaningful theme. The Rocky Mountain Quilt includes blocks for the victims of the Columbine school shooting and the Aurora theater shooting, but it also memorializes people in the area killed by domestic violence or victims of suicide.

The Not One More quilt was dedicated to the memory of Christopher Michael-Martinez, killed during a shooting rampage near the campus of the University of California, Santa Barbara, where he was a student. Shortly after his death, his father's impassioned statement to the media touched many hearts when he said, "When will this insanity stop . . . we don't have to live like this . . . we should say to ourselves, not one more."[95]

If you follow politics, you may be aware that Congresswoman Lucy McBath of Georgia was elected in 2018, running on a platform strong on gun control, supported by the Moms Demand Action group as a gun sense candidate, and driven to run by the murder of her son Jordan in 2012. One of the Mother's Dream quilts contains a block she placed for her son. The quilt was presented to her to hang in her DC office.

When I first saw the Mother's Dream quilt from Cincinnati and viewed others on the website, I noticed that from a distance you see a colorful overview of the homogeneous pattern, each square following the same template, much like observing a crowd from a distance, seeing only a blur of humanity. It is not until you zoom in that you see the individual squares, people, or stories, and notice how each one is unique from another, special for its own reasons, with nuanced colors, textures, personalities and stories to tell.

Quilted Responses to Police Brutality

Police brutality existed long before the *Age of Trump*, but like a category 1 hurricane gathering strength in the Gulf, he gave it more power as he blatantly "rallied" violence from his base, and sometimes the message was specifically aimed at law enforcement. There was no call for restraint or reform. But thanks to body cams and cell phone cameras, public awareness spread. I am well aware that the majority of police officers are competent, decent, caring people. But their ranks are infected with too many who feel they have a license to be brutal, often fed by racism, with accountability a rare occurrence. Given the history of quilts as described in this book, what better way to create a visible, public-facing way of personalizing some of the victims and those who loved them, while opening a dialogue that too many wish to ignore?

Sewing circles and quilting bees have always served more than one purpose. They can make a massive job feel smaller when the work is shared, and perhaps more importantly, they create a sense of community with common goals. So, it should be no surprise that so many social justice crafters and artists have turned to quilting as a tool that enhances visibility and awareness. Quilts have "been a way for women to gather and have political discourse and get away with it."[96]

xxxxxx

Gone But Not Forgotten was a collaborative quilting project created by Rachel Wallis to "make a memorial quilt for individuals killed by the Chicago Police Department or while in police custody since 2006." The collaboration between Wallis and the grassroots group We Charge Genocide "planned and organized a series of 15 peace-quilting circles where participants could read

"In a time of destruction and chaos, create something."

the victims' stories aloud, while creating a hand-embroidered quilt in their memory." The circles provided a safe space where more than two hundred people from vastly different neighborhoods and backgrounds could come together and discuss transformative justice, police accountability, and community safety. The quilters created six quilt panels nearly forty feet in length to honor 144 victims.[97] Using data from official police records, media coverage, and information from victims' families, these craftivists publicly documented the names, ages, and dates of death of each victim. More information was featured near the displayed quilt panels.

Using the known power of sewing circles and quilting bees, participants were encouraged "to engage in radical empathy, remembering that victims of police killings are more than statistics or another headline on the nightly news. No matter the circumstances of their death, each of these people had someone who loved them and mourned their deaths."[97] The goals included helping participants process their loss and the trauma of police violence, while exploring ways to end the history and cycle of violence in Chicago.

xxxxxx

Years later, members of the national Women of Color Quilters Network and the Textile Center in Minneapolis presented their first such exhibition, *Gone but Never Forgotten: Remembering Those Lost to Police Brutality*, in late 2020 at seven sites in the Twin Cities area, some of which ran through spring 2021. Quilt titles included "Dear White People," "Somebody's Child," and "Ode to George Floyd." Carolyn Mazloomi, the network's founder and curator of

"I Have Known Injustice All My Life,"
by Ed Johnetta Miller.

these exhibitions, recognizes the power of quilted craftivism. "When people think of quilts, they think about warmth and security . . . so, they can be a kind of soft landing—a way to tell the story of difficult topics."[96] (A common thread in this chapter.)

A *Call to Needles* went out to "about 500 quilters—mothers, grandmothers and great-grandmothers (average age 74)" after the death of George Floyd. More than four hundred quilts were submitted for these exhibits. *Again, so many voices with so much to say.*

The pandemic resulted in the deaths of eighteen members of the network, which led to a very different *Call to Needles*, as other members hit the pause button on their quilting to make thousands of masks for hospitals and frontline workers.⁹⁶

One Last Quilt Metaphor

This "story of a story quilt" appeared in the oddest of places when in September 2020, Tyler Perry received the Television Academy Governors Award for his achievements in television and the opportunities he has provided for marginalized communities through programs of inclusion, engagement, employment, and other initiatives.

His acceptance speech, given in pandemic mode, without a live audience, was a passionate anecdote and metaphor about a quilt! When Mr. Perry left home at 19, his grandmother gave him a quilt she made, and for years Mr. Perry was not hearing what she was saying in that quilt, and he admitted to being embarrassed by it—so many different colors and patches. Not his taste. Nothing special. Years later, he stopped when he saw a similar quilt on display in the window of an antique store. The shopkeeper told him the story of the maker, a freed slave, and the meaning of the patches in the story quilt. Mr. Perry was ashamed and embarrassed at how he had dismissed his grandmother's story and skills, simply because he wasn't a fan of how it looked. It is what he said next that gave me pause and touched my crafty heart:

> *Now, whether we know it or not, we are all sewing our own quilts with our thoughts, our behaviors, our experiences, and our memories. I stand here tonight to say thank you to all of the people who are celebrating and know the value of every patch, and every story, and every color that makes up this quilt that is our business, this quilt that is our lives, this quilt that is America.*⁹⁸

A CALL TO NEEDLES

10

ARPILLERAS

"God chose the humble to shame the powerful. It's for that reason we make the arpilleras so this kind of thing will never happen again."

—Marjorie Agosín's *Scraps of Life*

Arpilleras typically reflect the regional culture of the makers, using bright colors, with mountains, sun, and farm life, often finished with a red crocheted border.

Arpillera, translated from Spanish, to English, means "burlap." The term expanded to mean a small tapestry, typically done using appliqué and embroidery techniques on the background of a fabric like burlap. It is widely believed that arpilleras may have originated in Peru. They are often quite colorful, reflecting the life and times of the areas from which they originate. Arpilleras took on a new persona when they became a way of communicating messages and a tool of craftivism in a time of political upheaval in Chile.

Chile

I became a fan of author Isabel Allende when I saw the 1994 movie *The House of the Spirits*. Jeremy Irons, Meryl Streep, Glenn Close, Winona Ryder, and my first Antonio Banderas sighting! If you've ever been disappointed in the movie version of a book, it can be a game-changer to reverse the process. See the movie first and then read the book. For me, seeing this movie and reading the book created an interest for reading anything Ms. Allende writes. I think she is a brilliant storyteller. Ms. Allende drew on her own memories of family and a country experiencing political turmoil for much of this novel. *The House of the Spirits* brought a specific part of the history of the Americas to life.

Born to a life of privilege in Peru, Ms. Allende and her mother moved to Chile when she was a child to live with her grandparents after her parents' divorce. Her uncle was the democratically elected Chilean president Salvador Allende, the first Marxist president elected in the Americas, which of course was not acceptable to the United States. It was a domino that could not be left standing. In 1973, Allende was assassinated during a US-backed military coup. The man who stepped in to take over was Augusto Pinochet. CIA documents released in 2000 stated that the United States, under President Nixon, appeared to condone the 1973 coup, but there was "no evidence" of US participation. That debate continues. You can learn more about the life and works of Isabel Allende from the HBO documentary *Isabel*.

General Pinochet, the self-proclaimed president of Chile, operated as an authoritarian dictator. He soon went after anyone who was perceived as uncooperative or unwilling to acknowledge his leadership. Chilean people, mostly men, were rounded up and imprisoned, tortured, and often killed, usually with family members unaware of what had happened to them.

Reading about Chile's violent history and discovering an arpillera on a visit to New Mexico triggered my curiosity as a crafter with intent. That curiosity led me to the writings of Marjorie Agosín, a passionate advocate for women's rights in Chile. Agosín is an American author and poet whose grandparents emigrated from central Europe and Ukraine to Chile.[99] Her childhood memories include the wool in the "house at the end of the world," her grandparents' home in Chile. Her early introduction to the wonder and beauty of crafting with wool, even as an observer, likely influenced and drew her to the crafters about whom she now writes.

Scraps of Life and *Tapestries of Hope, Threads of Love* are books by Marjorie Agosín that detail the creative and often desperate efforts of the Chilean arpilleristas. In the prologue to *Scraps of Life*, Agosín chilled my blood with the following statement, because it sounded so familiar in the *Age of Trump* (not uncommon in authoritarian regimes, just unfathomable to most of us in the US):

> *In 1970 my native Chile was converted into a divided country, infected by fear and suspicion. Social and political groups that had lived together in relative harmony suddenly became fierce and violent antagonists. People around me began to distrust not just others but also themselves. (p. vii)*

He soon went after anyone who was perceived as uncooperative or unwilling to acknowledge his leadership.

Arpilleras

LEFT: Displayed at the Michigan State University Museum, on loan from the Marjorie Agosín collection. RIGHT: *¿Dónde está?* by Violeta Morales.

With more in common to our times, those targeted as the enemy of Pinochet included the poor, artists, writers, and intellectuals. In the United States under Trump, we often heard that certain groups of immigrants were to be feared and rejected, we should not believe the scientists, and journalists were the enemy of the people. *Straight from the authoritarian dictator's manual.*

Wives and other family members in Chile could find no answers, nor learn the fate of their loved ones, in spite of numerous visits and pleas to officials and prisons. At some point they had to navigate how to survive without them, always hoping, praying, and believing that they just might show up one day or the family would discover their fate. The arpilleristas did not start making these tapestries as *Acts of Craftivism* or political protest. They found other women in the same situation and began making them as a way to deal with their fear and grief, and hopefully, create a product that could be sold outside of their country, bringing a modest survival income into their lives. Often organized by the local Catholic churches, these groups met in safe, nurturing environments, and these women eventually began including messages embedded in their work that might be recognized by someone who had knowledge of their missing loved ones. A message may have been as discreet as a scrap of a husband's shirt that someone who knew him might recognize, now used to depict a woman's skirt in a tapestry, or a missing son's picture somewhere in the background of the arpillera. Words and phrases were also sometimes included.

×××××

The *¿Dónde está?* arpillera was created by Violeta Morales, the sister of a Chilean desaparecido (disappeared). According to Margaret at www.cachandochile.wordpress.com, Morales became a very active member of the Conjunto Folklórico of the AFDD: la Association de los Familiares de los Detenidos Desaparecidos (the

Association of the Families of the Detained and Disappeared). The 1987 Sting song "They Dance Alone" was about the women of this group. Morales based this arpillera on Dalí's painting, "Young Woman at a Window," because the arpilleristas were cultured and talented.

By the time Pinochet was removed from office, the thousands of Chileans taken away without leaving a trace were appropriately labeled "the disappeared." Tens of thousands survived imprisonment and torture.[99]

USA

I see many parallels between the Chilean arpilleristas, the *disappeared* of the 1970s, and the many people from Central America attempting to legally seek asylum in the United States today. Relying on credible sources, the news during the Trump administration was grim for people of color, immigrants, and all who love our democracy. Most of us were aware that the status of undocumented, *employed* immigrants was often ignored by their American employers (Trump included). But soon we began hearing Mexican and Central American women in the United States speak of not knowing where their husbands were after being taken by ICE agents, as well as children who had no idea what happened to their parents. These raids happened in Ohio, where I live, as well as other states, with one raid resulting in 680 immigrants being arrested by ICE agents on the first day of school in Mississippi in August 2019.

People taken from work while their children were at school sounds eerily similar to the disappeared in Chile and the women who had no idea what happened to husbands, fathers, brothers, and sons. I'd like to believe that, because this is America, all 680 detainees in Mississippi received due process under our law, unlike Chile in the last decades of the twentieth century, but evidence seems to indicate otherwise.

There is ample evidence that child detainees, separated from their parents, died or were abused in American custody. Parents were deported without their children and children without their parents. Hundreds of children literally disappeared from US detention facilities, and no one seemed able to account for them. In the United States of America. In 2019. Not in Pinochet's Chile.

What American *Acts of Craftivism* might arise from this mess? Cell phones, the internet, and social media make it much easier to get the word out to the world, unlike Pinochet's Chile. But we also know that crafted art can speak loudly and profoundly and can be amplified by social media. At the risk of being accused of cultural appropriation, what would an American version of an arpillera look like today? Consider the works of many of the quilters and craftivists in previous chapters. I would never want to endorse an *Act of Craftivism* that would in any way minimize or take away from the work of the incredible women of Chile, but I feel like permission to explore this idea has been given by Roberta Bacic in *Stitching Resistance: Women, Creativity, and Fiber Arts*, when she wrote this about arpilleras:

> *Their simplicity also means that they open up the possibility for reappropriating them for new contexts. They allow anyone willing to take the time to pick up a needle and thread to relate*

their own stories through cloth and stitches—a reality visible in the continuation of the arpillera tradition into other Latin countries and more recently far beyond. (p. 69)

Trump and those emboldened by him, including many ICE agents, Cabinet members, staff, and members of Congress, acted out and proudly violated our Constitution in plain sight daily, while he attempted to hypnotize us into believing him, with the sound of screeching helicopter blades, as he shouted answers to unheard questions from the press. While we may not need messages hidden in needlework to be smuggled out to alert the world what is going on here, I maintain that a few publicly facing, modern versions of the arpillera could speak volumes about what has happened to people seeking asylum in the United States since Trump was elected. Maybe something like this?

Social Justice Sewing Academy, "Love Means Nothing Without Action."

Although Marjorie Agosín's words chilled my blood earlier in this chapter, she warmed it back up in the closing of chapter one in *Scraps of Life*. It perfectly closes this chapter on arpilleras—not an ending, but a continuation:

But now our own history obliges us to speak, to loose words of fire. Thus welcome out of the silence and darkness to show ourselves as we are: free women, fighting women. We are washers of clothes, teachers, lawyers, journalists, poets. We are mothers, sisters, wives, daughters. We throw ourselves into the abyss of uncertainties with new-found strength; we are not afraid to dive into the hell of lies, into the visible and invisible machinations of the dictatorship. We wage our war every day in the country called Chile or Guatemala or the United States. We are new women with new stories to tell. (p. 16)

A CALL TO NEEDLES

Part III

CRAFTED COVID KINDNESS

We long to return to normal, but normal led us to this.
—Ed Yong, 2020

T**HE CORONAVIRUS PANDEMIC** put all Americans (all the world) on the front lines of battle in a war for which none of us had any training—so different from any previous conflict. This invisible enemy called for an entirely different approach to battle that seemed beyond the comprehension of our leadership and military complex, which has always been prepared to attack a human enemy or their possessions with weapons of destruction. In this war we needed to rely on science and medicine rather than bullets and bombs, a concept that a large number of Americans seemed incapable of comprehending.

One of the most insane and dangerous decisions made during the transition from an Obama White House to a Trump White House *(many options to choose from in this category)* now appears to be the decision to ignore the guidelines turned over to the incoming administration that included how to deal with possible pandemic scenarios (a "Pandemics for Dummies" paper, according to Susan Rice). The new administration ignored the recommendations and quickly disbanded the existing Pandemic Response Team.

The real heroes and frontline soldiers in this war became the doctors, nurses, first responders, and all involved in caring for those infected with the virus. How many of us worried for friends or family employed in the medical sector, sent into battle without enough of anything needed to do their job—and early on, with little understanding of the virus. Our other heroes were bus drivers and transit workers, grocery store employees, sanitation workers, truck drivers, mail and delivery services, and those left staffing restaurant carryout and delivery orders. Many people finally noticed that the people making the lowest wages among us were the ones making sure we had the basics, like food and medicine. They represented the essential services that were permitted to stay open and doing so put these essential workers at great risk for becoming victims of the virus.

One thing that will reverberate for a long time to come is the unexpected, surreal way most of us participated in

133

this war, compared to all the conflict experienced before. Stay home, self-isolate, and avoid crowds and close proximity to anyone. This was the task assigned as the best way to protect ourselves and those on the front lines dealing with increasingly overwhelming numbers of COVID-19 infected patients. The biggest risk was believed to be for people with existing health issues, and those over the age of sixty-five. The virus began evolving and mutating as it spread, and we saw too many otherwise healthy younger adults die after being infected or experience odd side effects, like blood clots. Some people with COVID were asymptomatic, and others had mild cases, which often made them unintentional super spreaders. But many of those who had COVID-19 were classified as long-haulers, left with chronic health conditions or damaged lungs.

In many states, at the direction of governors and their health experts, we hunkered down and stayed at home, only going to pharmacies and grocery stores for necessities, in our masks and gloves, when we couldn't arrange home deliveries. We were unable to surround ourselves with loved ones for life's celebrations, and even funerals were postponed or witnessed by immediate family only. One of the cruelest realities was knowing that so many COVID-19 patients were dying alone, because loved ones could not enter the hospital COVID wards.

The Mask Makers

Acts of Crafted Kindness, often emerging in times of crisis, became a gigantic response to the feeling of helplessness and isolation felt by so many during the pandemic.

When people learned that frontline medical personnel were running low or working without enough personal protective equipment, out came the sewing machines, and much like the Red Cross in World War I, a call went out to home sewists, who undoubtedly had a stash of fabric, to make masks. Children, grandmas, and many in-betweens were making masks from home. Over the years I've picked up fat quarters of fabric and a yard here or a yard there for quilts I would someday make. I could not know in those shopping moments that I would someday use those fabrics to make protective masks. *Let's be real here—those quilts were not likely to ever get made, and this is a far better use of the fabric. What is the saying? Life is what happens while you're busy making plans.*

×××××

Before getting into the unprecedented homemade mask phenomenon, I want to discuss an article posted on Vox.com in April 2020 that really struck a nerve. "The 'Women's Work' of the Pandemic" discussed the

Out came the sewing machines, and much like the Red Cross in World War I, a call went out to home sewists.

incredible mask-making efforts, but also what was described as "the cognitive labor" of the household—and both have become predominantly the work of women. *(So, here we are again.)* I was well aware that whether a manufacturer employing people who sew converted their skilled labor to making masks, or we who were sheltered at home were making masks on our home sewing machines, it was a task being done mostly by women. Not surprising since "whenever there's an emergency in the United States, women have always been called to make or create things." The article pulled the lens back to look at the bigger picture, which showed us that the bulk of the work of caring for others was also still being done by women, whether in a hospital or a grocery store. "Across the board, women seem to be doing a disproportionate share of the work to keep people safe, fed, and cared for during this pandemic."[100]

×××××

Of course, the homemade masks don't meet the standards of the KN95 or N95 medical masks, but the shortages were so severe in the beginning of the pandemic that medical professionals were told a bandanna is better than nothing. Later, as mutations like Omicron proved to be exponentially more contagious, cloth masks were not up to the task by themselves but could be doubled up, accompanied by filters, or used with the more expensive medical-grade masks to extend their usage.

In 2020, large numbers of mask patterns became available online. I opted to make a 100 percent cotton version that could be washed or sanitized and reused, with wire in the top to pinch around the nose and a pocket to insert an additional filter. These could be worn alone or over more protective masks, allowing those to last longer. A quilt shop in my area had an ongoing effort to provide masks made from this pattern to frontline workers without PPE. And since this was going on around the world, narrow elastic became rarer than kryptonite (supply and demand). Masks could also be made with two sets of ties made from fabric, which would hold up better in laundering and sanitizing than elastic. I started slowly, making a few masks for my daughter, the nurse; my grandson, the cancer survivor; and the rest of my family, since it was strongly recommended that we wear masks anytime we left the house. I was stunned to learn that our niece, working as a patient coordinator on the "rule out COVID" floor of a local hospital, had *no* PPE, so she received a few of my homemade masks.

I saw many kindred spirits on craftivist social media groups who, like me, had converted their dining room tables into mask-making shops, and I know that as isolated as we all were, we became part of an army of mighty mask-makers. I made approximately one hundred masks, but one of my friends made more than one thousand. Some mask-makers advertised on neighborhood sites, charging five to ten dollars for their masks, which bothered me not, because they may have been trying to pay bills with that bit of income. I also saw many on social media in need of masks, some for protection at work, but many for protection as they navigated shopping for necessities. Half of the masks I made in May 2020 went to a friend's construction company as they headed back to work after a six-week shutdown, adhering to union requirements that workers have PPE.

A CALL TO NEEDLES

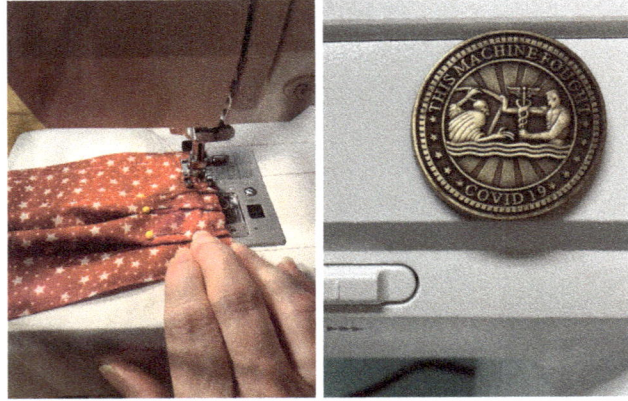

A mask maker and her hardworking sewing machine.

As I worked on these masks, I often thought of my mother, who left high school to become an essential worker in a textile mill during World War II. I was careful and precise with my stitching, making sure to backstitch at the beginning and end so the stitches would not come loose over time. That became my hug, my concern, my love, to embed in the mask for the person it would protect.

I found myself pressing foot pedal to the metal on the straightaway areas because of the sense of urgency I felt for those people needing masks. Some days, as I worked on them, I sang along to a favorite Pandora offering, some days mindless reruns on TV kept me going, and other days I just worked through the tears.

As states began lifting their stay-at-home orders in May 2020 under widely varying guidelines, a culture war developed over the wearing of masks. Falling along party lines, a disturbingly large number of Americans scoffed at wearing masks, seeing them as a sign of . . . weakness? Or unnecessary? Or an infringement on their personal freedom? *(The question marks reflect my befuddlement at the idea of making the wearing of a mask during a pandemic your personal freedom hill to die on. Literally and figuratively.)* When President Trump, Vice President Pence, and most in the administration refused to wear masks, or were ordered not to in public, it became much more challenging to convince their followers to wear them. But most Americans adjusted to the slight discomfort and intrusion in their lives as a new reality, required by most businesses, to protect themselves and others.

Eventually, idle factories, large and small, retooled to make N95 medical masks, surgical masks, hoods, and protective clothing, which meant many of us were able to slow down the homemade mask-making efforts. If factories could meet the need for PPE for doctors, nurses, and first responders, then the homemade masks could become the private personal protection we would likely all be required to wear for the foreseeable future. Masks became fashion, fandom, or political statement, as people made them with team logo fabrics and added statements on their masks like "Vote" or "BLM." The president gave out red MAGA masks at rallies for the few who chose to wear them.

xxxxxx

The more I looked at what was going on, though, the more I was reminded of the impressive nature of the human spirit in troubled times. The pandemic put an exclamation mark on that point. We found a mix of emotions that included fear, anxiety, and dread, but also, as always, grit, determination, hope, and *acts of kindness*.

Community mask trees became part of the home sewist's efforts. Facebook groups like "Community Mask Trees" in the UK and "The Mask Tree—Covid Masks Arizona" left homemade masks hanging on trees for the taking. The UK group included maps for those in need to find the nearest tree. The Arizona group posted this statement in their "about" section: "My heart is telling me to help in the best way I know how . . . I will hang masks I've made on the tree for the community to have as an act of love from me." Individuals often did the same, hanging a bag of masks on a front door, laying them on a table, or clipping them clothesline-style across a driveway or yard, offering them up for those in need.

xxxxxx

One of many more comprehensive efforts to coordinate the homemade mask movement was created by Jayna Zweiman, cofounder of the Pussyhat project and creator of the Welcome Blanket project, after people in her network of pink hatmakers reached out to see if this powerful community could help provide desperately needed masks. Masks for Humanity became the hub for people who needed face masks and other handmade PPE to connect with individual people and groups who could make face masks. On its first day, the site received requests for over 175,000 homemade masks. You might assume the requests came mainly from doctors, nurses, and first responders, but other groups put in the majority of requests, including homeless and domestic violence shelters, caregivers, workers in essential businesses, neighborhood health associations, and teachers anticipating the need for masks for students as many districts attempted to reopen—over two hundred facilities, each requesting hundreds of masks.[101]

Summing it up well for all of us, Zweiman stated, "This situation is infuriating, devastating, and there are some things we can do to help. Let's channel the anxiety and despair to help one another." *As always*. People found roles in this effort in the following categories:

- All of us as connectors—using every tool available, from phone calls to social media, as a means to get the word out that this organizational tool is available

- Front liners—those in need of PPE could make requests

- Makers—specific patterns and criteria listed on the site for those who made PPE at home

- Maker-groups—working remotely, of course, but organized to work "together" in this effort, often connected virtually

- Craft suppliers—most were closed or only doing online or curbside orders for much of 2020 but stocked everything needed to make PPE and were ready to help

- Materials donors for the makers or actual PPE to be distributed through this site

A page on the Masks for Humanity website titled "Patterns, Materials and Best Practices" provided patterns to fit different skills and ability levels and gave advice on prewashing fabrics and sharing an encouraging message for the recipients. Some of the maker-groups listed on the hub included these kindred spirits:

- A Merry Band of Sewers in Alabama
- LA Fabric Masks in California
- Just Me. Just Starting to Make Them. (California)
- Woven Women Collective in Florida
- Washington DC Mask Sewing
- Coalition of Old Capitol Quilters in Iowa
- Masks for Love in North Carolina
- The Nevada Mask Warriors

Another massive effort to coordinate mask-making was Stop the Bug: Nationwide PPE Task Force. Its Facebook page had 2,566 members by mid-2020. This massive undertaking had six divisions, including 3D makers, three thousand home sewists, manufacturing and business, collection and nationwide distribution, tribal outreach, and homeless outreach. Stop the Bug prioritized the need for PPE into tiers, with tier 1 for medical, military, and first responders. Tier 2 included specialty clinics, senior care facilities, police, corrections, isolation and quarantine units, and homeless shelters. Tier 3 covered public transportation workers, social service, and grocery workers.[102]

As the pandemic ground on, this PPE task force expanded to meet the need. The focus shifted to Indigenous communities, where "the bug" was able to deliver more than 1.5 million dollars' worth of PPE to the Navajo nation, Hopi, Paiute, Pueblo, and more. They also partnered with Doctors Without Borders to supply PPE and monitor the ongoing needs. This nationwide initiative did not forget the home base in Seattle, Washington, coordinating and hosting "Gratitude Feed," honoring their local first responders, providing them with gourmet meals, coffee, masks, sanitizer, and more.

××××××

Other giving groups refocused or added on to their mission statements for this emergency. Days for Girls, an international organization discussed in chapter 8, has long functioned under the mission of "turning periods into pathways" by collecting home sewn menstrual pads to distribute as part of a kit for girls in countries where young women often miss school when they can't pick up a pack of pads or tampons each month at a corner store. During the pandemic, the Days for Girls site, like so many others, included a COVID-19 response, reminding us that "periods don't pause for pandemics" and including a Masks 4 Millions effort. There were opportunities to volunteer, donate, or make requests.

××××××

Ashley Lawrence, a senior at Eastern Kentucky University, is an example of an individual doing what she could with the skills she had to fill a specific need. Her efforts brought attention to a portion of the population (forty-eight million in the United States) that need adaptive masks in medical settings. Lawrence, an education major who was planning to work with deaf and hard of hearing students, knew that many in this demographic rely on lip-reading, and even those who use sign language rely on facial expressions as well as signs. That becomes difficult when communicating with someone behind a mask. Medical professionals found it difficult to obtain enough communicator masks during the pandemic.

The deaf community knows that the world is made with hearing people in mind. Lawrence and her mom created a homemade version of a communicator mask using cloth and clear vinyl, then began making them and giving them to those in need. Hearing aids and cochlear implants mean the elastic straps that typically go around the ears can also be a problem, which required further adjustment. When the need and requests became overwhelming, Ashley set up a GoFundMe page to offset the cost of materials. Once the goal of $3,387 was attained, and people still wished to donate, Ashley closed the donations and suggested people give, instead, to the Hands and Voices Organization or support a teacher next year.[103] You will find many patterns and video tutorials online for communicator masks if you are interested. Because of the plastic window these masks do not meet the CDC's strictest standards and cannot be laundered, but they can be sanitized after use.

Finding Community in a Pandemic

Crafted Acts of Kindness related to the pandemic included ways to be kind to ourselves and help each other endure the stay-at-home orders and the isolation from family and friends.

I belong to several craft and knitting-themed Facebook groups, including Addicted to Knitting and Resistance Knitters, but by far the most endearing one I found was the "We Don't Need to Be Scared Alone MKAL," sponsored by Aberdeen's Wool Company in Lindsay, Ontario, created in mid-March of 2020, just as the stay-at-home orders started rolling across the country. "MKAL" is a "mystery knit-along." It is not a new concept, and there were similar groups for most types of needlework, even some sponsored by large companies like JOANN fabrics and craft stores, but this one was a specific response to the isolation factor. Nearly five hundred members from around the planet participated, using up a large amount of their yarn stash in the process, eagerly awaiting each clue and set of instructions. Approximately three thousand yards of worsted weight yarn in multiple colors was required for each of us. Creator Heather Breadner introduced the Facebook group with this message:

This group is intended to be a safe, happy place for us all to hang out together during social distancing. We came up with a project that is easy to do (our brains are all pretty full and overwhelmed at the moment so why make this stressful) . . . [W]e just don't want anyone to feel alone or isolated, and knitting is a community.

Clues and instructions were released every Monday and Friday, and options were always available to adjust colors or techniques for knitters of all levels. The first day's instructions closed with "let's have some fun, send virtual hugs, say hi to old and new friends, and embrace the calming click of the needles . . . and enjoy some community despite being in our homes." Personally, I looked forward to sitting down each evening and working on

My MKAL in progress, being checked by my quality-control expert.

memorialized in this blanket. Each yarn has a unique story to keep close.

××××××

The mask making and the MKALs are only a couple of examples of pandemic *Acts of Crafted Kindness*. There were group projects available for your choice of needles, with emphasis on community to help support us all emotionally and mentally during these disturbing times. Most of us were *not* okay, whether we admitted it or not. Watching the death toll and case count rise daily was hard to accept—and it was equally difficult not to become numb as a coping mechanism.

××××××

this presumed blanket. The sense of belonging to a community during a time when I could not hug my children or grandchildren brought a needed level of comfort, as intended. I was also impressed at the number of participants who, like me, were using this as a well-deserved break or reward from making cloth masks during the day. Some people ordered new yarn in thoughtfully selected colors for this MKAL, but it was also a great way to use up the stash of leftover yarn that most crafters possess. And, much like my grandmother's quilts, the pieces of which I could identify from their previous lives as her dresses and aprons and my grandfather's shirts, I'm going to look at this MKAL blanket for years to come and see the yarn I used to make matching cardigans for my granddaughter and her doll, the pinks that were knitted into Pussyhats for the Women's March in DC, and the yarn used for the baby afghan I made for our first grandson, all now

One of the more impressive *Acts of Crafted Kindness* related to COVID, due to its scope and intent, was Stitching the Situation (StS), launched by interdisciplinary artist Heather Schulte, of Boulder, Colorado. What began as a

"collaborative creation" intended to "provide a space for connection and healing" grew into an enormous communal public art project, documenting our unexpectedly long, difficult journey through COVID by the numbers. Intended to display, in stitches, the numbers of daily American COVID cases and deaths, as reported by the Johns Hopkins Coronavirus Resource Center. Some of those numbers became the faces of real people stitched into our collective hearts and minds. Heather describes the aim of this project in her own words on the StS website (www.stitchingthesituation.com):

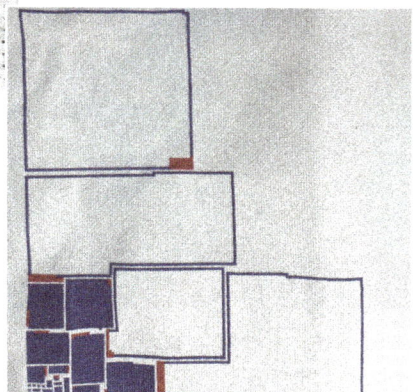

ABOVE: February 10, 2020. The single blue square in bottom left corner represents the first COVID case diagnosed in the United States on January 20, 2020.

RIGHT: March 20, 2020.

This project provides space and time to contemplate, grieve and cope with the impacts of COVID-19. It connects individuals through making a collective material expression of this time, creating new communities and relationships in the process. The work is a memorial to those lost, and a complex record of diverse pandemic experiences held in careful tension with one another.

Following COVID safety protocols in 2020, Schulte first included neighbors in StS, supported by a local grant. As protocols evolved and we found more ways to safely gather, she held stitching groups online and in other community spaces, expanding the effort outward. The concept for StS began as a simple cross stitched banner, a blue stitch for each case of COVID and a red stitch for each COVID death on a particular day in the US. The first 40-foot banners covered COVID cases and deaths from January 20 to June 25, 2020.

Schulte's goals were modest, in the beginning. She intended to take the banner to "sites of care and places deeply impacted by COVID to offer space to reconcile our experiences and reconnect our communities." It quickly became apparent, as cases replicated exponentially, that more stitchers would be needed. Funded by individual donations, Schulte was able to broaden the scope of the project to meet the increasing numbers and involve more than two hundred stitchers across the country. She created kits to send out and instructional videos on YouTube teaching participants to cross stitch and how to create a cross stitch pattern that would tell their story. That endeavor was made possible by a partnership with a local library's maker space, which provided funding for filming. StS is now fiscally sponsored by the Boulder County

Stitching the first banner with the neighbors, April 2020.

The work of Katie Brennan of Cleveland, Ohio, using data from August 5, 2020.

Arts Alliance, allowing StS to receive tax deductible donations. This assistance means the project will continue to evolve and people can find many ways to participate.

I chose one stitched piece to share here, from so many beautiful, inspiring pieces, because I found the quote so powerful (and the maker Katie Brennan is from my neck of the woods, Cleveland). She had never cross stitched before joining this project. Her work represents the data from one day, August 5, 2020. You can listen to the rationale for her design, along with several other participants at www.stitchingthesituation.com/en/project-overview-1.

×××××

Schulte formulated another goal for StS. A second grant, this one a community project grant from the Boulder Arts Commission, gave her the ability to expand access to the project. Working with a translator, Schulte had the entire website translated into Spanish, to include a portion of the American population that was disproportionately impacted by the pandemic.

For many of the projects in this book, I have described the need for financial support, typically sourced from individual donations people made from the heart, necessary to sustain the work. Here, I want you to notice that it is possible to look beyond to the community for financial and other forms of support. As an educator, I was always painfully aware that monies designated for grants, scholarships, improvements, and the like often went unused (or misused) because people did not know they existed. So, if you have an idea that requires funding, don't underestimate the power of the greater community. Get online and begin searching. Help is out there.

You have read about several organizations and their detailed efforts in this chapter, to make the point that when you observe the magnitude, the logistics, planning, coordination, and intelligence that have brought these forth, you have to wonder why the same effort never emerged at a national level in the United States at the start of the pandemic, early in 2020.

×××××

Crafters do have an unfair advantage, though. We have a particular set of survival skills that give us purpose, soothe and comfort us, allow us to help others in a variety of ways, and, let's admit it, have stashes of tools, fabrics, threads, and yarn worthy of an apocalypse.

12

THE WHITE ELEPHANT IN THE CRAFT WORLD

*Wherever we may be on the continuum of seeing
and addressing racism, we are not at the end.*

—Robin DiAngelo, *Nice Racism*

I AM A VISUAL LEARNER, and one lesson I still remember from my middle school art class is about the color spectrum. We were taught that white is the absence of color and black is a combination of all colors. (I don't recommend consulting Professor Google on this unless you have some time on your hands—seems it's a bit more complicated than the middle school art curriculum and involves physics, etc.)

I am old enough to remember white elephant gift exchanges, now often referred to as a Yankee swap or Secret Santa, but the term "white elephant" goes back to the King of Siam. The king was the only one permitted to own the rare and treasured albino elephants. If a courtier displeased him he would gift them a white elephant, knowing the upkeep would ruin them financially. Consult a dictionary and you will find meanings like "something of little or no value . . . an object no longer of value to its owner but of value to others" (Merriam-Webster). Phrase Finder has the timeliest description: "a burdensome possession: one that is more trouble than it is worth . . . any doomed enterprise."

Another elephant idiom, "the elephant in the room," represents "an important and/or enormous topic, question, or controversial issue that is obvious or that everyone knows about, but no one mentions or wants to discuss because it makes at least some of them uncomfortable or is personally, socially, or politically embarrassing, controversial, inflammatory, or dangerous" (Cambridge Academic Content Dictionary).

You may see where I'm going here when I combine the two idioms to introduce the subject of racism in our craft world. The intersection of analogy and metaphor here strikes me as appropriate because how could there possibly be a more burdensome, yet all-too-often ignored, possession than racism, wherever it exists?

Whether we talk about knitting, crochet, embroidery, quilting, sewing, spinning, or dyeing, it is quite ironic, but perhaps historically predictable, that an industry that thrives on colorful fibers has had so little awareness of the lack of color and diversity among those who participate in these crafts, especially at the level of pattern design, production, and merchandising of materials. When I say historically predictable, if America has marginalized people of color and immigrants in other aspects of life, why would the craft world be left out of that seriously flawed formula?

It is not to say that people of color have not been actively engaging in these crafts, but they have, too often, not been recognized for their contributions, or even included in conversations about the industry. "Black People Were the Original 'Craftivists'" is the title of an article written by Ruth Terry in 2019. She reminds us that "for centuries, Black people were the most proficient spinners, knitters, weavers, and sewists in America. And we were skilled on arrival."[104]

I was reminded of Charlotte, the enslaved seamstress in *The Invention of Wings* mentioned in chapter 9, when Terry added, "White people intentionally purchased slaves from regions known for expertise in textiles and natural dyes like indigo. Enslaved girls learned to knit as early as five, and women made fine garments for their masters, as well as clothing and blankets for themselves."[104] I believe the craftivism aspect has two components here. The first is a thread common to all races and cultures, where needlework has a social and emotional component that brings some comfort to traumatized lives. The second is the variety of ways that enslaved people found to tell their stories through their crafts.

Let's first take a look at knitting, a segment of the craft community where racism was called out publicly, resulting in some of the top influencers accepting responsibility and instituting (what we hope will be) significant changes. When a knitting controversy makes it to a major news site like the *New York Times*, maybe it deserves a closer look.

I recently reread a favorite book titled *Beyond Stitch and Bitch, Reflections on Knitting and Life* by Afi-Odelia Scruggs. I was a fan of her regular articles in the Metro section of the Cleveland *Plain Dealer*, so discovering that she was an avid knitter made her a kindred spirit. In this 2004 book, she discusses the fourth grade teacher who taught her to knit, the spiritual and meditative aspect of knitting that she values, and some of her experiences with knitters and yarn shops as her education, career, and personal life moved her to different parts of the eastern United States.

Scruggs does not specifically discuss the issue of race in relation to craft, but she does briefly mention how welcome she felt in one New England yarn shop, and then later hesitating, while hoping for the best, as she ventured into a yarn shop in Mississippi, where she was from, wondering if she would be the *first* or feel welcome. It became one of her favorite yarn shops, but it says a lot that she could not be sure until she crossed that threshold.

One can see Scruggs's African American heritage in the colors she used and the geometric patterns in the hats she designed, the patterns often emerging organically, as they grew on her needles. Several of her patterns are included in the book, including one hat that was an homage to Nakunte Diarra, a woman Scruggs felt had influenced her own art. Diarra made patterned cloth in Mali by applying fermented mud to strips of specially treated handwoven cotton, a technique called bogolan. Some of her work hangs in the *African Voices* exhibit at the Smithsonian National Museum of Natural History. As a common thread many people can identify with, Diarra had to find time for her art as only one aspect of the things that life required of her daily. Scruggs translated some of Diarra's fabric designs and charted them into knitting patterns. One of those became a knitted black and white hat, gifted to Diarra as a memento from her new American friend.[105]

The time Scruggs spent as a journalist for a major US newspaper, combined with her personal experiences as a knitter of color in a very pale craft world, may have informed her how to write a book that told her story. But in 2004, did she feel there were lines not ready to be crossed?

xxxxxx

Early in 2019, social media, especially Instagram, become a place where Black knitters began speaking out about their personal experiences with racism and prejudice in the knitting community. Frustration at seeing few people of color and little diversity among models pictured in knitting magazines, on websites, in blogs, and at knitting shows and conferences had built to a point that demanded wider recognition. As so often is the case with injustice, racialized people found they had to raise their voices first, to get the attention of those who need to be part of the solution and who, since they had not been personally impacted, are usually the last to notice.

Robin DiAngelo, author of *White Fragility* and *Nice Racism* might call this "racial arrogance" and a "lack of humility." In *Nice Racism*, DiAngelo states, "Because most white people have not been educated to think with complexity about racism, and because it benefits us not to do so, we have a very limited understanding of it. We are the least likely to see, comprehend, or be invested in validating racialized people's assertions and being honest about their consequences."[106]

Like a drop of color added to the dye pot, the ripples spread outward and into the craft world in ways that appear to be leading to change, slowly but surely. I share a few examples here, with the following reminder:

Knitting has always had political undertones and overtones!

I have already discussed how our crafted art can open conversations that are otherwise difficult to impossible to have. In response to violence and police brutality in Ferguson, Missouri, a group of (mainly) Black women formed a collective in 2014 called the Yarn Mission, which met every other Sunday in parks or coffee shops on the south side of St. Louis to knit.

Black knitters began speaking out about their personal experiences with racism in the knitting community.

Founder CheyOnna Sewell, a PhD student in criminology, wanted to provide an outlet of comfort for weary activists, through knitting, while engaging people in conversations about race and police brutality. "The women who participate . . . view it as a form of activism, but it is one that helps relieve stress. They cannot escape structural racism but coming together to knit offers solace in a community exhausted by police brutality."[107] (The two components of craftivism I mentioned earlier.)

Exemplifying the very definition of craftivism, they "use yarn to promote action and change to eradicate racism, sexism and other systems of oppression." Like so many other areas of life, women knitting on TV or in movies or customers in a local yarn store are predominantly white. The idea of having leisure time for knitting has historically been a white construct. Black women in the Yarn Mission, accustomed to feeling invisible, found that knitting together in public was a way to get people's attention and open a conversation. They were not on the street holding protest signs, they were engaging in an activity that looked enjoyable and interesting, rather than confrontational. "People consistently underestimate the power of knitting. They don't recognize its radical properties. They're always surprised when they talk to us about what we're knitting, like, 'Is she talking about racism right now? Did she really just say 'police brutality?' "[107] Some observers became part of the conversation; others walked on by, not ready for that.

Another great example for this conversation is Morgan Bame, who was approached by Joëlle Storet, the new manager of Arkansas's Fayetteville Underground Art Gallery, now ArtVentures, and the first young Black woman to manage the gallery. Storet asked Bame to be a guest artist and create a piece for display during Black History Month in 2017. By then, Bame, a self-taught knitter, was creating original designs in both fashion and nonwearable art. She accepted the challenge and decided to create an illusion or shadow-knit piece of art, a technique described in chapter 6. After five hundred hours of charting and using two thousand yards of yarn, Bame had created an 8' x 3.5' piece of fiber art that she titled "Anxiety of the Unseen." As people entered the gallery, the first piece they saw appeared to be simply a large rectangle of knitted stripes in two contrasting colors, but as they roamed the gallery looking at other displays, if they turned back toward Bame's display at just the right angle they would see the likeness of Martin Luther King Jr., *unseen* from the front straight-on view.

You can see the image appear on the ArtVentures Facebook page at www.facebook.com/artventuresnwarkansas. Use the name of this extraordinary work in their page's search tool.

Morgan Bame is a Black woman married to a white man, and she grew to dread discussing racism with white people. Often unwillingly drawn into these conversations, if Bame spoke her truth, it made participants uncomfortable to the point of pushing back, race-splaining *(shouldn't that be a term?)* to a Black woman why racism wasn't really the problem she thought it was. It led her to enter such conversations defensively, editing her tone and feeling censored.

Bame found that speaking through her art was different. She found it easier and safer to speak about her art, which represented her truth, at the gallery opening and "felt listened to" for a change, "genuinely heard . . . and THEN we talked about racism in America."

After creating this impressive piece of art, Bame's life journey took her in a different direction that involved looking inward and developing a more committed relationship with Christ. Her perspective changed, and she saw the world differently, much like a piece of illusion knitting. She realized that "Anxiety of the Unseen" was really about her own feelings of being unseen at the time. "I *try* to be slower to accuse and point fingers nowadays, and I have found that I receive much more mercy and patience over my own shortcomings. It's incredible that when you are slow to speak, people are quick to listen." Let's remember that we are all on a journey, and one project, one moment in time, cannot define our entire lives. This *Act of Craftivism* was Bame's contribution to this conversation in 2017, and it was only the beginning of her personal journey. Our art lives on, independent of the creator, always open to different interpretations.

After my communications with her for this chapter, I see someone who recognizes the need for and importance of self-care for creatives (see chapter 13). After suffering through "watershed moments of sorrow and strife," Bame now focuses on her own healing, including over issues of racism and sexism in America. Going forward, she intends to write and create art and "to be kind and forgiving to everyone." Let me take a breath here and remind us all, as activists and craftivists, to attempt the same.

Karen Templer of the Fringe Association unintentionally opened the creaky old racism door a little more when she blogged in January 2019 about her upcoming trip to India, referring to the journey as part of her "year of color," and describing the journey using language that made it sound like large amounts of personal courage would be required and would result in amazement and awe. People of Indian heritage found her statements hurtful and insulting, with colonialist vibes, and let her know, because people tend to feel emboldened to speak their truth on social media. It feels much less risky than in-person conversations.

Templer apologized in another post, saying, "It took women of color pointing this out for me to see it . . . which is not their responsibility, and I am thankful to them for taking the time."[108] She committed to continue raising the visibility of people of color and their fiber work. This was another small ripple in the water, but it started a broader conversation about racism and prejudice in the fiber world. Those ripples continue to spread outward. Knitwear designer Grace Anna Farrow of Unfinished Object pointed out that many knitters of color were frustrated that Templer's post was what it took to blow up the conversation. Farrow observed that "to say that white women noticed it when it happened to Karen Templer is more accurate." She goes on to say "The white community has left a lot to be desired. BIPOC (Black, Indigenous and People of Color) are left doing most of the work, facing most of the backlash, receiving the least recognition."[108]

UnfinishedObject.com deserves a closer look for those who want to better understand white privilege in the craft world and its impact. Grace Anna Farrow and several other self-described "makers, writers and disrupters" write in this forum about their experiences and observations with an unvarnished honesty will take you from your comfort zone to a place of possibility and better understanding. Blog post titles include "Calling Out and Calling In," "On Tone Policing," and "On Self-Knowledge and Honesty."[109]

×××××

Jeanette Sloan, a knitwear designer in the UK with a degree in textile design, specializing in hand and machine knitting, is another early influencer. As a Black woman in the fiber industry, she felt "representation was essential." She wrote an article for the November 2018 issue of *Knitting* magazine titled "Black People Do Knit." Black knitters have talked about being followed around by staff in yarn shops, asked if they can afford the expensive yarns, or overhearing comments of surprise that they knew how to knit, because "I thought Black people crocheted, I didn't know they knit."[110] Sloan also wrote "A Colourful Debate" for *Knitting* in August 2019. In this article, Sloan wrote about a conversation regarding the lack of diversity that exploded into an "intense discussion about the less palatable, but very real issue of racism in the knitting community."[111] This and other conversations led the Edinburgh Yarn Festival to add a diversity and inclusion panel at its most recent show and, in the United States, the *Vogue Knitting* LIVE events set up a diversity advisory council. (Encouraging, but still small drops in a very large dye pot.)

When Sloan posted a question on her Instagram account, asking followers "How many black knitwear designers can you name?" the response was more than 150 comments with names. Jeanette created the POC Designers & Crafters List that became a resource for those trying to be more inclusive. This included individuals, publications, companies, and fiber event sponsors. That led Sloan, in collaboration with several others, to create BIPOC in Fiber in 2019, to "showcase the talents of BIPOC in the global fibre community and work towards a more inclusive fibre industry. One that's as diverse as the community it serves."[112] You can explore this more at www.jeanettesloandesign.com. (In addition to BIPOC, you may also see the UK's term BAME, for Black, Asian and Minority Ethnic.)

"Can we just go back to making pretty things?"

When I came across this quote in the FAQ section on Unfinished Object as an often-asked question, I was reminded how difficult it can be to pry people free from their comfort zones. One part of the site's response was that pretending that it is just too much to think about is simply another form of "violence, silencing, or erasure." People accustomed to white privilege will have to get uncomfortable. More of the response: "Being an ally is tough work. Shining the light on your subconscious racism by asking yourself the hard questions needs to be done honestly and frequently . . . It is too easy to say I see you and I hear you. It is harder to ask, what can I do to help? . . . It's the second thought that counts—the first may be your subconscious talking, the second one is there for you to reflect upon."¹⁰⁹

A variation on this theme came from Gaye Glasspie when she shared her pain after the murder of George Floyd, in a post to her blog titled "Why I Can't 'Just Knit': The Story of a Black Knitter during Civil Unrest." Known as the Iconic Orange Lady, Glasspie, an avid knitter and blogger, uses her favorite color and her social media platform to share knitting and wisdom. She is open about the fact that knitting brought her through a rough time in her life, and she likes to encourage others to share in all the possibilities and benefits inherent in the knitting process. In this post, though, Glasspie addressed the reality that she cannot accept the "just knit" advice, because it feels like a slap in the face—a trivializing of her feelings, "when . . . there is an overall disregard for black lives. I canNOT just knit." She admits that between the pandemic and the social unrest, finding the usual joy and comfort in knitting has been difficult.¹¹³

So, when people in the fiber community ask what they can do to help, her answer is "stand in the gap," which she describes as "the space where inequality lives and breathes" and represents the area blocking diversity and inclusion. In that space "Black makers, designers, dyers, bloggers, podcasters, and YouTubers didn't exist." In collaboration, Glasspie is "asking non-Black people to stand in the gap," because "together we become a force."¹¹⁴ Some of the actions mentioned in this chapter have helped shrink the size of the gap, but for Glasspie and others, the murder of George Floyd and so many other injustices felt like a giant leap backward. In addition to collaboration, she believes the other essential tool for closing the gap is communication. Talking *to* each other, which involves actually hearing (processing), instead of just listening, even when the subject is uncomfortable, even if you don't understand, *yet*, why the conversation matters, is how you will learn to be an ally. And it moves everyone in the same direction, forward.

Personally, I think we're capable of multitasking on this one. We can "make pretty things" while we fight for fairness and equity for all.

"The road to change is paved with yarn"

—Melissa Gingras

In 2020, we observed parallels in the craft world to what was happening outside of it, even if a bit behind the curve. Social media, a twenty-four-hour news cycle, the Black Lives Matter Movement (at odds with those determined to "Make America Great Again," under their definition of "great") brought social justice issues front and center, as I discussed in the chapter on quilts. I have mentioned before that, like many other baby boomers, I came of age during the late sixties and early seventies, which is the last time I can remember so many white people actively participating in civil rights and women's rights efforts, marching together toward the same goal. For those of us old enough to remember, the Black Lives Matter movement made sense to us—a collective outrage against police brutality. The surprise, four decades later, is that if the backlash and the pushback have been less common, and less violent than the sixties, it sure hasn't been by a very large margin. To many of us, it feels like moving backward.

When the ripples from BLM spread to the fiber world, it resulted in many long-established leaders of the online crafting community, determined to be allies, examining the way they did business and attempting to make important changes. Much will be written on this subject, but I will mention a few agents for change here who are trying to "stand in the gap."

×××××

If you knit, crochet, weave, spin, or dye yarn you are more than likely a registered participant on Ravelry. It is a free community site, launched in 2007, with the emphasis on community. For someone like me who loves to knit but occasionally crochets, I can find patterns for most anything I want to make. Many are free, but for those that come with a charge, I'm sure I've never paid more than eight dollars for a pattern, and 98.7% of the payment goes to the designer with the rest used to support the site and the team who works to make it possible. Ravelry is now often referred to as the "Facebook of knitting." By 2020, they were approaching nine million registered users.

Ravelry has leveled the playing field while elevating craft as art. Traditions, by definition, have endured over long periods of time. And what needlework tradition tells us is that recognized designers using traditional fibers and techniques were always the ones featured in traditional knitting magazines and books. *Vogue Knitting* magazine has long been the one that pushed the edge of acceptable styles, colors, and variations on techniques more than most, and it survived and thrived, coloring just a bit outside the lines. But Ravelry opened a portal for any designer, first-time or prolific, whether for hobby or livelihood, to upload and promote their patterns.

We know the internet changed everything and that is no less true for needleworkers. I can search any needlework technique and find multiple YouTube videos showing step-by-step instructions and countless ideas and inspiration on Pinterest. Etsy was the first widely successful centralized site I remember where crafters could sell their finished work, tools, patterns, or supplies, but it was much broader than just needlework. The vastness of the internet made it harder and more time consuming to find something specific. The information we sought was all out there in cyberspace, just not in one convenient place until Ravelry created that place.

What does the "Facebook of knitting" do next in the *Age of Trump*? Play it safe or take a calculated risk? Stand as an example to Facebook and Twitter? If you are Ravelry you take a stand, counting on your community to understand and support the decision. On June 19, 2019, Ravelry posted this statement on their site:

We are banning support of Donald Trump and his administration on Ravelry.

Ravelry posted a lengthy explanation, with policy changes that included this statement:

> *We cannot provide a space that is inclusive of all and also allow support for open white supremacy. Support of the Trump administration is undeniably support for white supremacy.*[115]

Surprising no one, the reaction was immediate and extensive, showing up beyond the borders of the crafting world, becoming a story on mainstream news outlets such as the *New York Times* and *BuzzFeed News*:

> *The announcement led to a swift and intense reaction from all corners of the knitting world, whose denizens range from twentysomethings in Brooklyn to grandmothers in the Midwest. Some people condemned the policy as liberal bias and promised to delete their accounts, while others said they had "never been prouder to be part of this community."* [115]

Some conservatives called it censorship and an effort to limit free speech, but Ravelry is a private company and has the right to ban content it deems unacceptable. Not all critics were Trump supporters. Even my liberal, nasty woman self had a tiny twinge of anxiety over the risk they were taking, upsetting a community united in love of all things yarn. Predictably, devotees of Ravelry who felt violated, vented their anger in the forums with comments like "kill yourselves," "I don't support thought police," and "boycott Ravelry." Moderators of the forums responded accordingly by deleting some comments and archiving others. Many who had been loyal to the site made it clear in social media posts that they were done with Ravelry and would take their yarn love elsewhere.

Ravelry took a calculated risk from the apex of the yarn world and for the most part received overwhelming appreciation and support. And remember, knitting, especially, can trace its political involvement extensively through history.

Clara Parkes is a wool expert and author of several books on the subject of yarn. She believes this is a watershed moment for the industry. "Ravelry is 8 million members strong. I've been with them since 2007, and believe me, they do not take these steps lightly."[116]

※※※※※※

Knitty.com is an online blog for the knitting magazine of the name same created in 2002 by Amy Singer. For years, its philosophy, like many other online venues, was "no religion, no politics." But when the ripples in the dye pot reached the people behind *Knitty*, they responded with a clearly stated new policy on diversity, discrimination, and racism, which they stated clearly "is not up for debate":

> *Knitty will not condone or tolerate any form of racism and discrimination. We believe in being an inclusive and welcoming publication where all people can see themselves in our pages. Our staff are working on their own to become good anti-racist allies.*

> *Knitty actively encourages people of all skin colors, body sizes, heritages, abilities, gender identities, and ages to participate in Knitty. We have recently reached out to specifically encourage Black knitters, crocheters, and spinners to consider sending their work to Knitty, and are actively scouting Black contributors and models.*[117]

Notice that the first paragraph shows an awareness of the problem and a commitment to change, but would be hollow without the second paragraph, taking actions that prove the intent stated in the first part of the policy—words in action. Many other online craft companies posted similar statements rejecting discrimination of all types, which seems like a good place to begin. We have to face it to fix it. And the burden now is on white people to step up as allies and push the changes that will work for everyone.

Many sites like Knitty now list and recommend Black-owned companies for yarns, patterns, and instructions as well as places to become more informed, not just on the subject of social justice and racism, but on how to become advocates and talk to others about the white elephant we have allowed to take up so much space in our favorite crafts.

Part of the reason I take these commitments seriously is that in addition to bringing attention to people of color who are designers and vendors in the field, such sites also include links to books and other resources to better understand racism, along with organizations working for change that you can participate in, or to which you can donate. These efforts are especially important in bringing along people who are reluctant to acknowledge their white privilege and react reflexively that they "don't have a racist bone in their bodies" (a.k.a. "credentialing," *Nice Racism*, p. 58).

xxxxx

Another leading voice is Needlework, a fabric shop and creative workspace in Hamilton, Ontario. In June 2020, the owners of this shop posted a declaration on their website in solidarity with the Black Lives Matter movement and a commitment to the work of anti-racism. Part of the statement reads:

> *Took a break from sharing shop updates on social media to make space and amplify Black voices. We spent time reading, listening, and learning about the experience of Black and Indigenous in America . . . the result . . . we're critically looking at our white privilege and how the color of our skin has no consequence on how we move through the world . . . we commit to sharing our privilege to create equal opportunities for BIPOC in our communities.*[118]

This statement was followed by a detailed plan for achieving those goals and can be viewed on the Needlework website, as we also saw with Knitty's commitment. I have committed the above phrase, "how the color of our skin has no consequence on how we move through the world" to memory, as a personal reminder of my own privilege.

I was already a fan of Donna Druchunas of *Sheep to Shawl Knitting Studio*, and I have featured some of her hat designs in chapter 8. But she is included in this chapter because of her long-standing commitment to this conversation. Druchunas created a blog series in 2017 titled "We Knit Too: Diversity in Knitting." Each month that year, the site hosted a guest writer who was a person of color or otherwise underrepresented in the craft industry. The series is no longer available on the website, but I mention it because contributors included not only BIPOC, but also a physically handicapped knitter who represented a minority that is also often overlooked. The words of one of the series writers, Fatimah Hinds, a designer on Ravelry, stood out to me as a good observation of the progress to date: "Today I see more and more faces of all colors in knitting magazines, on Ravelry searches, and in yarn catalogs. But there is still work to be done . . . We all benefit from seeing people of all backgrounds, looks, abilities, and genders represented in the things we buy, because the knitting world includes all of those people."

xxxxxx

Other members of the fiber arts world have also noticed a lack of diversity and representation. When Shannon Downey of Badass Cross Stitch engaged volunteers from the quilting community, a world previously foreign to her, in her effort to get Rita's Quilt completed so Rita's soul could rest peacefully (**chapter 6**), she was amazed at the quilting world so white. When the *Washington Post* noticed a rift in the quilting community, it was clearly time to pay closer attention. Peggy McGlone wrote an article for the *Post* early in 2020 titled "Now, even quilters are angry: How a social-justice design started a feud." The National Quilt Museum's Block of the Month Club stirred up a controversy about the January square "No. 2 Pencil Power" inspired by the Social Justice Sewing Academy (**chapter 8**).

No. 2 pencil power.

When some members objected to what they saw as introducing politics into an apolitical world, with a left-leaning message, they were accused of being intolerant. Frank Bennett, the museum's chief executive, tried to calm the ripples by encouraging tolerance—"Let's be an inclusive community and consider voices different from our own." But are those voices really different? And is that statement heavy with white privilege? And was that phrasing intentional, knowing his intended audience? Bennett reminded members of the historical connections between quilting and the movements to end slavery, promote suffrage, and eradicate AIDS. "Let's embrace our diversity and show the world our humanity." Injustice is not typically a trigger word for people trying to hide from politics or controversy.[119]

Social Justice Sewing Academy founder Sara Trail was surprised by the controversy, which continued for weeks after Bennett's plea. The dustup made Trail wonder if it was the message in the quilt block or the group behind the design that ruffled so many feathers. It was created by a teen from Baltimore and as Trail stated in the article, the block "is 'G-rated' if using a movie rating scale."[119] Attempts to whitewash the block design angered the other side as being dismissive and reflecting the white fragility of the quilting community. Eventually, members decided it was time to move on, as a new quilt block pattern was released the next month. "There are no quilt police." An uneasy truce for the sake of the art? *So, the fiber dust settled but did any attitudes really change?*

"Let's become anti-racist stitchers."

×××××

In the embroidery realm, Natalie Naito of the Stranded Stitch maintains a website, www.thestrandedstitch.com where she sells her "collection of irreverent cross stitch designs," kits, supplies, and tools. She has recently added several free patterns for anti-racist stitchers and requested ideas for patterns from Black stitchers. Her message:

> *I want us to stitch for Black lives with the same enthusiasm we had when we stitched for feminism in 2016. Black lives matter. They matter in every aspect of our everyday existence—even in the patterns we use and the stitches we make! Let's keep our craftivism going for the long haul. Let's display our art, gift it, and share it. Let's use our stitches to build community, spark conversation, and live in discomfort.*[120]

The embroiderers in **chapter 6**, Subversive Cross Stitch, Badass Cross Stitch, the Tiny Pricks Project, and many others, also have designs that support Black Lives Matter, the LGBTQ and BIPOC communities, and other social justice issues.

Let us temper these efforts with a reality check. Recognizing racism in the craft world should not have taken this long or required so much effort. And making the needed changes, going forward, will take more time and require more commitment from all.

As a Black business owner, Diane Ivey, creator of the indie-dye yarn company Lady Dye Yarns, is an important voice in the struggle for equity and equality in the craft world. She found success online long before Instagram and social media brought attention to the whiteness of the crafting world. She has seen "extraordinary growth" in her business since 2019 and believes it is the result of more industry influencers promoting lists of businesses owned by people of color.

Ivey posted powerful advice for those committed to being allies in her May 2019 blog post "Perspective," reminding us that the online community does not include all crafters:

> *As much as we think there are tons of crafters on Instagram, I promise you for every 1 person on Instagram, there are 5 that are not. I think it's important to spread the message to a broader audience. I believe one way is to talk with your local knitting group. If you do not have a local knitting group, consider hosting a forum at your local library, opening it up to anyone to come who wants to engage in this conversation. Or ask a yarn store to host a talk about it.*
>
> *I just want people to stop and listen to what's going on in their community. If you are part of a knitting and crochet group, ask people if they know what's going on around our discussion on racism and inclusion. If they are not, engage in conversation.*[121]

Lisa Woolfork is a powerful voice in this conversation. She was one of the organizers of the Black Lives Matter Charlottesville protest and found herself in harm's way as the opposing Unite the Right torchbearers marched through the town in opposition on August 11, 2017. After spending part of that day locked in a local church, the next day she was at the intersection where an Ohio man drove a car through the peaceful BLM protestors.

Woolfork, a college professor, lives, works, and sews in Charlottesville, and while the sight of neo-Nazis marching through the streets and the violence they brought was traumatic and disturbing, a bigger surprise for Woolfork was the reaction of her sewing community. "The white sewists and quilters she had known and sewed with for decades rejected her—bitterly, abruptly, and completely—when she tried to bring her whole self as a Black woman and activist into what she thought was her community."[122] This informed Woolfork that hidden behind a facade of acceptance, there is a place in the craft world where acceptance and inclusion for some is conditional.

In a very personal *Call to Needles*, Woolfork was determined to create spaces where Black sewists could meet and connect. So she created Black Women Stitch, "the sewing group where Black lives matter." She describes the group as a values-led project that centers "Black women, girls, and femmes in sewing." You can learn more and see her beautiful work at www.blackwomenstitch.org, follow her on social media, and listen to *Stitch Please*, the Black Women Stitch podcast.

✕✕✕✕✕✕

I have attempted to bring some light and awareness to the efforts of people in the craft industry to reject racism, bring more people into the conversation, and initiate the work needed to continue. These are only a few examples and I do not feel I was able to give any of the social justice warriors enough space to speak all of their truths here, so I encourage white readers to do more research, on your own, or through the many links available in this book. Even if (especially if) it makes you uncomfortable. And learn to speak up and out as an ally, even if your voice is shaky. Think of it as muscles that need to be flexed and challenged to grow stronger.

Seeing the start of important conversations has empowered those with other issues of equality and equity to find voice to discuss a wide range of discrimination issues, beyond specific techniques, from cultural appropriation to size shaming, to fiber brand elitism, to accessibility for the disabled. We will continue adding drops to that dye pot and the ripples will continue to spread outward, as they must!

Learn to speak up and out as an ally, even if your voice is shaky.

SELF-CARE FOR THE WEARY CRAFTIVIST

Self-care is not selfish. It's actually one of the greatest gifts we can give ourselves and others, because we cannot give from an empty well.

—Michelle Maldonado

Moderation. Balance. Because too much of a good thing . . . tends to have a negative impact on our health and well-being. I am not sure this philosophy fits comfortably into most crafters' paradigms. There are plenty of cautionary tales—too much ice cream will give you a tummy ache, too much alcohol can cause a variety of problems, too much exercise can risk physical injury, but who would advise less needlework and for what reason? Perhaps if it became an obsession and resulted in neglecting self, family, or work. But, in my experience, most who work with needles and fiber, even passionate craftivists creating for a cause, manage to function as responsible humans and may function better for having needlework as an outlet. To quote Shannon Downey from chapter 6, "Stab it until you feel better."

Taking care of ourselves in times of crisis can include simple creature comforts like indulging in favorite comfort foods, spending time in nature, exercising, meditation, lotions, scented candles, getting enough sleep, escapist TV watching, games, reading, and making healthier food and beverage choices (alas—often in direct conflict with those comfort food options).

On his website, Stuff That Needs to Be Said, author and pastor John Pavlovitz wrote on April 7, 2021, a post titled "Kind People Are Suffering from Cruelty Sickness." He described the affliction using terms like "emotional weariness" and "a low-grade hopelessness." Reading the article did not leave me feeling hopeless, though; that's not the Pavlovitz way. He left us several threads of hope, in statements like, "We tether ourselves to one another" and "Now, more than ever, good and tired people need to cultivate community, to stay connected . . . and to carry one another through the fatigue when it comes." You can read the full article at www.johnpavlovitz.com.

We can make choices that can bring us respite from the daily onslaught of disturbing news without giving in to an urge to completely withdraw and hide from reality. We need to temper real-world calls to action with self-care, because democracy is not a spectator sport, and we are all needed to make it work for all. When you need a break, take one, while others carry the burden, and come back refreshed and renewed, while someone else rests. And, maybe, create something beautiful for yourself, or someone else, in the process. Either can be satisfying, and I consider it a form of self-care that assists me as I prepare for the work ahead, putting belief into action, like putting your own oxygen mask on first.

As the flow and movement of our needles lulls us into Zenlandia, though, we sometimes ignore our body's signals, reminding us that it may be time to get up and move a bit or hydrate more. Just "one more row" or "one more stitch" is a strong mantra in an era when sitting has been dubbed the new smoking, for the negative effects on our health and well-being that can result from hours of seated work. I applaud those who have found ways to work at a standing desk or replace their office chair with an inflated ball to develop balance and core strength, but needlework does not always lend itself well to standing or squirming as part of the process.

So, what is a committed craftivist or leisure crafter to do? First, let's take a look at the benefits of needlework and crafts in general on our physical, mental, and emotional health. But then, I am going to try to get you to put those needles down (occasionally, and I promise, for not too long) and leave that chair often enough to reap all the benefits of movement, while avoiding self-harm through unintended physical neglect.

The Cognitive Impact of Crafting

When I complete a project, whether a knitted hat or a full-size blanket, it provides great satisfaction, but many of us have come to realize it's really about the process and the journey. That journey begins, like all works of art, with an idea or concept. It involves the goal of an imagined outcome or finished product, as well as choices to be made about method, materials, and cost. Shopping and sorting through fibers or fabrics is often as pleasurable as seeing that finished product.

For an imagined piece to have the intended outcome, it benefits crafters to be visual as well as logical and verbal

We need to temper real-world calls to action with self-care, because democracy is not a spectator sport.

learners. All the patterns I have read and followed in my life make me the one in the room who can always figure out the directions for putting together anything IKEA can throw at us or any Christmas toy. The latest trend in putting furniture together seems to be *no* written directions, just illustrations. *So, visual learners, step up!*

Learning styles aside, it's only been in recent years, I've come to realize, that if the real joy is in the journey, that would include the *act* of crafting. My husband has referred to my needlework as an "obsession." But one night, several years ago, my needles were clicking away on an afghan as we watched TV. My husband learned transcendental meditation in the 70s and continues to meditate almost daily. He observed that my knitting seemed to be like meditation for me. I would soon be retiring from teaching and was in the process of becoming a certified yoga teacher and therapist, so his comment was a moment of realization for me, since I was learning meditation techniques in my yoga teacher training. That led to me do more reading and research on the meditative benefits of knitting. My husband's observation was correct. The process of knitting and other forms of needlework can be meditative, and therefore, therapeutic. That assumes you are working on something with a simple repetitive pattern and you are not checking pattern instructions frequently or learning a new technique. It needs to be a process that has been relegated to the autonomic part of your nervous system. Someone just learning to knit would likely not feel that meditative effect. But they can get there rather quickly. (More on this ahead.)

xxxxxx

This is not to say that mindful benefits only come from mindless knitting. Challenging yourself with a difficult lace pattern or a new technique (the baroque stitch was my most recent challenge) will fire up those brain cells and absorb you in a way that will make everything else irrelevant for a while. Who wouldn't find that beneficial sometimes? Psychologist Mihaly Csikszentmihalyi describes this as flow: "A period of time when you are so completely absorbed by an activity that nothing else seems to matter . . . when someone starts creating, his existence outside that activity becomes 'temporarily suspended.'" Csikszentmihalyi also believes crafting is unique because it can engage so many different areas of the brain. "It can work your memory and attention span while involving your visuospatial processing, creative side, and problem-solving abilities."[123]

Most crafters understand the restorative and relaxing nature of working with needles and fiber. But the craft process is also "exercising" our brains in ways we don't notice while making. PBS Learning Media shares a weekly educational YouTube video about how the brain works. One week's lesson, titled Brain Craft, reinforces the flow theory and describes our needlework as something that involves the entire brain. When we are paying attention to what we are doing (counting and following a pattern, even if memorized) the frontal lobe of the brain is involved. Planning and processing visual information (choosing patterns, techniques, tools, fibers, fabrics and following the progress of stitches) uses the parietal and occipital lobes. Storing memories (memorizing the repeat or steps of a pattern, recognizing abbreviations for different stitches) happens in the temporal lobe. And the coordination of movement and timing (technique, tension, method) is the job of the cerebellum. Lighting up all these areas of the brain as you knit, for example, stimulates the firing of neurons and the interaction between all areas of the brain, working as a team to improve and protect brain function.[124]

Engaging in any craft you enjoy can help with anxiety, depression, chronic pain, PTSD, inflammation, and even slowing the aging process of the brain, which ample science now backs up with results from multiple studies.[123] (The truth is out there . . . and it's science-based.)

As one example, NYU researchers gave subjects simple sewing projects and fitted them with blood pressure cuffs and fingertip electrodes. On average, heart rates dropped eight beats per minute for beginners and eleven for experienced sewists.[123] Notice that the experienced sewists had a stronger benefit than beginners, supporting the concept that the benefit increases when you are past that learning stage and don't have to overthink each step and movement.

"Creating—whether it be through art, music, cooking, quilting, sewing, drawing, photography, or cake decorating—is beneficial to us in a number of important ways."[124] This may explain why adult coloring books are so popular, as well as cooking shows, and why I have dubbed my annual Christmas cookie madness as liquid embroidery. It's just another form of coloring, and once the basic skills of royal frosting are mastered, a very calming activity. Many roads lead to Zenlandia.

Gingerbread therapy.

Knititation— Meditation in Motion

The meditative aspects of knitting have more research behind them than any other form of needlework, so that will be the focus here, as we examine some of the evidence and best practices for using knitting as a tool of healing.

If you google "knitting as meditation," you will get over eighteen million hits. Books and blogs on the subject are plentiful, and many include the research data to back up the theories. Most seem to agree that it is the repetitive, rhythmic motion that triggers the relaxation response or a meditative state, even if the goal is to make a scarf for someone as a gift.

Watch or *listen* to someone knitting. The click of the needles and the motion of the hands may even benefit the one watching, perhaps explaining why so many observers have asked the maker, "can you teach me to do that?"

Knitting is meditation. The steady click of the needles is a rosary, a mantra, chanting monks. This unprofitable chore is therapy worth $60 an hour. I cannot afford not to knit. (Chris Carusi, The Knitting Way, *p. 6*)

Betsan Corkhill worked professionally as a senior physiotherapist in the UK until a completely different career path led her to become a freelance production editor on a range of leisure-based magazines. Corkhill came across "a large amount of anecdotal evidence on the therapeutic benefits of knitting and stitching. Large numbers of people from different backgrounds and cultures around the world told similar stories of using knitting and stitching to successfully self-manage a variety of medical conditions—in particular, stress, depression, and long-term pain."[125] This became her own *Call to Needles*, inspired by her excitement at the potential she saw, leading her to conduct more research. She saw the possibility of approaching health and well-being in a way that would incorporate creative therapies as alternatives or partners to enhance traditional Western medicine approaches, especially for chronic conditions. And a way to look at quality of life issues in a more holistic fashion—addressing the whole person.

In 2005 Corkhill launched stitchlinks.com as "a central hub which could always be trusted and relied upon to give accurate information" because she realized, "even at this early stage, 'the media' would undoubtedly sensationalize research findings."

Stitchlinks provides information, research updates, and a forum for support. There are posts in the form of flyers, for example, titled "25 Ways Knitting and Stitching Can Help _____." You can fill in that blank for tips on pain, depression, stress, addiction, or dementia—even a guide to good posture and one for those with hand, arm, and neck problems. I believe no matter what ails you, you can find testimonials on this site that can inspire you, as well as inspiration and support for setting up and conducting effective groups for therapeutic knitting. This site is a rich, full source of science-based information. *(Quite refreshing in the Age of Trump.)* If you prefer a book in your hands to reading on a screen, I recommend Corkhill's *Knit for Health & Wellness: How to Knit a Flexible Mind and More*. I promise, wherever you are on the health or pain spectrum (even those who are at 0, lucky enough to be enjoying good health), you will find something enlightening in this book to improve your well-being.

Mary Maddux came to a significant realization while knitting through a stressful time in her life and wrote about it one day in the blog she shares with her husband, Richard, *Meditation Oasis*. As she knitted and pondered the similarity between meditation and knitting, she realized "you can't worry and knit at the same time!" When you worry, your emotions get involved in a way that creates or increases anxiety. Knitting engages your brain in a way that breaks that pattern. Maddux challenges us to test the theory by letting those worrisome thoughts enter while knitting, and you may notice there is "no emotional juice" or rise in anxiety levels.[126]

××××××

There are two other books I recommend on this subject if the thought of eighteen million Google hits seems overwhelming.

The first is *The Knitting Sutra: Craft as a Spiritual Practice*, by Susan Gordon Lydon, which is an "Eat, Knit, Love" type memoir of Susan's personal journey, healing from a serious arm fracture. Her doctor agreed that knitting, already a skill and passion for her, would be important to her healing process. The following are my three favorite takeaway quotes from this book:

- "How you do anything is how you do everything." (p. 151)
- "Like the counting of the rosary, the motions of needlework are singularly well-suited to the practice of contemplation." (p. 4)
- "Some cultures describe the mind as a drunken monkey, reeling from place to place with no rhyme or reason. Like meditation, knitting calms the monkey down." (p. 143)

The second book is *Mindful Knitting: Inviting Contemplative Practice to the Craft*, by Tara Jon Manning. A completely different approach, but it shares the same message about the connections between knitting and meditation. Tara draws on her foundation in fine arts and textiles, as well as her daily knitting practice and includes several patterns that lend themselves well to the meditative quality of knitting, like the "Deliberate Focus Garter Stitch Scarf" with instructions for using this simple, repetitive pattern for a meditation session. Manning compares the commonalities between knitting and mindful meditation:

- Both require light attention to the environment.
- Both allow the mind to rest.
- Both have a natural object of focus that contributes to a rhythmic quality. (p. 3)

The needleworker's self-care toolbox contains a variety of tools. I discovered the Commit to Knit 30 Challenge hosted online by Becky Stewart, while looking for fresh ideas to start the new year of 2020, instead of another list of resolutions. Knit Om is Stewart's website where you can learn more about her work as a therapeutic knitting and wellness coach. She repeats the challenge each January and usually again midyear in an ongoing effort to "show you how to cultivate a daily mindful knitting practice so that you can leverage therapeutic benefits of knitting and experience more peace, joy, and improved overall well-being!"[127]

After registering for the free thirty-day challenge, you are welcomed to the Commit to Knit Facebook page, where you can share the experience with kindred spirits on the same journey.

Participants are encouraged to create a space for their daily practice, where you can find some peace and quiet and really engage your mind in the experience without distraction. You can choose what you knit for the challenge, as well as how much time you commit to each daily session. Some choose to finish a long-abandoned project with fresh intent. Others choose something simple with no pattern required, to allow more mindfulness. Becky is there for every one of the thirty days, with an email to inspire you with ideas for finding focus and reminders on how to stay in the moment.

I created my space in our spare bedroom. A chair that belonged to my parents, a good lamp or two, a childhood pal, in this case Lamb Chop, my beach shawl, a book by Barbara Kingsolver (a favorite author, who also knits) and propped in the table lamp, a picture of the

My mindful space.

grandmother who taught me to knit and love all things needlework. I found the hoped-for peace in the early days of the pandemic and was reminded each day of the value of my knitting practice to my mental well-being.

One participant shared a quote on the group's Facebook page that reminded us of another powerful way to contemplate as we knit.

> When we engage in fiber arts, we are creating something, but we're also participating in historic traditions, tens of thousands of years old. You are not only making art for your soul and for future generations, you are embodying the work of our ancestors. —The Woven Road *[blog]*

As I participated each day of January, with an intention to meditate, I often thought about my grandmother's skills, used for necessity as well as for gift giving, community, satisfying a need for beauty, accomplishment, and peace in her hardworking life. She shared this gift with me, and I honor her and the grandmother who symbolically placed the needle in my hand with every stitch I make, consciously or not.

You can create your own meditative space for knitting mindfully, with or without guidance from sites like Knit Om. You know best what will work for you. I saw one suggestion (lost now in those eighteen million hits) to dedicate a meditation time and a small, random length of yarn, to knit mindfully, with no planned outcome, until the yarn runs out. During that time, try to focus on the movement of your hands, the needles, the feel of the yarn, or the yarn itself and the journey it made to get to you. Focusing completely on the task cannot help but clear and relax the mind. Then unravel and rewind the yarn for next time.

Counting can also deepen the meditative aspect of knitting. Not counting to find out if or where you made a mistake, as all knitters must, but counting as its own mantra or rhythmic means of focus, using your breath as part of the counting process. (Inhale as you knit two, exhale as you purl two, for example.) This is a common technique in yoga and meditation to increase mindfulness, often counting mala beads held in the hands, like a rosary. Knitting needles, crochet hooks, embroidery and quilting needles, or any crafting tool can act as your mala beads. In the bigger picture, keep in mind that anything done mindfully, with intention, is beneficial as a form of meditation.

Wrap Yourself or Someone Else in a Shawl

I recently saw a post on a knitting group's Facebook page asking why everyone was so into making shawls, adding that the purpose of a shawl always seemed unclear.

In my mind a shawl is really an adult swaddle. There is something unique about wrapping oneself in a shawl. One cool early autumn day, I grabbed a large scarf instead of a jacket (because a jacket would be an admission that summer was over, and I wasn't ready) and kept myself swaddled in it all evening. It was comforting in a light, weighted blanket kind of way.

The popularity of handmade shawls is enjoying a dramatic resurgence. Patterns, shapes, and techniques abound. According to the Roving Crafters website, Ravelry alone contains almost thirty thousand knitted shawl patterns and over six thousand crocheted shawl patterns. Roving Crafters provides a complete history of shawls if you crave more information.[128]

Knitted and crocheted shawls first caught my attention (and intention) when Janet Bristow and Victoria A. Cole-Galo created the Prayer Shawl Ministry in 1998, after participating in a women's leadership institute where their compassion and spirituality merged with their needlework skills—their *Call to Needles*. It has been a massively successful effort with Prayer Shawl Ministry groups still active around the country.

In yoga and meditation, participants are often encouraged to set an intention for their practice. An intention is meant to be a reminder throughout a yoga session, to return to when your mind wanders or your body wants to come out of a pose, when maybe you could stay a little longer. Setting an intention means deciding and committing to something you want to bring attention to, either on the mat or in your life. An intention can also be something you would like to bring into your life, such as positive energy, gratitude, or patience.

Chapter 3 mentioned a counted cross stitch picture I completed as a prayer for a child. Early Christians, Muslims, and Hindus stitched altar cloths and robes for their respective faiths, with every stitch considered a prayer.

You can find many prayers to use while making a prayer shawl on their website, www.shawlministry.com. I have chosen to share a portion of one of them here. It mentions the crafter on a mission, and it also reminds me of the underappreciated work of the frontline and essential workers during the pandemic:

> *Bless my hands . . . often just appendages at the end of my arms . . . workers doing their job without appreciation . . . looked at, yet not really seen. These instruments of love have done mundane tasks, yet also create beauty. They reach out, touch, stroke, scrub, lift, grasp, gesture and guide. These hands, my hands, gifts of great importance, blessings be on them and in them as I begin. May the fruits of their labor be good!*[129]

If we as crafters consider our hands "gifts of great importance," perhaps we will be inspired to take better care of them, which is the focus of the next section.

As you endeavor to take better care of yourself, consider making a shawl for someone you know who may be dealing with cancer, grieving the loss of a loved one, or trying to overcome an addiction, a mental or physical illness, loneliness, or depression, or to serve as a reminder to them of your love or friendship. There is an endless supply of patterns, ideas, and great inspiration out there, or you can create your own.

The pattern I am recommending as a good fit for all I have written about in this book is the "Moving Forward Wrap" designed by Denise Bayron, available on Ravelry. This shawl is made to resemble an arrow and serves as a great metaphor for this time in so many of our lives, when moving forward may feel like equal parts desperately necessary and terrifying, all at once. Wrapping yourself in this proverbial arrow can be a tangible reminder to keep moving forward, no matter how small the steps. The symmetry and balance of the design can remind us to look for those qualities in our lives as tools in the march onward out of our dark days. In the words of the designer:

> *I designed it during a time of personal transition when I had to make important and difficult decisions in order to move my life forward. They say that art imitates life. In this case, I translated my need for life balance into the stitches of this wrap. Wearing this big arrow is an external reminder that I am solely responsible for guiding my life in the right direction.*[130]

This is also a fun pattern to knit, with clear instructions and links to tutorials. I chose to make mine with a yummy Georgia Pecan hued yarn from Lady Dye Yarns in Boston.

Yoga for the Needle Clenchers

As a lifelong needleworker, I still find myself clenching my needle(s) sometimes, especially when trying something new or hurrying to finish a project. One Christmas comes to mind. I decided, rather late in the season of giving, that my go-to gift that year would be a bottle of wine wearing a knitted sweater complete with a cable down the center. They worked up rather quickly, so what could go wrong? I made more than a dozen and was frantically knitting right up to a Christmas Eve gathering. Even though I was enjoying the process, I remember the pain that would shoot through my shoulders, arms, and wrists as my body screamed, "Have you lost your damned mind?"

My version of the Moving Forward Wrap.

At other times, I become so engrossed in my craft that I sit too long in the same position, regretting that decision when I have to get up and move on. *I know you've been there as well—don't deny it.*

I recently discovered and highly recommend the book *Knitting Comfortably: The Ergonomics of Handknitting* by Carson Demers. The book has received high praise from some big names in the knitting world. Demers is a knitter, spinner, designer, and a physical therapist specializing in ergonomics. He realized there was a need for this book after working with clients who had *injured themselves knitting*. Demers covers everything from the chair you use to the needles and other tools and how you use them—even minding your posture when blocking that finished project or sitting at your computer looking for the next project. Knitting is in the title but much of this valuable information would translate well to other types of needlework and includes many helpful stretches, exercises, and advice on the mechanics.

Betsan Corkhill's book *Knit for Health and Wellness* and the Stitchlinks website mentioned earlier describe the importance of posture to knitting and other forms of needlework. One chapter in the book is titled "Sit Well, Improve Your Knitting Posture."

Demers and Corkhill make the case for preventing health and pain issues caused by too much sitting, especially (as we tend to do) in poor posture, focused on our needlework. Let's consider our audience here for a moment. Most stitchers, myself included, have long-established (mostly bad) habits—partially reclining, dog(s) or cat(s) nestled close, the right light and tools for the effort, in reach of our favorite beverage. It's about relaxing into the work and feeling comfortable—our moments of Zen. Few of us sit in straight-backed chairs with our feet on the floor (the described ideal). We tend to think of these mechanics as something important when working at a desk or computer, but for our needlework, it is rarely a consideration.

Teaching computer skills to middle and high school students in the 1980s, we were sure we needed to teach our students keyboarding skills at the computer. Districts like ours invested heavily in *Mavis Beacon Teaches Typing*. We tried, but eventually realized that we were too late. By then, they were self-taught hunters and peckers, some using two fingers, some using more, and had habits too difficult to change. It was now in the muscle memory. I see that in our stitching as well. That is why my focus here is to look at ways to undo some of our self-inflicted damage (pain). Some of you may decide to take on the challenge of improving your ergonomics, and I applaud those efforts.

xxxxx

I turned to yoga (also about posture and ergonomics) for a very achy lower back over twenty years ago. Job stress, anxiety, and, I now know, fibromyalgia often left me bent over, walking like a frail, elderly woman, in my forties. The amazing results I experienced from a consistent yoga practice made me a believer for life. As my public school teaching career wound toward retirement and I contemplated my next life phase, I decided to become a yoga teacher. I loved teaching, I could take on as few or as many classes and clients as I deemed retirement-worthy, and it would be refreshing to teach people who were in class by choice and, as adults, had fully functioning frontal lobes. I became a certified yoga teacher and yoga therapist a few months before retiring from teaching high school.

I taught a yoga class that I called "Yoga for Cranky Backs" with a small, loyal group of (mostly) women in my age range with achy backs, looking for relief. A year later I changed the class name to "Yoga for Healthy Backs and Bones" because those who attended the class regularly no longer had cranky backs! I also taught "silver sneaker" yoga (seated on a chair, rather than on a mat on the floor) at a local rec center. I firmly believe everyone can benefit from some form of yoga and meditation, ideally on the floor on a good yoga mat. But, for those with mobility issues, chair yoga can be incredibly beneficial.

I have come to think of yoga as the answer to many questions concerning pain and overall wellness. One of my yoga teachers, Judi Bar, was hired by the Cleveland Clinic to manage the yoga program in its Center for Integrative Medicine. She was one of the first in the country to hold such a position with a major medical institution. The Clinic was able to see the wisdom of using multiple approaches to wellness, combining western medicine with alternatives like yoga, meditation, and other traditional paths to healing. You can find several of Judi's yoga videos available on the Cleveland Clinic website under Wellness and Preventive Medicine. Each video is under three minutes and targets specific needs.[131]

Movement Matters

When you're young, synovial fluid flows freely through the body to lubricate the joints. But as with so many things in life, that changes quickly after you enter those adult years. Sometime in your twenties, your body gets stingy with the synovial fluid and requires that you move those joints in order to get a delivery of natural lubrication to the area. Yoga helps this process and has the added benefit of being a weight-bearing exercise, so important for maintaining healthy bone structure. A fairly simple, traditional yoga pose like warrior works most muscle groups in the body and is a full body, weight-bearing stretch.

If you're not a regular yoga practitioner, you don't have to be flexible to start. Yoga helps you become more flexible. And I don't recommend you plop yourself into just any yoga class, because American yoga has increasingly become a "workout" rather than a "practice" in the traditional yoga sense, and it often results in injuries. If you're starting out, be sure to look for a beginner class, a gentle yoga flow, or consult with someone at the studio, rec center, or gym for the class that would best suit your needs. Look for yoga teachers who are certified with the RYT (registered yoga teacher) designation. For a home practice, search "yoga for _____" and fill in the blank with what bothers you most (arthritis, neck pain, anxiety, PTSD, etc.). There are plenty of resources, but as with any internet search, screen for credible sources and begin slowly.

If you are expecting to find yoga for hands, arms, shoulders, and neck in this chapter, you will, but it is more complicated than that because our body parts are all so interconnected. For example, lower back pain may have nothing to do with your spine or back muscles. The sciatic nerve and the piriformis and iliopsoas muscles (a.k.a. hip flexors) all connect from muscles in the front of your upper thighs and fit nicely through those holes in your hip structure, on their way to connecting to your lower back muscles. That means that flexing your knees and stretching your hamstrings and quadriceps may ease back pain if they are indeed the culprits. Second to the quads in neglect are the hamstrings, which are actually a small group of muscles at the back of the thigh. The majority of Americans have extremely tight hamstrings from too much sitting and inactivity. I have included a few simple stretches to reach these neglected areas.

Breath Matters

Any good yoga practice begins with the breath. There are many yoga breathing methods with specific focus, but I will keep it simple with ways to improve the ability of your lungs to obtain and hold air and release all that needs to leave you when you exhale.

We tend to spend too much needle time hunched over our work. The process of holding two needles, or a needle in one hand and a hoop in the other, tends to bring both hands to the center of the chest and close the front, upper body inward, at the same time rounding the shoulders and back, the head tilting forward. Even when you are accustomed to sitting in good posture, needlework is going to somewhat restrict a full opening of the chest. Another problem is that our working posture, and sometimes the nature of the work itself, combined with stress or anxiety, may cause us to fall into a breathing rhythm that consists of somewhat constricted shorter breaths, encouraged by that forward closed position—especially when following an intricate pattern or trying a new, challenging technique.

A yoga session should always include breath work to begin and end, with prompts for inhaling and exhaling at appropriate points in any pose. I enthusiastically encourage a regular yoga practice, but breath work can also mean pausing throughout the day to consciously take a few deep breaths. My Fitbit is set up with a reminder ten minutes before each hour if I have not taken at least 250 steps in that hour. There are other ways to set up such reminders, like setting the timer on your phone or asking Alexa or Google to alert you when it's time to move. I encourage you to find a way to remind yourself to stop, set the needle(s) down, and focus on your breathing, even while seated. Standing up to take a few deep breaths only improves the process if your standing posture includes rolling shoulders and head back and lengthening your spine with a gentle stretch to make room for your breath.

Imagine you've settled into your favorite knitting spot with your preferred beverage in reach and you are about to pick up your needles. Before you do that, try a mini-practice of a few deep breaths to clear your mind and lungs. If you have a regular yoga practice (yay, you!), and a favorite yogic breath, like ujai or alternate nostril, or you prefer adding an "om" on the exhale, go for it!

To begin, evaluate your typical deep breath. Take one deep breath without thinking about the process. Did your chest and shoulders lift vertically? If so, let's work on that first:

- With one hand on your chest and the other hand on your lower abdomen, make sure your spine is lengthened and you are not hunched over in any way.
- Exhale completely (*figure 1*).
- As you begin a slow inhale, let your lower abdomen lead by expanding out (this will allow the diaphragm to drop lower and make more room for your lungs to expand).
- Inhale deeply and you will feel the lungs expand.
- Don't be surprised if this feels uncomfortable or awkward at first—you may even cough reflexively, as you send air into neglected areas.

Figure 1

In these photos, I am sitting on the edge of a folded blanket to rotate the hips forward, lengthening the spine.

Keep in mind that breathing is normally an autonomic process. I am asking you to make it a conscious process here. Take several slow breaths, with eyes closed, making your exhales slightly longer than your inhales. One way to do that is to slowly count 1, 2, 3, 4 each time you inhale, hold briefly at the end of that inhale, then exhale as slowly as possible to a count of 6 or 8. Follow these intentional breaths with several normal breaths, hands still in place to monitor the process. Practice this often enough, and the autonomic process will accommodate this improvement.

Needle(s) up and go! Check your breathing occasionally or pause your work intentionally for a few deep, cleansing breaths, especially if you get frustrated with a pattern or someone interrupts your counting.

In yoga poses, the breath is extremely important. A good yoga teacher will remind you to breathe, because when we are "posing" and fighting gravity, we tend to hold our breath. But there should also be prompts on how to use inhales and exhales within a pose for maximum benefit. Any pose that opens the chest or extends muscles is usually done as you inhale, while poses that bend you forward or inward are typically done on the exhale, often taking you deeper into a pose than you thought possible. Yogic breathing takes practice, but the benefits are profound. Let's practice this concept of moving with the breath in mind, in a simple seated pose on a mat or seated on an armless chair:

- Lift the head a little and roll the shoulders back into an open-chest posture with both hands resting on the upper chest (*figure 2*).
- As you inhale slowly, open the right arm straight and to the side, parallel to the floor. As you slowly exhale, bend the right elbow and bring the hand back to the chest. Repeat with left arm, following the inhale to open and exhale to close (*figure 3*).
- Repeat on each side, but this time, inhale a little longer, and take the arm further back. Match the length of the exhale as you return hand to chest.
- Repeat one more time, taking each arm as far back as you comfortable (or slightly uncomfortably) can go. Enough to feel a good stretch and opening of the chest.

CHALLENGE: After each pose, notice whether you feel any changes in the area stretched—a warmth or tingling that may not have been there before.

Figure 2

Figure 3

There should be no pain in yoga. Let go of the old and dangerous "no pain, no gain" mantra. In yoga, you gain incrementally, by listening to what your body is trying to tell you, using the breath to challenge yourself to hold a pose a little longer or go a little deeper than is comfortable. Notice here that there is a difference between discomfort and pain. Discomfort is how we grow and improve (whether in exercise, relationships, life, yada-yada) but pain is never the goal. And of course, if you have any serious health issues, you should never begin any exercise practice without checking with your doctor. Some health conditions are not compatible with certain yoga poses. For example, if you have glaucoma, you should not be doing deep forward bends or any inversions that would increase pressure in the eyes.

For the Neck

Consider how fragile our necks are, supported by the upper end of the spine (the cervical spine) and tasked with holding up the huge, heavy sphere that contains the control center for the body. Now think about how much time your head spends bent forward. We need to counter that occasionally.

On the mat or in a chair

Bring your chin up and let the head tilt back, just a tiny bit, as if someone is gently pushing on your chin, to bring the head more in line with your spine. It may help to consult a mirror once or twice until you know how that alignment looks and feels. (On a mat, it may help to sit on the edge of a folded blanket, legs crossed in a simple seated pose. If you're using a chair, it should have a firm seat and straight back with no arms, for all seated poses in this chapter.)

- Relax the shoulders (always a good first step), because stress and life tend to make them shrug.
- Inhale, lifting the head and lengthening the spine.
- Exhale, bringing your chin toward your chest until you feel a good stretch in the back of the neck. Hold there for another breath.
- Repeat, lifting and lowering your head several times, slowly, following your natural breathing pattern.

- On an exhale, tilt right ear toward right shoulder and hold for a breath or two, inhaling as you lift head back to center. Repeat on the other side, taking left ear toward left shoulder on an exhale.

- Pause on an exhale and roll the head from one side, down and across the chest to the other shoulder. Roll back slowly, and repeat a few times, breathing naturally.

Relax the shoulders (always a good first step), because stress and life tend to make them shrug.

For the Shoulders

Carrying the weight of a world in disarray means the shoulders need extra TLC. Travel over the shoulder to that shoulder blade area of the back and you will find very few people without a cranky knot or two lurking in that area, because we tend to carry more of our stress in that part of the body. A good massage therapist can loosen those stress magnets, but yoga can also help.

On the mat

- Lie flat on your back, knees bent, feet flat on the mat, arms outstretched to either side, palms up.
- Pushing down into the feet, lift your hips ever so slightly and scooch them a few inches to the left for better spinal alignment in the coming pose.
- Bring knees to chest and roll them to the right, until bent legs rest on the floor, arms still outstretched (*figure 4*). Breathe into the pose for a few breaths before we massage those shoulders. If your legs can't comfortably rest on the floor, try propping with a pillow or folded blanket. Less bend in the knees may also help.
- Keeping your left arm straight, lift it off the floor and across the body to rest on the right arm, as if drawing a rainbow over you.
- You should now be lying on your right side, knees bent, palms together with arms stretched out. As the left arm moves across to meet the right arm, you should feel a little "massaging" of the right shoulder blade area (*figure 5*).
- Inhale as you bring the left arm straight up and back across to beginning position. Repeat this sequence slowly, 4 to 5 times.
- Bring the knees back to center with feet flat on the floor, lift and scooch the hips a bit to the right, and repeat the entire sequence on the other side of your body. Bent knees now roll to the left, with the right arm drawing the rainbow, massaging the left shoulder blade.

Figure 4

Figure 5

Self-Care for the Weary Craftivist

Seated (or on the mat)

- If seated on a chair, keep feet flat on the floor. If you choose the floor and a mat, sit in simple seated pose with legs crossed.
- Bring hands to top of shoulders, or as close as possible (*figure 6*).
- Make large forward circles, leading with the elbows (4–5 circles, normal breath).
- Reverse the direction and number of repeats.

- -

- Starting in the same beginning pose (*figure 6*), bring elbows together in front, upper arms parallel to the floor (*figure 7*). Then inhale as you return to beginning position (*figure 6*), taking the bent arms as far back as possible without strain or pain to maximize the opening of the chest. Exhale as you bring the elbows back together. Repeat several times, as comfort level allows.
- Keeping hands on shoulder tops, inhale and drop elbows down to sides, letting the head stretch back as you look up (*figure 8*). As you exhale, lift elbows up toward the sky, dipping head forward out of the way. Repeat several times (*figure 9*).

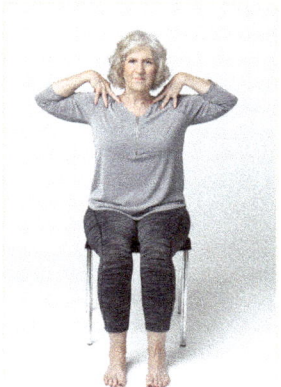

Figure 6

Figure 7

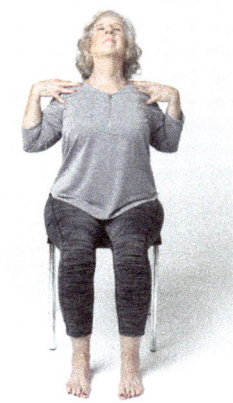

Figure 8

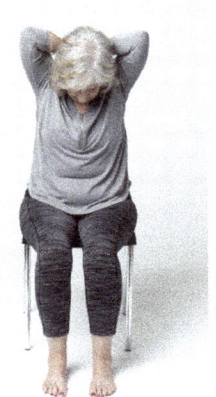

Figure 9

Additionally, simple shoulder rolls in both directions (arms relaxed, at side) should be part of your daily routine. You can do them without unrolling a mat or moving to a more rigid chair. Add a few "shrug, hold, and release" moves. Remember, we're lubricating the complicated shoulder joint, relaxing tension points, and stretching muscles, tendons, and ligaments with these moves.

The 4 Motions of the Spine

The amazing, life-supporting, yet rather fragile backbone! When we aren't taking it for granted, let's remember that the spine has four directions of movement. A good yoga sequence will work all four. The spine can move forward and back, bend side to side, curve forward or arch back, and twist side to side.

Repeat each of the following poses several times, if possible, without strain or pain.

Figure 10

On the mat

If you are a regular yoga practitioner, the recommended poses to target all four directions: Cat–cow, cobra, or sphinx, seated twists and forward bends, child's pose, or even a sun salutation sequence.

Seated Modifications

Motion 1: Forward & Backward

Figure 11

- Sitting at the front edge of the chair, bring your feet wide apart and flat on the floor, hands hanging loosely at your sides. Inhale to a long spine as you bring arms straight up overhead. Bend forward, hinging from your hips, without curling the back. If you are doing this pose for the first time, or have chronic back pain, you may find it more comfortable to place your hands on your thighs, elbows bent, as you hinge forward (*figure 10*). *(To be clear, this is not a sumo wrestling pose; there is a chair under me in the picture.)*

Self-Care for the Weary Craftivist

- Bend ONLY as far forward as you comfortably can, bringing hands toward or to the floor, between the open legs (*figure 11*). Hold for a breath or two before finding an inhale to bring you back up without curving the spine.

- Back in simple seated pose, still on the front edge of the chair, hold the sides of the chair seat and inhale as you lean back in the chair, still keeping the spine long and straight. You should feel your core engage. Exhale as you come back.

Motion 2: Side Bends

- OPTION 1: Hold edge of chair seat with left hand. Feet are together and flat on the floor. Inhale and bring the right arm straight up, lightly touching right ear. As you exhale, bend toward to the left, keeping the right arm aligned with the right ear to maximize the bend. You can hold in the bend for a few breaths or create a flow in and out of the bend. Remember to use your breath, exhaling into the deepest part of the bend, inhaling on the way up. Repeat for other side (*figure 12*).

- OPTION 2: Inhaling, lift both arms straight up overhead, in-line with ears. As you exhale, hold right wrist with left hand and bend to the left. Hold for a breath or two. Repeat for other side (*figure 13*).

Figure 12

Figure 13

Motion 3: Front Arches and Back Curls

- OPTION 1—Simple Arches & Curls: Sitting straight and a little forward in the chair (leave some space between your back and the chair back), inhale, lengthening the spine and lifting the head up and back slightly. Hinge forward as you exhale, curl the back, stretch the arms forward and lift back up to center as you inhale (*figure 14*).

- OPTION 2—Deeper Arches & Curls: Sitting tall in the chair, still slightly forward on seat, bring both hands to the back of the chair, arms straight, holding each side as high as possible on the outer edges of the chair back. Keeping your spine long and straight, pull your upper body forward as you inhale, back slightly arched, as if trying to pull away from the chair back. This is a great chest opener! Hold for a few breaths (*figure 15*).

Figure 14

Figure 15

- Alternate this stretch with letting go of the chair back and sweeping the arms, parallel to the floor, out in front of you, on an exhale, curling the back, while stretching the arms forward.

Motion 4: Twists

- OPTION 1: Inhale to a long spine. On an exhale, twist (turn) to the left, taking left hand across the back as far as slightly uncomfortable, without collapsing the spine, and hold for a few breaths. Your left hand can hold the back of the chair seat. Place your right hand on the outside of the left knee to help hold the pose and deepen the twist. As you hold this pose, notice that in order to inhale fully, you will untwist ever-so-slightly, and as you exhale, you will ease back into the deeper version (*figure 16*).

Figure 16

- OPTION 2: Less intense, but equally effective. Sit sideways on the chair. Inhale to a long spine. As you exhale, twist toward the back of the chair, and hold each side of the chair back. Same advice as above, as you hold this pose for a few breaths. Turn 180° to sit facing the opposite direction and repeat, twisting to hold the back of the chair for a few breaths (*figure 17*).

Shake it off!

Sometimes, the best way to release some stress is to literally shake it off. Seated or standing, shake your hands, your shoulders, your entire upper body, like no one is watching.

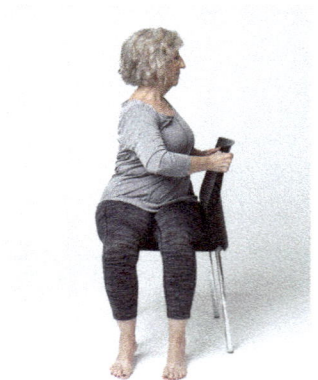

Figure 17

STRETCH THOSE HAMMIES

The chronically tight hamstrings deserve and desperately need daily stretching. This sequence will be a multitasking yoga flow, opening the chest, bringing the breath, and stretching the entire body, especially the hamstrings.

Half Sun Salutation
(standing flow)

- Stand on the floor or on a mat, preferably barefoot, and take a breath or two as you consider your posture. This is called mountain pose and deserves as much focus and consideration as any yoga pose.
- Roll the shoulders back slightly to align with the sides of the body.
- Lift chin slightly and pull it in and back a bit, to bring head in proper alignment with the spine.
- Imagine your feet are the roots of a tree, holding you upright in soft strength.
- Soften the knees a little and bring palms together in front of the chest. Pause here for a few focused breaths, eyes closed.

- Inhale. Lower the arms and sweep them up from the sides to bring palms parallel overhead. Arch back slightly (*figure 18*).
- Exhale, sweeping arms forward and down as you hinge forward from the hips into a forward bend. Modify as needed. Your hands may not reach the floor and that's okay. As long as you feel the stretch in the back of the thighs, you are where you need to be. If there is any back discomfort as you bend forward, change the sweep of the arms from straight forward to out and down at the sides. Then bring them forward once you have hinged the spine forward. That should feel better.
- From the forward bend, place your hands on the front of the legs and inhale part way up until your spine is parallel to the floor (*figure 19*). Lift your head up as you inhale, then exhale back into the full forward bend.
- On an inhale, sweep the arms up on the sides as you lift yourself back into mountain pose, arms overhead, palms parallel to each other.

Figure 18

Figure 19

- On an exhale, bend both arms, bringing the palms together and the hands down toward your upper back. You should feel a yummy stretch in the back of the upper arms (the triceps) (*figure 20*).

- Inhale the arms back up toward the sky, bring the palms together and lower them back to the front of the chest where you began the sequence. Take a few breaths here and consider how and what and where you "feel."

- Repeating this half sun salutation flow, at least a few times, will increase the benefits.

Seated Modification

- Stretch the hamstrings first. Seated toward the front edge of the chair, straighten one leg out in front, resting on the heel, the other foot flat on floor as anchor. Inhale to a long spine, hands resting on the thigh of the bent leg, exhale, and hinge forward until you feel a stretch in the back of the extended leg. Hold for a few breaths and repeat on the other leg (*figure 21*).

- For the upper body portion of the half sun salutation to stretch the spine and work the shoulders, lift the arms overhead on an inhale bringing palms together. Bend the elbows and bring the hands (still together) down toward your upper back (as shown in *figure 20*). Hold for a breath or two. Inhale arms back overhead and bring down to your heart's center in front of your body.

Figure 20

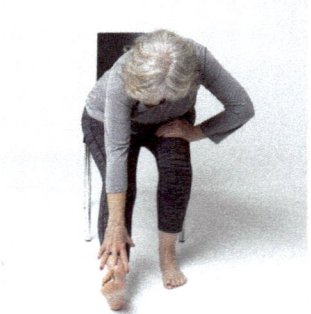

Figure 21

QUADRICEPS STRETCHES

If you sit for long periods, the quadriceps in the front of your thighs (top of thighs while seated) actually shorten as you sit. Stretching the quads is not as easy as stretching other areas of the body so we tend to neglect them.

On the mat

Traditional yoga poses like camel, dancer, hero, pigeon, bow, sugar cane, and crescent lunge are all excellent for stretching the quadriceps. There are modifications for each.

Simple modification on the mat

- Sit on the mat with legs extended forward. (Reminder—if this is not comfortable, use a cushion or folded blanket under the hips.) Bend the knees and bring both feet to the left, resting the right foot against the left upper leg. (*figure 22*).

Figure 22

- Bring your upper body down to the right, resting on your right forearm, on the floor.

- If you can, hold the top of your left foot with your left hand, then lift slightly off the ground and pull the bent left leg back until you feel a good stretch in the left quadriceps. Keep the leg parallel to the floor. Hold for about 30 seconds (*figure 23*).

Figure 23

- Release your hand and counter-stretch by straightening and sweeping the left leg across the front of the body, parallel to the floor. Repeat a few more times.

- Come back to seated with legs straight out in front of you and stretch the right quadriceps by repeating these steps on the other side.

Seated modification

- Sit completely sideways, toward the front edge of the chair, turned to the right, with right hand holding chair back for stability. Drop the left leg, with knee bent, off the chair. If you can tolerate it, rest top of left foot on the floor. (If that is not comfortable, place the weight of that leg on a bent left foot, weight on the toes, foot arched. That should feel better.)

- At this point, your quadriceps are already getting a mild stretch. To deepen the stretch (the goal) bring the left foot back as far as possible on the floor and with a long, straight spine, gently and slowly, tip your upper body back a few degrees. You will feel a deeper stretch. Hold for 20–30 seconds (*figure 24*). Repeat, seated sideways to the left, stretching the right quadriceps.

For the Hands

Our most important and often neglected tools. The shoulders and arms are intended to be tools of strength. The hands are more about dexterity, flexibility, and finesse. Our hands can be used:

Figure 24

> *As a tool, as a symbol, and as a weapon. A whole literature of legend, folklore, superstition, and myth has been built up around the human hand. As an organ of performance, it serves as eyes for the blind, the mute talk with it, and it has become a symbol of salutation, supplication, and condemnation. The hand has played a part in the creative life of every known society, and it has come to be symbolic or representative of the whole person in art, in drama, and in the dance.*[132]

> "Because of their ubiquitous utility, the hands . . . are prime prey of a disease based on wear and tear. Yoga is useful in its characteristic ways: improving range of motion, enhancing the health of the many joints, providing stretch and calm to inflamed parts."[133]

We ask so much of our hands. Let's show them some appreciation and love, like any well-cared for tool, to help them function longer and more efficiently. Let's begin this portion of self-care by bringing more awareness to our hands. Notice during the day when and where are you gripping too tightly—the steering wheel, your phone, *your needle(s)*? That kind of tension will affect not just the hands, but the arms and shoulders, and even the lower back.

Let's begin this portion of self-care by bringing more awareness to our hands.

Self-Care for the Weary Craftivist

There are 14 phalanges (finger bones), 5 metacarpals (palm bones), and 8 pebbly-looking carpal bones (in the wrist).[134] How often do we bring our awareness to the anatomy of our hands? Let's pause to consider that our hands are overworked and overused on a daily basis.

In yoga, we often begin any session, meditation, or breath work by carefully considering the position of our hands. In a simple seated pose, we may rest our hands lightly on our knees (or thighs if seated in a chair) palms up to receive energy, or palms down to release excess energy. If you practice any of the poses or stretches mentioned here, I encourage you to bring light attention to relaxing your hands and try a *mudra* to see how it feels.

AWARENESS AND MUDRAS

- Think of a mudra as a yoga pose for the hands. There are hundreds of mudras from Eastern religions and the practice of yoga. An internet search will show you many options. It is a way to center yourself and bring focus. *(TBH—I can make a good rationale for that role being played by my knitting needles, as long as my grip is relaxed and mindful).*
- Palms together in front of the chest in mountain pose is one mudra. Thumb to forefinger, other fingers lightly extended is another mudra (*figure 25*).

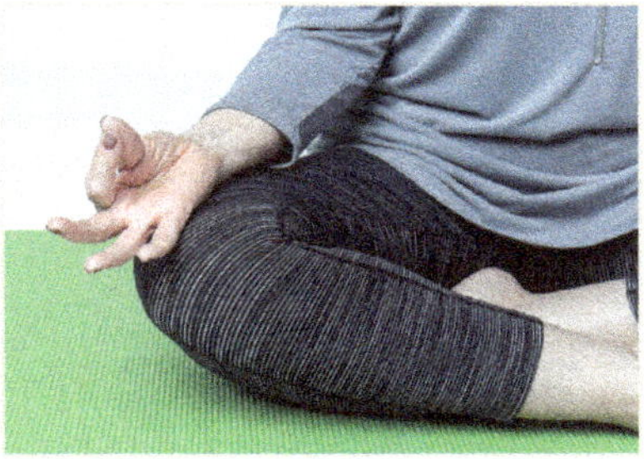

Figure 25

MUDRA IN MOTION

- Seated or standing—lift the hands slightly and tap and hold each thumb to the forefinger on the same hand (right thumb to right index finger, left to left).
- Slowly move the thumbs, simultaneously, to tap middle fingers, then to ring fingers, then to the pinkies (*figure 26*).
- Reverse the motion by tapping the pinkies again, then travel back to original thumb to index finger position.

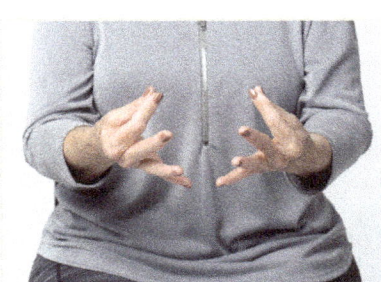

Figure 26

- You can repeat this multiple times and try speeding the movement up at your own pace. Chanting can help you focus, by saying a word on each finger tap. In kundalini yoga the chant is often "Sa, ta, na, ma," which in Sanskrit represents birth, life, death, and rebirth, but collectively they represent one's true essence or identity.[135] It can be very meditative. But your chant could be anything that works for you, even knit, one, purl, two.

- Wanna really get crazy? Try starting one hand at the index finger and the other hand at the pinkie, each hand tapping it out in opposite directions (*figure 27*).

Yoga for the Hands and Wrists

Remember how small the bones, ligaments, and tendons of the hand are compared to the larger structures in the body. They lend themselves well to stretching, but be careful not to overdo it. Most muscles that move the wrist, hand, and fingers are not located in the hand, but in the forearm. Many of the muscles in the hand attach to tendons of the longer muscles in the forearms, giving more strength to the hands.

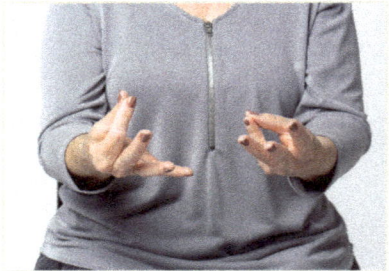

Figure 27

The following hand yoga poses come from the book *Yoga for Arthritis*, by Loren Fishman, MD, and Ellen Saltonstall.[133] I've used them in my own teaching and personal practice. The wording here is my own. When repeats are mentioned, I want you to repeat only as many times as you can, comfortably, without causing pain. Start slowly, and, when possible, increase the number of repeats or the time held, for continued benefit.

This Mudra in Motion may not seem like you're doing much to benefit your weary hand warriors, but remember that dexterity, used in craft, involves coordination with the eyes and brain. Some of this dexterity we accomplish any time a needle is in our hands, but it can be enhanced and strengthened with fresh challenges. Another beneficial challenge is to use your nondominant hand occasionally for daily rituals, like brushing your teeth. Or take some scrap yarn and needles or hook—imagine you are teaching a lefty (if you are a righty) to knit or crochet—you'll quickly fall out of your comfort zone!

Thumb and Finger Stretches

- Remember to use gentle stretches on these digits.
- Pull the thumb gently down toward the side of the wrist, away from fingers.
- Stretch each finger gently, separately forward and back.
- Bend each finger gently, at each joint, forward only, of course, and hold for a few seconds (*figures 28, 29*).
- Make a loose fist with both hands, then open the hands, spreading the fingers as far apart as possible. Repeat several times, then shake the hands gently at your sides.

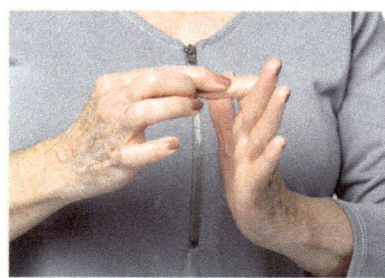

Figure 28

Digital Roly Poly

- Sitting or standing, breathing normally, bring hands to front of chest and interlace your fingers.
- Make small figure 8 driven by your wrists, with fingers as relaxed as possible. Keep upper arms at the sides, keeping them out of this move. Repeat 10 times. Then reverse the direction of the figure 8 for another 10 repeats (*figure 30*).

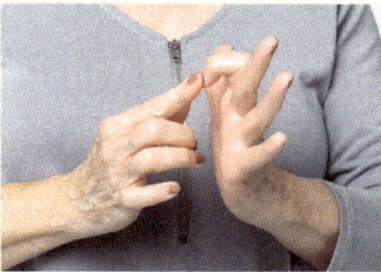

Figure 29

Prayer Pose

- Seated or standing, with normal breath, put palms together in front of the chest. Press the hands together firmly enough to maximize the amount of contact between fingers and palms. Check that forearms are parallel to the floor, which will bring elbows up and out a bit. Engage the 4 corners of the palms.
- Keeping the hands together as if you could not separate them if you wanted to, raise the hands over the head and pause there.

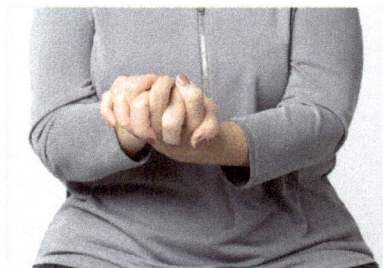

Figure 30

- Slowly bring the hands, still in a purposeful prayer pose, straight down in front, taking them as low as you can go, without the palms separating at the base. Repeat this up and down sequence several times, slowly.

- Bring hands back to chest level, still in prayer pose. Keeping the matching fingers together, fan the fingers and thumbs apart and bring them back together several times.

- Holding hands in prayer pose, turn hands and fingers away from your body and downward, keeping the wrists close to you (*figure 31*). Hold for several seconds and release slowly. Rotate back up and bring the hands down toward the chest, as far as you can, comfortably (*figure 32*). Hold for several seconds and release slowly.

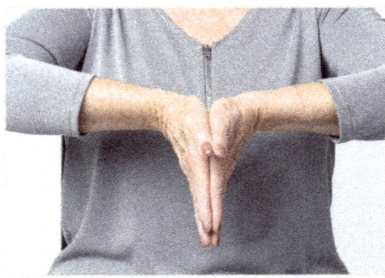

Figure 31

Aikido Wrist Stretches

- Aikido is a Japanese martial art practice that trains one to absorb the energy of your attacker and redirect it back at them. The peaceful, dignified philosophy and training is compatible with yoga, and your wrists will thank you.

- For ease and clarity, I am going to refer you to *Yoga for Arthritis* co-author Ellen Saltonstall for visual instructions on these two stretches. www.youtube.com/watch?v=Lz69qwqw2kU

Figure 32

ADDITIONAL HAND CARE

Once you have tried these basic moves, trust your instincts. There are so many ways you can move and stretch your hands and fingers for optimal benefit. Play that invisible piano—try it with fingers straight and then with bent fingers. Rotate those wrists like they are holding castanets, and dance like no one is watching. Use a wall or tabletop to bend the fingers or entire hand (from the wrist) forward or back in a gentle stretch. If it's fun, you'll be more likely to stay with it.

Massage:

- Take a break occasionally to massage your hands or make it a pre- or post-needlework routine. Lotion adds a nice "touch."
- Massage the dense area between the thumb and forefinger, the webbing between the fingers, each finger joint, and the thumbs, individually.
- Massage the palm with slightly more force than used on the fingers.

Pause for a minute after doing any or all of the hand movements. Rest your open hands, palms up, on your lap, and assess how they feel.

Fondle That Fascia

Fascia (not to be confused with a fascist, which has a very different cell structure) is the substance in our body that holds us all together, so it seems important. It is collagen rich, and a layer of it surrounds and supports every organ, bone, nerve, blood vessel, and muscle in its rightful place in the body. It should stretch when you move, but stress, trauma, surgery, injury, lack of movement, or repetitive movement that overworks one part of the body day after day (*hello, needleworkers*) can cause the fascia to tighten up and become thick, sticky, and binding, a problem that can then referred to as adhesions, depending on the level of severity.[136] Tight, inflexible fascia is going to be a problem because it can limit mobility and cause those pesky knots to form. Fascia can be quite sensitive and fussy, causing people to think they are experiencing muscle pain, even fibromyalgia, when the culprit may be the fascia.

So, what's a dedicated needleworker to do? Keep your fascia in tip-top condition by moving more, and more often, even if only a couple of minutes every hour, stretching regularly and maintain good posture, standing or sitting.

There are medical options available, but you may not need them if you practice more self-care. Exercise like yoga, massage, foam rollers, and heat therapy are all effective. One overlooked tool is to avoid inflammatory foods like too much sugar, white flour, and the additives found in overly processed foods. Try avoiding these inflammatory triggers for a week and see if you notice a

Keep your fascia in tip-top condition by moving more, and more often.

difference. And if the home remedies and preventions don't work, consult a doctor for more help. You're worth it!

Yay you, for engaging in some well-deserved self-love and care! Give yourself a big hug, right arm crossing over left, with hands reaching your upper back shoulder area. And while you're there, dig those fingers into the flesh between the shoulder and shoulder blade (lovingly, of course—no nails), and see if you notice any tender areas, which might indicate that the fascia needs a little more consistent love in that area (*figure 33*).

Inhale and open the arms wide and back until you've opened up your chest (and heart). Repeat the hug with left arm crossing over the right and dig in again.

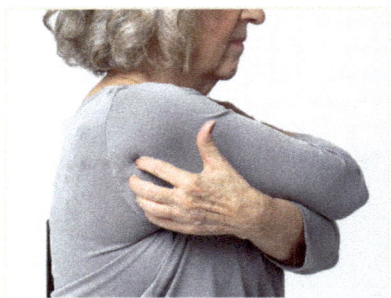

Figure 33

14

SEEKING CLOSURE

Even though the calendar will turn,
2020 will be with us for a long, long time.

—Harry Smith, NBC News 12/27/2020

Closure means finality. When we lose a loved one or an important relationship ends, we grieve the loss, and that looks different in different people. Experts say there is no one right or wrong way to grieve, because it is a very individual process with no easy path or time limit. As this book comes to an end, I am not sure how the same grief response for losing a loved one or a relationship fits the need for closure that so many of us have experienced at this point in history. It seems so much bigger than one individual, personal loss. I know 2020 will be remembered as the first year of a particularly challenging time for a multitude of reasons I will not attempt to list here, since I am confident you keep your list close. And it felt like a turning point when we elected Joe Biden and Kamala Harris near the end of that historically significant year. But when history looks back at the origins of the *Age of Trump*, it may find a disturbance in the force (worldwide) that took more years than we realized at the time to propel Trump into office in 2016. If we look back to examples of criminality in the past, we should realize that it takes years to investigate, litigate, prosecute, and hold accountable all the people who violated our constitution in this era.

Even as life has continued to hit us with the loss of one love, one job, one stage of life, one relationship, or one constant in our lives, whether through death, disagreement, estrangement, or other factors, by conscious choice or against all hope, there is a bigger picture of grief now, due to the COVID pandemic. Too many of the losses have become shared grief, and the number of losses is so enormous that most of us have no frame of reference for comparison. That means the traditional advice seems inadequate for what it will take to move beyond the *Age of Trump*.

According to *Psychology Today*, on the subject of closure:

The ending of a significant piece of one's life . . . may be difficult and even painful for many of us. Something that you once counted on as very important to your life is over and done. Finding closure implies a complete acceptance of what has happened and an honoring of the transition away from what's finished to something new. In other words, closure describes the ability to go beyond imposed limitations in order to find different possibilities.[137]

After rereading this quote a few times, I think that the shared and individual experiences of 2020, the four years of the Trump presidency, and the fallout that followed us well beyond 2020, will take time to process. It will take time just to understand what happened and the imprint it left on us. But traditional advice might still help us find our way back to normal.

xxxxxx

The following "5 Ways to Find Closure from the Past," from a *Psychology Today* blog, was posted several years before Trump was elected and follows mainstream psychological tenets, but it may hold clues for these times as well. For each of the five ways listed here, I have included the detail points that seem to speak the loudest to these times and how I see them at work in my own life. I have included space for you to consider how they might apply to you, how you choose to deal with the concept of closure, and where your personal *Call to Needles* may fit into the formula.

1. Take full responsibility for Yourself

- If you're willing to let go, what does that really mean?
- What will you have to do?

My response: *Will my needles call me to continue making what often feels like subversive statements, hoping someone will listen? Or will I go back to making fun, functional items? (Ideally, a healthy blend of the two.) Will craftivism continue to be a necessary, ongoing tool for change? For as long as craftivism has existed, even before the term, I can't conceive that the need will disappear, so I will keep those needles at the ready, to respond when needed while trying to let go of the need for my constant vigilance.*

Your response?

Seeking Closure

2. Grieve the loss

- Take plenty of time to do this.
- There is no set amount of time and no prescribed way; it's totally up to each person to find that for themselves.
- However, grieving should not go on for years. That's just being stuck, still heavily invested in the past.

> **My response:** *I fear we became numb to the constantly rising death count from COVID-19, as well as the continuous crimes against democracy, committed in plain view by Trump and so many loyalists. I worry that at some point the reality of the numbers for both will impact us like an explosion, leaving us in a collective pool of grief, like nothing we have experienced before. Will the tested advice for dealing with trauma and grief work when that happens?*

Your response?

3. Gather your strengths

- Surround yourself with people who know you well and will encourage and support you.
- Define and affirm what you're able to do something about now.

> **My response:** *I got this one! In spite of the unbearable loneliness and loss felt while isolating at home during a pandemic, we found ways to connect with others. I regularly Zoomed with friends, old and new, including a group of like-minded crafters from various parts of the planet as we stitched, and bitched, and laughed, and lifted each other up. The craftivist efforts felt like a superpower that some of us used to attempt to protect democracy, doing what we could with the skills we possessed. And crafting itself, with all its healing power, helped make well-being sustainable for me.*

Your response?

4. Make a plan for the immediate future

- Determine what's most important for you moving forward.
- If you can't find a path, make one!

My response: *The first things that I knew I would need moving forward were a vaccine (done!) and a functioning government that upholds the Constitution and represents all its people fairly and equally—too much? Too soon?*

I also desperately need the hugs and physical presence of family and friends. The vaccine and new treatments got that box checked. The rest may take a little time. Personally, making a path forward may involve a learning curve for being in a crowd or sitting close to someone in a theater or restaurant.

Your response?

5. Create a ritual

- Performing a ritual is a powerful tool to help gain closure.
- Ritual is driven by intention and action. A "symbolic enactment" allows you to utilize your creativity and intuition in order to bypass the intellectual, logical part of your brain.

My response: *Needlework and yoga are only two of the daily rituals that helped me survive the early twenties and I count on them to help me get through the next phases, good, bad, or ugly, which will include the need for healing on a massive scale.*

A "symbolic enactment" might involve setting the previous year's calendar on fire or ripping it to shreds, although in reverse order I could do both.

Your response?

A final thought on closure from the *Psychology Today* article:

Finding closure allows you to move into your future, unencumbered, and optimistic.

And hopefully, you'll find that when all is said and done, you will have learned something valuable from all of the significant events and people in your life — even if they didn't work out the way you thought they would.[137]

I understand this statement, and while it wasn't written with this era in mind, it makes great sense, especially for the value of what many of us will hopefully learn, but I hit a snag with the term "unencumbered." For those who felt greatly "encumbered" moving forward, it may turn out to be a form of PTSD or PTTD (Post-Traumatic-Trump-Disorder.)

I hope that one takeaway from this book is that in addition to being a powerful tool for relaxing and healing body, mind, and soul, our needles can be powerful tools for putting what is often perceived as controversial or difficult messages in a slightly softer package for people to ponder and discuss, persistently chipping away at outdated, patriarchal constructs that impede progress and keep some of our fellow humans oppressed and in pain. Keep in mind, we can "make pretty things" and at the same time, find and get into some good trouble with our chosen needles.

And, if I may say it one more time—*Onward*—because we refuse to go backward.

A different take on Trump's often used misogynistic insult (nasty woman) on a mug that states my preferred definition:

A confident, independent female who gets shit done.

A CALL TO NEEDLES

CITATIONS

[1] Christopher Joyce. 2010. "Study: Neanderthals Wore Jewelry and Makeup," NPR Morning Edition, January 12, 2010. https://npr.org/templates/story/story.php?storyId=122466430

[2] Kate McLaren. 2015. The Sewing Needle: A History through 16–19th Centuries. National Gallery of Victoria, Melbourne, Australia, June 13, 2015. https://ngv.vic.gov.au/the-sewing-needle-a-history-through-16-19th-centuries/

[3] Knitsbyjenn. 2015. "Knitting for a Living—The Medieval Knitting Guilds." Roving Crafters: A Place to Share Knitting, Crocheting and Spinning Adventures [blog], June 17, 2015. http://rovingcrafters.com/2015/06/17/knitting-for-a-living-the-medieval-knitting-guilds/

[4] Beth McLaughlin. 2019. Crafting Democracy: Fiber Arts and Activism, edited by Juilee Decker and Hinda Mandell. Rochester Institute of Technology Press, p. 17.

[5] Pat Ashforth and Steve Plummer. 2020. "In Pursuit of Crafty Mathematics." Woolly Thoughts. http://woollythoughts.com/aboutus.html

[6] Victor Tangermann. 2020. "Scientists Grow 'Yarn' Out of Human Skin Cells So They Can Literally Stitch People Up." Science Alert. (Originally reported in New Scientist) https://sciencealert.com/scientists-grow-yarn-out-of-human-skin-cells-so-they-can-literally-stitch-people-up

[7] George Land. 2011. "The Failure of Success." TEDxTuscon. https://youtube.com/watch?v=ZfKMq-rYtnc

[8] Renee Ghert-Zand. 2019. "Knitters Worldwide Recreate Sweater Worn by Girl Who Survived Holocaust in Sewer." Times of Israel, October 22, 2019. https://timesofisrael.com/knitters-worldwide-recreate-sweater-worn-by-girl-who-survived-holocaust-in-sewer/

[9] Lea Stern. 2019. "The Knitted Green Sweater Project: A Holocaust Survival Story." PieceWork magazine, November 11, 2019. https://piecework-magazine.com/knitted-green-sweater-project-holocaust-survival-story/

[10] Paula Becker. 2004. "Knitting for Victory—World War I." HistoryLink, August 17, 2004. https://historylink.org/File/5721

[11] Paula Becker. 2004. "Knitting for Victory—World War II." HistoryLink, August 19, 2004. https://historylink.org/File/5722

[12] Corinne Segal. 2017. "Stitch by Stitch, A Brief History of Knitting and Activism," PBS News Hour Weekend, April 23, 2017. https://pbs.org/newshour/arts/stitch-stitch-history-knitting-activism

[13] Natalie Zarrelli. 2017. "The Wartime Spies Who Used Knitting as an Espionage Tool: Grandma Was Just Making a Sweater. Or Was She?" Atlas Obscura, June 1, 2017. https://atlasobscura.com/articles/knitting-spies-wwi-wwii

[14] Clare Hunter. 2018. "Our History of Banner Making." Sewing Matters, Processions. https://processions.co.uk/story/history-banner-making/

[15] Elizabeth Crawford. 2018. "Suffrage Stories: 'Silk, Satin and Suffrage' and Digital Drama's '100 Banners' Project." Woman and Her Sphere, February 19, 2018. https://womanandhersphere.com/tag/suffrage-banners/

[16] Encyclopædia Britannica. "The Third Wave of Feminism." https://britannica.com/topic/feminism/The-third-wave-of-feminism

[17] Beth Ann Pentney. 2008. "Knitting and Feminism's Third Wave." Third Space, A Journal of Feminist Theory and Culture, 8 (1). https://journals.sfu.ca/thirdspace/index.php/%20journal/article/view/pentney/210

[18] Shannon Downey and Denise LeBlanc. 2021. "Disrupting Craftivism: Reducing Harm and Creating Greater Impact." Fuller Craft Museum (Panel), YouTube, March 19, 2021. https://youtube.com/watch?v=uXtKgcwNvbg

[19] Melissa Kossler Dutton. 2017. "Craftivism: Melding of Crafting, Activism Is Having a Moment," AP News, Lifestyle, November 21, 2017. https://apnews.com/article/cc32f1c2e3aa49c5a3580645b95e50a8

[20] Katy Winter. 2013. "She Didn't Learn THAT at WI: "'Vaginal knitter' spends 28 days making scarf from wool stored inside her." Daily Mail, December 5, 2013. https://dailymail.co.uk/femail/article-2518107/Vaginal-knitter-artist-Casey-Jenkins-makes-scarf-wool-stored-inside-vagina.html

[21] Jeanette McDermott. 2015. "Sisters Create Baby Blanket Ministry." Sisters of the Good Shepherd, January 7, 2015. https://sistersofthegoodshepherd.com/sisters-create-baby-blanket-ministry/

[22] Steve Weatherbe. 2016. "Cross-Canada Pro-Life Knitting Bee Sends 6,978 Pairs of Baby Booties to March for Life." LifeSite News, May 12, 2016. https://lifesitenews.com/news/cross-canada-pro-life-knitting-bee-sends-6978-pairs-of-baby-booties-to-marc/

[23] Sarah Corbett. Craftivist Collective. https://craftivist-collective.com

[24] Sarah Corbett. 2019. "How a Gentle Protest with Hand-Embroidered Hankies Helped Bring Higher Wages for Retail Employees." Ideas.ted.com, January 24, 2019. https://ideas.ted.com/how-a-gentle-protest-with-hand-embroidered-hankies-helped-bring-higher-wages-for-retail-employees/

[25] Sandra Markus, Interview with Hinda Mandell. 2019. "Through the Eye of a Needle: Craftivism as an Emerging Mode of Civic Engagement and Cultural Participation." Dissertation, Teacher's College, Columbia University, May 22, 2019.

[26] Office of Elementary and Secondary Education. Protest and Patriotism: A History of Dissent and Reform: A Teacher's Guide. Smithsonian Institution. http://smithsonianeducation.org/educators/lesson_plans/protest_and_patriotism/si_protest-and-patriotism.pdf

[27] Jo Freeman. 2003. "Protest Is Patriotic." January 26, 2003. https://jofreeman.com/war/protestpatriotic.html

[28] Vickie Howell. 2019. The Knit Vibe, A Knitter's Guide to Creativity, Community, and Well-Being for Mind, Body & Soul, p. 58. Abrams.

[29] Elena Martinique. 2017. "What Is Yarn Bombing?" Widewalls magazine, February 18, 2017. https://widewalls.ch/magazine/what-is-yarn-bombing

[30] Lauren O'Farrell. Deadly Knitshade. https://whodunnknit.com

[31] Sayraphim Lothian. 2018. Guerrilla Kindness & Other Acts of Creative Resistance, pp. 61–63. Mango.

[32] Chinatown Yarn Circle Project STAND-SPEAK-SHAPE. 2021. Think! Chinatown, July 18, 2021. https://thinkchinatown.org/happenings/2021/7/18/chinatown-yarn-circle-project-stand-speak-shape-

[33] Nicole Nikolich. 2021. Yarnbombed Liberty Bell for Craftivism at the National Liberty Museum, by Lace In the Moon, October 2021. Instagram. https://instagram.com/p/CVYHDA_rMhw/

[34] Nicole Nikolich (@lace_in_the_moon). 2021. "yarnbombed the LIBERTY BELL." Instagram photo, October 22, 2021. https://instagram.com/p/CVWkcc-Dvoa/

[35] Leanne Prain. 2014. "On Yarn Bombing and Ethics." Co-conspirator blog and newsletter. http://leanneprain.com/2014/08/on-yarn-bombing-and-ethics/

[36] U.S. Department of Arts and Culture. https://usdac.us/revolution

[37] Kudzu Project. https://thekudzuproject.org

[38] Margo Smith. 2019. "The Kudzu Project: Vinebombing Virginia's Confederate Monuments." Crafting Democracy: Fiber Arts and Activism, pp. 32–37. Rochester Institute of Technology Press.

[39] Rachel Maddow. 2019. "Best New Thing in the World Today: Impeachment Embroidery!" The Rachel Maddow Show. MSNBC, November 23, 2019. https://youtube.com/watch?v=uh3ZA4mAAvs

[40] Julie Jackson. Subversive Cross Stitch. https://subversivecrossstitch.com/pages/about-us

[41] Shannon Downey. Badass Cross Stitch. https://badasscrossstitch.com

[42] "From Insta to IRL, How @Badasscrossstitch Is Bringing Craftivism (& Rita's Quilt!) to a Community Near You." No Kill Magazine. https://nokill-mag.com/articles/shannon-downey-badass-cross-stitch

[43] Allison Klein. 2019. "'I Had to Buy It and Finish It': Why 1,000 People Offered to Crowd-Stitch the Quilt of a Dead Woman None of Them Knew." Washington Post, October 25, 2019. https://washingtonpost.com/lifestyle/2019/10/25/i-had-buy-it-finish-it-why-people-offered-crowd-stitch-quilt-dead-woman-none-them-knew/

[44] Kristen Tauer. 2019. "Lingua Franca Teams with Artist-Activist Diana Weymar. Weymar's "Tiny Pricks" Series Is Going on Display at the Brand's Bleecker Street Boutique." Women's Wear Daily, June 10, 2019. https://wwd.com/fashion-news/fashion-scoops/lingua-franca-teams-with-artist-activist-diana-weymar/1203152343

[45] Sarah Cascone. 2019. "To Channel Her Frustration, One Woman Started Embroidering Donald Trump's Most Outrageous Quotes. She Inspired an Army of Needleworkers." Artnet.com, June 14, 2019. https://news.artnet.com/exhibitions/tiny-pricks-project-lingua-franca-1572865

[46] Knitting Nannas. https://knitting-nannas.com

[47] Betsy Greer. 2016. "The Knitting Nannas Stitch Together Activism and Community." Creative [blog]. https://creativelive.com/blog/the-knitting-nannas/

[48] Knitting Nannas Against Gas. Facebook. https://facebook.com/KnittingNannasAgainstGas/

[49] Pat Ashford and Steve Plummer. "The World of Illusion Knitting, Where Nothing Is Quite What It Seems." Woolly Thoughts. http://illusionknitting.woollythoughts.com/

Citations

[50] Emily Bradshaw. 2018. "Visible Mending: Punk's Not Dead, Just Patching Itself Up." The Conversation. April 11, 2018. https://theconversation.com/visible-mending-punks-not-dead-just-patching-itself-up-91226

[51] Sarah Kuhn. 2019. "Mending Our Clothing, Mending the World." Crafting Dissent, edited by Hinda Mandell, pp. 239–244. Rowman & Littlefield.

[52] Aram Han Sifuentes. 2020. "Protest Making: How Crafting Collectively Can Empower Disenfranchised People." Crafts magazine, Sept/Oct 2020 issue. https://www.craftscouncil.org.uk/stories/protest-making-how-crafting-collectively-can-empower-disenfranchised-people

[53] Aram Han Sifuentes. https://aramhansifuentes.com/protest-banner-lending-library

[54] Ellen Gadberry. 2018. "Cultivate Compassion through Contemplative Crafting." Compassionate Atlanta, March 16, 2018. https://compassionateatl.org/contemplative-crafting/

[55] "The Science of Compassion." Compassionate Atlanta. https://compassionateatl.org/the-science-of-compassion/

[56] Ryan Grenoble. 2017. "Australia's Oldest Man Knits Tiny Sweaters for Penguins Injured in Oil Spill," HuffPost, July 12, 2017. https://huffpost.com/entry/australias-oldest-man-sweaters-penguins-oil_n_6660962

[57] Penguin Foundation. https://penguinfoundation.org.au

[58] Warm Up America! https://warmupamerica.org

[59] "Made With Love." Warm Up America Foundation. https://warmupamerica.org/make/made-with-love

[60] Jan Householder. The Giving Doll. https://thegivingdoll.org

[61] "PGH HandMade Hearts." Facebook. https://facebook.com/events/contemporary-craft/pgh-handmade-hearts/309275376383174/

[62] Sarah Winsper. 2020. "Make Hearts for Hospitals: Charity Craft Appeal." Gathered, June 12, 2020. https://gathered.how/arts-crafts/make-hearts-for-hospitals-charity-craft-appeal/

[63] "Knitted Knockers: Bra Inserts Handmade with Love By Volunteer Knitters for Breast Cancer Survivors." 2017. Women You Should Know, February 14, 2017. https://womenyoushouldknow.net/knitted-knockers-bra-inserts-handmade-love-volunteer-knitters-breast-cancer-survivors/

[64] Knitted Knockers. https://knittedknockers.org

[65] Jayna Zweiman. Welcome Blanket. https://welcomeblanket.org

[66] Betsy Greer. "Making Change: The Art and Craft of Activism." https://museumofdesign.org/making-change/

[67] Mary Vaneecke. The Mourning Project. https://maryvaneecke.com (formerly https://themourningproject.com)

[68] Christopher Ingraham. 2014. "Our Infant Mortality Rate Is a National Embarrassment," Washington Post, September 24, 2014. https://washingtonpost.com/news/wonk/wp/2014/09/29/our-infant-mortality-rate-is-a-national-embarrassment/

[69] Centers for Disease Control and Prevention. "Infant Mortality." https://cdc.gov/reproductivehealth/maternalinfanthealth/infantmortality.htm

[70] "The Mourning Project." Facebook. https://facebook.com/TheMourningProject/

[71] Nadja Popovich, Livia Albeck-Ripka, and Kendra Pierre-Louis. 2020. "The Trump Administration Rolled Back More Than 100 Environmental Rules. Here's the Full List." New York Times. Updated January 21, 2022. https://nytimes.com/interactive/2020/climate/trump-environment-rollbacks-list.html

[72] The Tempestry Project. https://tempestryproject.com

[73] Ed Hawkins. 2018. "Warming Stripes," Climate Lab Book. https://climate-lab-book.ac.uk/2018/warming-stripes/

[74] Miriam Quick. 2020. "Making Data Physical Could Help Us Care for the Planet," Nightingale, April 21, 2020. https://medium.com/nightingale/making-data-physical-could-help-us-care-for-the-planet-64a3e8c22c29

[75] Rahel Wachs. "Patriotic Pussyhat" pattern. https://ravelry.com/patterns/library/patriotic-pussyhat

[76] Donna Druchunas. Sheep to Shawl Knitting Studio & Store. https://sheeptoshawl.com

[77] "Advancing Menstrual Equity in Malawi." 2021. Days for Girls [blog], August 21, 2021. https://daysforgirls.org/blog/advancing-menstrual-equity-in-malawi/

[78] Violet Protest. https://violetprotest.com

[79] Lory Hough. 2018. "Activism, One Stitch at a Time, When Social Justice and Sewing Come Together." Harvard Graduate School of Education Magazine, Fall 2018. https://gse.harvard.edu/news/ed/18/08/activism-one-stitch-time

[80] Social Justice Sewing Academy. http://sjsacademy.org/

[81] Paz, Aleesha. "Raise Your Needles: In Defence of Public Knitting." Public Books. January 17, 2020. https://publicbooks.org/raise-your-needles-in-defence-of-public-knitting/

[82] Mike Fussell. 2020. "Grandma for Breonna Taylor Arrested on Lawn of AG Daniel Cameron's Home." Wave 3 News, Louisville, KY, August 20, 2020. https://wave3.com/2020/08/20/grandma-breonna-taylor-arrested-lawn-attorney-general-daniel-camerons-home/

[83] Bonnie Black. 2019. "Quilting as Metaphor." The WOW Factor, Words of Wisdom from Wise, Older Women (blog). January 26, 2019. http://bonnieleeblack.com/blog/quilting-as-metaphor/

[84] Barb Bergquist. "The History of Quilting." A Block Away Quilt Shop [blog]. https://ablockaway.com/long-history-of-quilting-explored.htm

[85] Sarah Ives. 2005. "Did Quilts Hold Codes to the Underground Railroad?" National Geographic. February 4, 2005. https://nationalgeographic.com/news/2004/2/did-quilts-hold-codes-to-the-underground-railroad/

[86] Nikki Rhoades. "8 Places around Cleveland That Were Once Part of the Underground Railroad." Only in Your State. https://onlyinyourstate.com/ohio/cleveland/underground-railroad/

[87] "Underground Railroad Quilt Guide." 2005. Really Good Stuff Activity Guide for Teachers. https://page.reallygoodstuff.com/pdfs/154227.pdf

[88] Judy Anne Breneman. 2001. "Underground Railroad Quilts & Abolitionist Fairs." America's Quilting History. Womenfolk.com. http://womenfolk.com/quilting_history/abolitionist.htm

[89] "Quilts and Quiltmaking in The Invention of Wings, by Sue Monk Kidd." The Literate Quilter (blog). April 28, 2014. https://theliteratequilter.blogspot.com/2014/04/quilts-and-quiltmaking-in-invention-of.html

[90] Eleanor Levie. 2016. "The Invention of Wings, from a Quilter's POV." Inspiring Quilting, November 11, 2016. https://eleanorlevie.com/quilting-blog/?p=1424

[91] "World War Quilts for Relief and Comfort." World Quilts, QuiltStudy.org. https://worldquilts.quiltstudy.org/americanstory/engagement/worldwarquilts

[92] AmfAR, The Foundation for AIDS Research. https://amfar.org

[93] NAMES Project Foundation. The AIDS Memorial Quilt. http://search.aidsquilt.org/about/the-names-project-foundation

[94] Chrissy Callahan. 2020. "Teen Creates COVID-19 Quilt to Honor Those Who Have Died." Today Show, September 25, 2020. https://today.com/health/madeleine-fugate-made-quilt-honor-those-who-died-covid-19-t192406

[95] Mother's Dream Quilt Project. https://mothersdreamquilt.org

[96] Patricia Leigh Brown. 2020. "Gone But Never Forgotten in a Quilt." New York Times, December 16, 2020. https://nytimes.com/2020/12/16/arts/design/quilt-art-women-injustice.html?referringSource=articleShare

[97] Rachel Wallis. "Gone But Not Forgotten." https://rachelawallis.com/gone-but-not-forgotten.html

[98] Good Morning America. 2020. "Tyler Perry Accepts Governors Award at 2020 Emmy Award Ceremony." September 20, 2020. https://twitter.com/i/status/1307869263848407040

[99] Marjorie Agosín (ed.). 2014. Stitching Resistance: Women, Creativity, and Fiber Arts. Kent, England: Solis Press

[100] Anna North. 2020. "The Women's Work of the Pandemic—Who Sews the Masks? How Women are Shouldering the Burden of Pandemic Preparedness." Vox.com, April 30, 2020. https://vox.com/2020/4/30/21238454/coronavirus-face-mask-cooking-women-covid-pandemic

[101] Jayna Zweiman. Masks for Humanity. https://masks4humanity.org

[102] "Stop the Bug: Nationwide PPE Task Force Collaborating Efforts Nationwide to Stop COVID-19. http://stopthebug.org

[103] "College Student Makes Masks for Deaf and Hard of Hearing." 2020. LEX18, Lexington, Kentucky. https://lex18.com/news/coronavirus/college-student-makes-masks-for-the-deaf-hard-of-hearing

[104] Ruth Terry. 2019. "Black People Were the Original Craftivists." Zora Medium, September 25, 2019. https://zora.medium.com/icymi-bipoc-are-the-original-diy-craftivists-5ce6ae19742e

[105] Afi-Odelia Scruggs. 2004. Beyond Stitch and Bitch: Reflections on Knitting and Life, pp. 58–59. Hillsboro, Oregon: Beyond Words Publishing.

[106] Robin DiAngelo. 2021. Nice Racism. New York: Penguin Random House.

[107] Sarah Kendzior. 2015. "Ferguson's Radical Knitters: 'If Someone Asks Me What I'm Doing, I Say, I'm Knitting for Black Liberation'." The Guardian, August 6, 2015. https://theguardian.com/us-news/2015/aug/06/ferguson-radical-knitters-talk-justice-race-issues

[108] Jaya Saxena. 2019. "The Knitting Community Is Reckoning with Racism." Vox, February 25, 2019. https://vox.com/the-goods/2019/2/25/18234950/knitting-racism-instagram-stories

[109] "Meet the Makers; the Writers; the Disruptors [Grace Anna, Korina, Ocean, and Sukrita]." Unfinished Object. https://unfinishedobject.com/about

[110] Jeanette Sloan. 2018. "Black People Do Knit." Knitting Magazine, November 2018. https://jeanettesloandesign.com/written-articles.html

[111] Jeanette Sloan. 2019. "A Colourful Debate." Knitting Magazine, August 2019. https://jeanettesloandesign.com/acolourfuldebateknittingissue196.html

[112] Jeanette Sloan. "BIPOC in Fiber." https://bipocinfiber.com

[113] Gaye Glasspie. 2020. "Why I Can't 'Just Knit.'? The Story of a Black Knitter During Civil Unrest." GGMadeit. Knitting Life Blog, June 5, 2020. https://ggmadeit.com/why-i-cant-just-knit-the-story-of-a-black-knitter-during-civil-unrest/

[114] Gaye Glasspie. 2021. "Stand in the Gap: A Call to Action." GGMadeit. Knitting Life Blog, January 18, 2021. https://ggmadeit.com/stand-in-the-gap-a-call-to-action/

[115] Sarah Mervosh. 2019. "Knitting Has Always Been Political: Ravelry Bans Pro-Trump Content, and Reactions Flood In," June 24, 2019. https://nytimes.com/2019/06/24/style/ravelry-knitting-ban-trump.html

[116] Jane Lytvynenko. 2019. "A Popular Knitting Website Banned Posts Supporting Donald Trump, Accusing Him of 'Open White Supremacy'," BuzzFeed News, June 23, 2019. https://buzzfeednews.com/article/janelytvynenko/knitters-ravelry-trump

[117] "#Black Lives Matter: The Scoop from the Editors." 2020. Knitty magazine [blog], Fall 2020. https://knitty.com/ISSUEff20/editors.php

[118] "In Solidarity of Black Lives Matter: Our Commitment to Anti-Racism Work." Needlework Fabric Shop and Creative Workspace. Hamilton, Ontario, June 10, 2020. https://iloveneedlework.com/pages/in-solidarity-of-black-lives-matter-our-commitment-to-anti-racism-work

[119] Peggy McGlone. 2020. "Now, Even Quilters are Angry: How a Social-justice Design Started a Feud." The Washington Post, January 20, 2020. https://washingtonpost.com/entertainment/museums/now-even-quilters-are-angry-how-a-social-justice-design-started-a-feud/2020/01/20/0e9874be-3951-11ea-bb7b-265f4554af6d_story.html

[120] Natalie Naito. The Stranded Stitch. https://thestrandedstitch.com

[121] Diane Ivey. 2019. "Perspective." Lady Dye Yarns [blog], May 3, 2019. https://ladydyeyarns.com/blog/

[122] Lisa Woolfork. Black Women Stitch. https://blackwomenstitch.org

[123] Jacque Wilson. 2015. "This Is Your Brain on Crafting." CNN, January 2015. https://cnn.com/2014/03/25/health/brain-crafting-benefits/index.html

[124] "The Unexpected Benefits of Knitting." 2014. BrainCraft, June 5, 2014. https://pba.pbslearningmedia.org/resource/knitting-benefits-science-video-braincraft-1058/the-unexpected-effects-of-knitting-braincraft/

[125] Betsan Corkhill. Stitchlinks. http://stitchlinks.com/how_it_started.html

[126] Mary and Richard Maddux. 2009. "Knitting as Meditation." Meditation Oasis (blog), April 9, 2009. https://meditationoasis.com/blog/2009/04/09/knitting-as-meditation

[127] Becky Stewart. Knit Om. https://knitom.com/

[128] "A History of Shawls." Roving Crafters, a Place to Share Knitting, Crocheting and Spinning Adventures. May 11, 2016. https://rovingcrafters.com/2016/05/11/a-history-of-shawls

[129] Janet Bristow. Prayer Shawl Ministry. https://shawlministry.com/prayers.htm

[130] Denise Bayron. Moving Forward Wrap Pattern, Ravelry. https://ravelry.com/patterns/library/moving-forward-wrap?fbclid=IwAR0nggWISOJKGI-hfkShdP05hZ5yTIn52SUghua-dT2rkYQSGc3_iqPB7kSw

[131] Cleveland Clinic Yoga Videos with Judi Bar. https://my.clevelandclinic.org/departments/wellness/integrative/treatments-services/yoga

[132] Ethel J. Alpenfels. "The Anthropology and Social Significance of the Human Hand." Digital Resource Foundation for the Orthotics & Prosthetics Community. http://oandplibrary.org/al/1955_02_004.asp

[133] Loren Fishman and Ellen Saltonstall. 2008. Yoga for Arthritis: The Complete Guide, p. 217. W.W. Norton & Company.

[134] "Anatomy of the Hand." Johns Hopkins Medicine. https://hopkinsmedicine.org/health/treatment-tests-and-therapies/anatomy-of-the-hand

[135] "Sa Ta Na Ma Meaning." Yogapedia. May 26, 2020. https://yogapedia.com/definition/10781/sa-ta-na-ma

[136] "Muscle Pain: It May Actually Be Your Fascia." Johns Hopkins Medicine. https://hopkinsmedicine.org/health/wellness-and-prevention/muscle-pain-it-may-actually-be-your-fascia

[137] Abigail Brenner. 2011. "5 Ways to Find Closure from the Past." Psychology Today [blog], April 6, 2011. https://psychologytoday.com/us/blog/in-flux/201104/5-ways-find-closure-the-past

Websites

AFRIpads, https://AFRIpads.com

AmfAR. The Foundation for AIDS Research, https://amfar.org

Badass Cross Stitch, https://badasscrossstitch.com

Barefoot College Solar Mamas, https://barefootcollege.org/solution/solar/

BIPOC in Fiber, https://bipocinfiber.com

Black Women Stitch, https://blackwomenstitch.org

Cachandochile: Reflections on Chilean Culture, https://cachandochile.wordpress.com

Chart Minder, https://chart-minder.com

Cloth Menstrual Pad Database, http://clothpads.wikidot.com/patterns

Compassionate Atlanta, https://compassion.org

Contemplative Crafting, https://contemplativecrafting.com

COVID Memorial Quilt, https://covidquilt2020.com

Craftivism Manifesto, https://craftivism.com/manifesto

Craftivist Collective, https://craftivist-collective.com

Days For Girls International, https://periodaisle.com

Deadly Knitshade, https://whodunnknit.com

Dictionary, https://dictionary.com

Donna Druchunas Designs, https://ravelry.com/designers/donna-druchunas

Fandom Knits: A Geek Driven Blog, https://fandomknits.com

Fandom Knitting and Crochet, http://fandomknittingandcrochet.com/

Fibreworkshop, https://fibreworkshop.co.uk/

Franklin Habit, https://franklinhabit.com

Geek'd Out, https://geekd-out.com

GGMadeit, https://ggmadeit.com/

Green America, https://greenamerica.org

Harriet Powers Quilts, http://earlywomenmasters.net/powers/

I Support the Girls, https://isupportthegirls.org

Jeanette Sloan Designs, https://jeanettesloandesign.com

Knit in Public Day, https://wwkipday.com

Knit Om, https://knitom.com/

Knitted Knockers, https://knittedknockers.org

Knitty, https://knitty.com

Lace in the Moon, https://laceinthemoon.com

Lady Dye Yarns, https://ladydyeyarns.com

London Kaye, https://londonkaye.com

Luna Wolf, http://lunawolf.co.uk/wordpress/

Made with Love, https://warmupamerica.org/make/made-with-love

March for Science, https://marchforscience.org/

Marked by COVID, https://markedbycovid.com

Masks for Humanity, https://masks4humanity.org

Moms Demand Action for Gun Sense in America, https://momsdemandaction.org

Mother's Dream Quilt Project, https://mothersdreamquilt.org

Museum of Design Atlanta, https://www.museumofdesign.org/

My Make Do and Mend Year, https://mymakedoandmendyear.wordpress.com

Nanze, https://nanze.org

National AIDS Memorial Quilt, https://aidsmemorial.org/custom-templates/quilt

Penguin Foundation, https://penguinfoundation.org.au

Prayer Shawl Ministry, https://shawlministry.com

Project Knitwell, https://projectknitwell.org

Protest Banner Lending Library, https://aramhansifuentes.com/protest-banner-lending-library

Ravelry, https://ravelry.com

Roving Crafters, https://rovingcrafters.com

Sew in Peace, http://sewinpeace.blogspot.com/2013/08/feminine-cloth-pad-tutorial.html

Sheep to Shawl, https://sheeptoshawl.com

Sister Mountain, https://sistermountain.com

Social Justice Sewing Academy, https://sjsacademy.org

Stitch Fiddle, https://stitchfiddle.com

Stitching the Situation (StS), https://stitchingthesituation.com

Stitchlinks, http://stitchlinks.com/index.html

Stop the Bug, Nationwide PPE Task Force, http://stopthebug.org

Subversive Cross Stitch, https://subversivecrossstitch.com/blog/

Textile Beat (Slow Clothing), https://textilebeat.com

The Eco Friendly Family, https://theecofriendlyfamily.com/2011/06/mama-cloth-plus-free-patterns/

The Giving Doll, https://thegivingdoll.org

The Knitting Nannas Against Gas, https://knitting-nannas.com

The Kudzu Project, https://thekudzuproject.org

The Mourning Project, https://maryvaneecke.com

The Period Aisle, https://periodaisle.com

The Pussyhat Project, https://pussyhatproject.com

The Spruce Crafts, https://thesprucecrafts.com

The Stranded Stitch, https://thestrandedstitch.com

The Tempestry Project, https://tempestryproject.com

The Woven Road [blog], https://thewovenroad.com

The WOW Factor, Words of Wisdom from Wise Older Women, https://bonnieleeblack.com/blog

The Violet Protest, https://violetprotest.com

Think! Chinatown, https://thinkchinatown.org

Tiny Pricks Project, https://tinypricksproject.com

Unfinished Object [Blog], https://unfinishedobject.com/blog

US Department of Arts and Culture, https://usdac.us/revolution

[USDHHS] National Institutes of Health, https://aidsinfo.nih.gov

Visible Mending, https://visiblemending.com

Warm Up America!, https://warmupamerica.org

Welcome Blanket, https://welcomeblanket.org

Women's March, Feminism for the Now, https://womensmarch.com

Woolly Thoughts, https://woollythoughts.com

Yarn [Documentary], https://yarnfilm.com

Other Resources

Abrams, Kathryn. "Sweater Curse: Folklore or Fact." All Free Knitting. https://allfreeknitting.com/Mens-Knit-Sweaters/Sweater-Curse/amp

Agosín, Marjorie. 2008. Tapestries of Hope, Threads of Love, The Arpillera Movement in Chile, 1974–1994. 2nd ed. Lanham, MD: Littlefield.

Amina. 2020. "How many Black embroidery artists do you know?" Stitch Floral, Breaking Down Hand Embroidery. June 3, 2020. https://stitchfloral.blogspot.com/2020/06/how-many-black-embroidery-artists-do.html

Bryan-Wilson, Julia. 2017. Fray, Art + Textile Politics. Chicago & London: The University of Chicago Press.

CDC. 2020. "Infant Mortality." U.S. Department of Health and Human Services. https://cdc.gov/reproductivehealth/maternalinfanthealth/infantmortality.htm

Cole, Diana. 2007. "Were Quilts Used as Underground Railroad Maps?" June 24, 2007. U.S. News & World Report. https://www.usnews.com/news/articles/2007/06/24/were-quilts-used-as-underground-railroad-maps

Conserve Energy Future. "11 Strong Reasons to Switch to Reusable Menstrual Products." https://conserve-energy-future.com/strong-reasons-switch-reusable-menstrual-products.php

Deep Recovery. 2016."Understanding Fascia: The Bands That Bind Us." August 23, 2016. https://deeprecovery.com/understanding-fascia/

Feldman, Loren. 2021." A Black Dyer Shakes Up the White-Dominated Yarn Industry." Finurah by Bloomberg. October 8, 2021. https://finurah.com/2021/10/08/a-black-dyer-shakes-up-the-white-dominated-yarn-industry/

Giusti, Marianna. 2020. "How Embroidery Became a Political Power Player, Whether Stitching Slogans or Calming Anxious Hands, Needlework Is Gaining Many New Fans." Financial Times. May 30, 2020. https://ft.com/content/52a6cfb7-0dbf-4e7d-9767-9462cddcf005

Guest Chick, Those London Chicks. 2020. "8 Reasons To Switch To Reusable Menstrual Pads." July 10, 2020. https://thoselondonchicks.com/8-reasons-to-switch-to-reusable-menstrual-pads/

Hall, Stephanie. 2020. "Symbolism in the Women's Suffrage Movement." Library of Congress, Folklife Today [blog]. August 24, 2020. https://blogs.loc.gov/folklife/2020/08/symbolism-in-the-womens-suffrage-movement/

Harkey, Allyson. "The Battle Against Cancer Metaphors," Martin Nugent [blog], Hager Sharp. https://hagersharp.com/the-battle-against-cancer-metaphors-a-case-for-people-first-language/

Kaminoff, Leslie. 2007. Yoga Anatomy. Champaign, IL: Human Kinetics.

Khan Academy. "Women in the 1950's." https://khanacademy.org/humanities/us-history/postwarera/1950s-america/a/women-in-the-1950s

Lin, Sharon. 2020. "Homemade Masks in a Time of Shortage." Hackaday. March 18, 2020. https://hackaday.com/2020/03/18/homemade-masks-in-a-time-of-shortage/

Long, Ray. 2006. The Key Muscles of Yoga. 3rd ed. Bandha Yoga.

Marsom, Sarah. 2020. "Crafting a Voice: The History of Suffrage Banners." Spoonflower [blog]. February 6, 2020. https://blog.spoonflower.com/2020/02/crafting-a-voice-the-history-of-suffrage-banners/

McKay, Sarah. 2014. "This Is Your Brain On Knitting." Drsarahmckay.com [blog]. April 27, 2014. https://drsarahmckay.com/brain-knitting/

McLaughlin, Katie. 2014. "5 Things Women Couldn't Do in the Sixties." CNN. August 25, 2014. https://cnn.com/2014/08/07/living/sixties-women-5-things/index.html

Milburn, Jane. 2017. Slow Clothing, Finding Meaning in What We Wear. Textile Beat.

Napoleoni, Loretta. 2020. The Power of Knitting, Stitching Together Our Lives in a Fractured World. New York: Penguin Random House.

National Museum of American History. "Harriet Powers's Bible Quilt, 1885–1886." Smithsonian Institution. https://americanhistory.si.edu/collections/search/object/nmah_556462

National Women's History Museum. "Women's Suffrage Timeline." https://womenshistory.org/exhibits/timeline-woman-suffrage

Nirode, Vanessa. 2020. "Black DIY Influencers Shine A Light on Prejudice in the Crafting Industry." HuffPost, August 18, 2020. https://huffpost.com/entry/black-diy-influencers-makers_l_5f31848ec5b64cc99fdc7a1b

Oprah. 2014. "Oprah Talks with Sue Monk Kidd about The Invention of Wings." Oprah Magazine. January 2014. http://oprah.com/spirit/Oprah-Talks-with-Sue-Monk-Kidd-About-The-Invention-of-Wings/2

Oprah. 2014. "Sue Monk Kidd Takes Readers' Questions on The Invention of Wings." Oprah's Supersoul Sunday Interview, OWN, April 13, 2014. https://youtube.com/watch?v=C60tTaOWsvg

Ortiz, Jorge L. "Women's March 2019: Activists Press on for Saturday Protest Despite Stiff Headwinds." USA Today. January 19, 2019. https://usatoday.com/story/news/2019/01/18/womens-march-2019-third-annual-march-faces-stiff-headwinds/2605361002/

Parker, Rozsika. 2010. The Subversive Stitch: Embroidery and the Making of the Feminine. NY: Bloomsbury Visual Arts. (Originally published 1984.)

Parsons, Vanessa. 2017. "Quilting in America—A Brief History." Textile Arts Center. May 1, 2017. http://textileartscenter.com/blog/quilting-in-america-a-brief-history/

Quilting in America. "History of Quilts." https://quilting-in-america.com/History-of-Quilts.html

Reagan, Gillian. 2009. "Web Site for Knitting Nuts Has New York Needlers in Stitches." February 2, 2009. https://observer.com/2009/02/web-site-for-knitting-nuts-has-new-york-needlers-in-stitches/2/

Sifuentes, Aram Han. 2017. "Steps Towards Decolonizing Craft." Textile Society of America, April 23, 2017. https://textilesocietyofamerica.org/6728/steps-towards-decolonizing-craft

Sulcoski, Carol J. 2015. Knitting Ephemera: A Compendium of Articles, Useful and Otherwise, for the Edification and Amusement of the Handknitter. New York: Sixth and Spring.

Textillia [blog]. 2019. "Our Stance on Racism and White Supremacy (in Craft)." March 16, 2019. https://textillia.com/blog/2019/03/our-stance-racism-and-white-supremacy-craft

Australian Associated Press. 2016. "Knitting Nannas Charged in NSW Coal-Seam Gas Protest." January 17, 2016. The Guardian. https://www.theguardian.com/environment/2016/jan/18/knitting-nannas-charged-in-nsw-coal-seam-gas-protest

Thomas, M. 2019. "Crafters Take Heart, Give Them to Others in Wake of Tree of Life Shooting." Pittsburgh Post-Gazette. February 11, 2019. https://post-gazette.com/ae/art-architecture/2019/02/11/pittsburgh-PGH-Handmade-Hearts-Tree-of-Life-mass-shooting-Randy-Barbara-Grossman/stories/201901070024

Tobin, Jacqueline L., and Raymond G. Dobard. 2000. Hidden in Plain View: A Secret Story of Quilts and the Underground Railroad. New York: Anchor Books.

Turney, Joanne. 2009. The Culture of Knitting. London: Bloomsbury.

Universal Class. "Knitting Tools and a Brief Knitting History." tps://www.universalclass.com/articles/self-help/knitting-tools-and-a-brief-knitting-history.htm

National Institutes of Health. "AIDS Info." U.S. Department of Health and Human Services. https://aidsinfo.nih.gov

Villarosa, Linda. 2018. "Why America's Black Mothers and Babies Are in a Life-or-Death Crisis." New York Times. April 11, 2018. https://nytimes.com/2018/04/11/magazine/black-mothers-babies-death-maternal-mortality.html?referringSource=articleShare

Warner, Geraldine. 2017. Protest Knits. New York: Bloomsbury and Herbert Press.

Webster's Knitting Needle Notions. "Century by Century—the Chronology of Knitting Needle." http://knitting-needle-notions.com.au/history-of-knitting-and-the-knitting-needle/

Wilson, Jacque. 2015. "This Is Your Brain on Crafting." CNN. January 2015. https://www.cnn.com/2014/03/25/health/brain-crafting-benefits/index.html

Zhang, Lisa. 2019. "How Knitting Became Entwined with Protest Art." Artsy. August 13, 2019. https://artsy.net/article/artsy-editorial-knitting-entwined-protest-art

Zimmermann, Elizabeth. 1971. Knitting Without Tears, New York: Fireside Books.

PHOTO CREDITS

p. v, author's collection

p. 7, author's collection

p. 23, courtesy of Diana Burk

p. 24, courtesy of Jenn Monahan

p. 25, top, courtesy of the US Holocaust Museum, Krystyna Keren Collection

p. 25, bottom, courtesy of Lea Stern

p. 26, author's collection

p. 38, courtesy of the Washington, DC Southwest Business Improvement District p. 47, courtesy of Voice of America and Brian Allen

p. 48, courtesy of Jayna Zweiman

p. 49, both images, author's collection

p. 50, both images, courtesy of The High Littleton and Hallatrow Yarnbombers p. 51, courtesy of Nicole Nickolich, Lace in the Moon

p. 53, top left, courtesy of Dave Loewenstein

p. 53, top right, courtesy of Margo Smith, Kudzu Project

p. 54, top left, courtesy of Margo Smith, photo by Tom Cogill

p. 54, bottom, both images courtesy of Margo Smith, photos by Tom Cogill

p. 55, author's collection

p. 56, author's collection

p. 57, both images, author's collection

p. 58, courtesy of Julie Jackson, Subversive Cross Stitch

p. 59, all images courtesy of Julie Jackson

p. 60, all images courtesy of Shannon Downey, Badass Cross Stitch

p. 62, courtesy of Shannon Downey, photo by Mark Germain

p. 64, courtesy of Diana Weymar, Tiny Pricks Project

p. 65, top left, courtesy of Diana Weymar, photo by Charlie Burlock

p. 65, bottom right, author's collection

p. 66, top left, Knitting Nannas Against Gas (KNAG)

p. 66, bottom right, courtesy of KNAG , photo by Gwilym Summers

p. 67, both images courtesy of KNAG, photos by Gwilym Summers

p. 68, top, both images from author's collection

p. 69, bottom left, courtesy of Pam Gabriel

p. 69, bottom right, author's collection

p. 70, all images from author's collection

p. 72, courtesy of Liz Haywood, www.lizhaywood.com.au, Oct 2018 archive

p. 74, bottom left, courtesy of Aram Han Sifuentes, photo by Virginia Harold

p. 74, bottom right, courtesy of Aram Han Sifuentes, photo by eedahahm

p. 76, courtesy of Penguin Foundation, Australia

p. 77, both images courtesy of Warm Up America Foundation

p. 78, both images courtesy of Warm Up America Foundation

p. 79, courtesy of Jan Householder, The Giving Doll Project

p. 80, both images courtesy of Jan Householder

p. 81, top middle, author's collection

p. 81, bottom right, courtesy of Barbara Demorest, Knitted Knockers

p. 82, both images courtesy of Barbara Demorest

p. 86, courtesy of Jayna Zweiman, Welcome Blanket Project

p. 88, courtesy of Jayna Zweiman

p. 89, courtesy of Mary Vaneecke, The Mourning Project

p. 90, top left, CDC, public domain

p. 90, bottom, both images courtesy of Mary Vaneecke

p. 91, top left, courtesy of Mary Vaneecke

p. 91, right, courtesy of The Tempestry Project

p. 93, both images courtesy of The Tempestry Project

p. 94, courtesy of The Tempestry Project

p. 95, author's collection

p. 96, top left, all images courtesy of Donna Druchunas

p. 96, bottom right, courtesy of Lynn Sosnowski

p. 97, courtesy of Yakoob Badat, Nanze Children Services

p. 98, all images courtesy of Yakoob Badat

p. 101, courtesy of Ann Morton, Violet Protest

p. 102, courtesy of Ann Morton

p. 103, top, both images courtesy of Ann Morton

p. 103, bottom right, courtesy of Sara Trail, SJSA

p. 104, both images courtesy of Sara Trail

p. 105, both images courtesy of Sara Trail

p. 111, author's collection

p. 112, author's collection

p. 118, both images, public domain

p. 119, all images courtesy of Madeleine Fugate, The COVID Memorial Quilt

p. 123, bottom left, courtesy of Rachel Wallis, photo by Christie Fail

p. 123, bottom right, courtesy of Rachel Wallis, photo by Martin Macias, Salome Chasnof

p. 124, courtesy of Carolyn Mazloomi

p. 127, author's collection

p. 129, top left, courtesy of Marjorie Agosín, and the MSU Museum, photo by Pearl Yee Wong p. 129, top right, courtesy of Margaret Snook, Cachandochile

p. 131, courtesy of Sara Trail, SJSA

p. 136, both images, author's collection

p. 137, courtesy of Jayna Zweiman

p. 138, courtesy of Stop the Bug

p. 140, top left, author's collection

p. 140, right middle, courtesy of Heather Schulte, Stitching the Situation (StS)

p. 141, all images courtesy of Heather Schulte, bottom photos by Brad Haynes

p. 142, courtesy of Heather Schulte and Katie Brennan

p. 153, courtesy of Sara Trail, SJSA

p. 154, courtesy of Natalie Naito, The Stranded Stitch

p. 157, author's collection

p. 160, author's collection

p. 163, author's collection

p. 165, author's collection

p. 169 – 186, all yoga images, author's collection, photos by Laurence Nozik

p. 191, author's collection

ACKNOWLEDGMENTS

Writing this book was undoubtedly the most ambitious and audacious thing I have ever done. It took a village to "raise" this first-time author. That village included supportive friends, family, and professionals, guiding me through the process.

My thanks and love to the following incredible humans:

All of the creative people I wrote about in this book, hoping to honor their work and inspire readers to action. I hope I represented you well. Many of them have teams of dedicated, hardworking people, expanding their efforts outward into the world, making sustainability possible. Hugs and gratitude to that extended network, as well.

My editor, Pam. How lucky I was to find someone who also stitches and understands the language and passion of needleworkers. I think it made our collaboration much more productive.

Laurence, the photographer, graphic artist, and miracle worker who helped me look professional in the headshot, took all of the yoga photos, designed the cover, and set the layout of the book.

Laura, the proofreader, who found all of the missed oopses and became an enthusiastic friend and ally in the process.

Emily and Claire at Hitchcock Media Group for all things publishing and publicizing.

Elizabeth, who read my first few pages and enthusiastically told me I needed to do this; Carolyn, friend, work colleague, business partner, and the first person who understood and shared my obsession with needlework, especially counted cross stitch; Karla, who will take shared confidences to the grave, for being an early reader and cheerleader; and Barb, dear friend and supporter, determined to plan the launch party.

Shannon Downey, for her support and encouragement. But especially, for bringing me back to embroidery, reminding me of my power, and introducing me to a new circle of friends.

My husband, for his patience (I'm trying to concentrate here!) and encouragement, in spite of not fully understanding my obsession with needlework. We grew stronger as partners during the isolation from the world during the pandemic. And when he said he was proud of me—well, that meant the world.

Our sweet Cavanese, who had my back during the long hours I spent at the computer, protecting the house while I researched and wrote, always ready for a mind-clearing walk or romp and a snuggle when day was done.

And finally, the grandmother who shared her needlework skills and instilled a reverence for making things; the other grandmother, who knew where I was headed, needle in hand; and my mother, who was always so proud and loving.